RENEWALS 458-4574
DATE DUE

GAYLORD			PRINTED IN U.S.A.

Hugo Riemann and the Birth of Modern Musical Thought

Generally acknowledged as the most important German musicologist of his age, Hugo Riemann (1849–1919) shaped the ideas of generations of music scholars, not least because his work coincided with the institutionalisation of academic musicology around the turn of the last century. This influence, however, belies the contentious idea at the heart of his musical thought, an idea he defended for most of his career – harmonic dualism.

By situating Riemann's musical thought within turn-of-the-century discourses about the natural sciences, German nationhood and modern technology, this book reconstructs the cultural context in which Riemann's ideas not only 'made sense' but advanced an understanding of the tonal tradition as both natural and German. Riemann's musical thought – from his considerations of acoustical properties to his aesthetic and music-historical views – thus regains the coherence and cultural urgency that it once possessed.

ALEXANDER REHDING is Cotsen Fellow at the Princeton Society of Fellows. He is co-editor of *Music Theory and Natural Order from the Renaissance to the Early Twentieth Century* (Cambridge, 2001). He was awarded the Jerome Roche Prize of the Royal Musical Society in 2001.

New perspectives in music history and criticism

GENERAL EDITORS

JEFFREY KALLBERG, ANTHONY NEWCOMB AND RUTH SOLIE

This series explores the conceptual frameworks that shape or have shaped the ways in which we understand music and its history, and aims to elaborate structures of explanation, interpretation, commentary, and criticism which make music intelligible and which provide a basis for argument about judgements of value. The intellectual scope of the series is broad. Some investigations will treat, for example, historiographical topics, others will apply cross-disciplinary methods to the criticism of music, and there will also be studies which consider music in its relation to society, culture, and politics. Overall, the series hopes to create a greater presence for music in the ongoing discourse among the human sciences.

PUBLISHED TITLES

Leslie C. Dunn and Nancy A. Jones (eds.), *Embodied Voices: Representing Female Vocality in Western Culture*

Downing A. Thomas, *Music and the Origins of Language: Theories from the French Enlightenment*

Thomas S. Grey, *Wagner's Musical Prose*

Daniel K. L. Chua, *Absolute Music and the Construction of Meaning*

Adam Krims, *Rap Music and the Poetics of Identity*

Annette Richards, *The Free Fantasia and the Musical Picturesque*

Richard Will, *The Characteristic Symphony in the Age of Haydn and Beethoven*

Christopher Morris, *Reading Opera Between the Lines: Orchestral Interludes and Cultural Meaning from Wagner to Berg*

Emma Dillon, *Medieval Music-Making and the 'Roman de Fauvel'*

David Yearsley, *Bach and the Meanings of Counterpoint*

Alexander Rehding, *Hugo Riemann and the Birth of Modern Musical Thought*

David Metzer, *Quoting Music within Music: Quotation and Cultural Meaning in the Twentieth Century*

Hugo Riemann and the Birth of Modern Musical Thought

ALEXANDER REHDING

PUBLISHED BY THE PRESS SYNDICATE OF THE UNIVERSITY OF CAMBRIDGE
The Pitt Building, Trumpington Street, Cambridge CB2 1RP, United Kingdom

CAMBRIDGE UNIVERSITY PRESS
The Edinburgh Building, Cambridge, CB2 2RU, UK
40 West 20th Street, New York, NY 10011-4211, USA
477 Williamstown Road, Port Melbourne, VIC 3207, Australia
Ruiz de Alarcón 13, 28014 Madrid, Spain
Dock House, The Waterfront, Cape Town 8001, South Africa

http://www.cambridge.org

First published 2003

Printed in the United Kingdom at the University Press, Cambridge

Typeface Palatino 10/12 pt   *System* LATEX 2$_\varepsilon$ [TB]

A catalogue record for this book is available from the British Library

ISBN 0 521 82073 1 hardback

CONTENTS

Acknowledgements   *page* ix

Introduction   1

1 Hugo Riemann's moonshine experiment   15

2 The responsibilities of nineteenth-century music
   theory   36

3 Riemann's musical logic and the 'As if'   67

4 Musical syntax, nationhood and universality   113

5 Beethoven's deafness, exotic harmonies and
   tone imaginations   162

   Epilogue   182

   Glossary: Riemann's key terms as explained in the
   Musik-Lexikon *(5th edn, 1900)*   186
   Bibliography   199

   Index   212

ACKNOWLEDGEMENTS

This project has incurred many debts over the years. First and foremost, this book would not have come into existence without the longstanding support of John Deathridge. In continuing acts of generosity, he helped me open up an intellectual world in which to situate Riemann's theories – especially those parts that seem at first utterly counterintuitive. And from the other side of the Atlantic, Brian Hyer has also watched over this project from its very inception to its final state. In hundreds of emails he has shared his thoughts and musical insights on Riemann's theories with me over the years. I could not have benefited from a better intellectual axis than John and Brian.

Scott Burnham and Suzie Clark must be thanked for indulging my interest in nature and legitimation in music theory, and for their patient reading of earlier drafts of the script. I have shared many interesting conversations with both Scott and Suzie – so many more than I expected after a hilariously unpromising start when I first met with Scott one sunny autumn afternoon in Princeton.

I have recently had the opportunity to share my interest in harmonic dualism at a workshop organised by Ian Bent at the first Summer School on historical aspects of music theory at the Mannes School of Music in 2001. Ian's conscientious reading of Riemann's article 'Das Problem des harmonischen Dualismus' happily coincided with my working of the final draft of this script. I am grateful to all the participants for stimulating discussions, and particularly to Edward Gollin, who read the entire script.

The list of friends and colleagues at Cambridge and Penn who have contributed in one way or another would be impossible to complete. Nevertheless, I shall make an attempt to name at least those who contributed in a more immediate way: Julie Brown, Bojan Bujić, Daniel Chua, Nicholas Cranfield, Martin Dixon, Daniel Grimley, Christopher Hasty, Richard Jones, Cristle Collins Judd, Anthony Gritten, Jeff Kallberg, David Kasunic, Larry Klein, E. Dean Kolbas, Roger Parker, Susan Rankin, Jim Samson, Lucy Shanno, W. Dean Sutcliffe, Simon Werrett and Paul J. D. Yates. Penny Souster has scrupulously watched over this project at all stages. The series editors have given me thoughtful

and careful advice, and my copy-editor Michael Downes must be thanked for his infallible hawk-eye scrutiny.

Some passages in this book have appeared in print: 'The Quest for the Origins of Music in Germany circa 1900', *Journal of the American Musicological Society* 53 (2000), pp. 345–85; 'Music Theory and the Human Touch', *Music Theory Spectrum* 24 (2002), pp. 283–93, and 'Wie können Untertöne in der Geschichte der Musiktheorie hörbar gemacht werden?', in *Musiktheorie zwischen Historie und Systematik*, ed. Ludwig Holtmeier and Clemens Kühn (in press). I am grateful to the original publishers for their permission to reuse material.

Like most projects, this one could not have been finished without financial support. I am grateful to the British Academy, the *Studienstiftung des deutschen Volkes* and Queens' and Emmanuel Colleges, Cambridge, for the supportive framework they provided. Support of an invaluable kind I received from my two families, Gabi, Wolf, and Gerardo, for whom I could find no better words than Riemann's own motto: *Amor constans vincit*.

Introduction

When Hugo Riemann died on 10 July 1919, only one week before his seventieth birthday, it was evident that the young discipline of musicology had lost one of its cornerstones.[1] A special issue of the recently founded journal *Zeitschrift für Musikwissenschaft*, which had been planned as a congratulatory volume for him, now had to double as his obituary. Its editor Alfred Einstein appraised Riemann's achievement, with what appears like uncanny prescience, in terms of its historic significance:

In Hugo Riemann, a piece of the history of musicological research of the past half-century is embodied. Of all the great names, if his is ignored, it becomes virtually impossible to conceive of this history.[2]

It goes without saying that the celebratory-commemorative occasion for which this eulogy was written called for a certain degree of honeymouthed exaggeration. But even if we treat Einstein's superlative assessment with some caution, what remains nonetheless is that even during his lifetime, Riemann's work was considered a milestone in the history of musicology. His prodigious output encompassed over fifty books, and countless articles and editions. His music dictionary – compiled entirely by himself – became the standard reference work for generations. And his theories of harmony and metre suggested that the basic codes of music had finally been cracked. In short, Riemann was a key player in what is easily stylised into a heroic pioneering age of the history of the discipline.

At the turn of the century, the academic discipline of musicology was a recent addition to the institutional landscape. After chairs were established in Vienna (Eduard Hanslick, 1870, succeeded by Guido Adler

---

[1] I am using the term 'musicology' as a translation of *Musikwissenschaft*, although the rigorous, scientific flavour of the German *Wissenschaft* is not fully captured in its English equivalent.

[2] Alfred Einstein, 'Hugo Riemann zum 70. Geburtstag', *Zeitschrift für Musikwissenschaft* 1 (1919), p. 569. 'In Hugo Riemann ist ein Stück Geschichte der musikwissenschaftlichen Forschung im letzten halben Jahrhundert verkörpert. Sein Name ist der, der aus dieser Geschichte am wenigsten, am unmöglichsten wegzudenken ist.' All translations are mine, unless marked otherwise. The original text of longer quotations is provided wherever possible.

1

in 1898), Strasbourg (Salomon Jadassohn, 1897) and several other universities in German-speaking countries that quickly followed suit, musicology was urgently in need of self-definition and a demarcation of its identity as an independent subject. Like Guido Adler before him, Riemann had offered a musicological syllabus covering a number of subdisciplines.[3] In Riemann's vision, this canon of subdisciplines covered five areas: acoustics, tone physiology and psychology, music aesthetics, practical music theory, and finally – as 'musicology's best part'[4] – music history. Riemann's subdisciplines present overlapping areas of study, from physical attributes to perceptual, pedagogical and ultimately historical concerns. At the same time the identity of the object of investigation shifts, almost seamlessly, from sound wave to musical structure, and on to musical style.

The systematic progression of this canon reflected Riemann's personal approach to his subject: the aspects that these subdisciplines examined all came together under the category of 'musical hearing', which Riemann defined and redefined throughout his career. In this sense, Einstein's eulogy noted that in the academic landscape Riemann 'occupies an exceptional position: he is the only [musicologist] who did not start specifically as a historian'.[5] Rather, in line with the idea of a 'bottom-to-top aesthetics', prevalent in the work of then fashionable thinkers such as Theodor Fechner and Johann Friedrich Herbart, he tried to capture an essential quality of music, starting with the most general and fundamental aspects and then going into the particular and specific manifestations.[6]

---

[3] Guido Adler, 'Umfang, Methode und Ziel der Musikwissenschaft', *Vierteljahrsschrift für Musikwissenschaft* 1 (1885), pp. 5–20. Hugo Riemann, *Grundriß der Musikwissenschaft* (Leipzig: Quelle & Meyer, 1908). On Adler's and Riemann's conceptions of musicology, see Barbara Boisits, 'Hugo Riemann – Guido Adler: Zwei Konzepte von Musikwissenschaft vor dem Hintergrund geisteswissenschaftlicher Methodendiskussionen um 1900', in Klaus Mehner and Tatjana Böhme-Mehner, eds., *Hugo Riemann (1849–1919): Musikwissenschaftler mit Universalanspruch* (Cologne, Weimar, Vienna: Böhlau, 2001), pp. 17–29.

[4] Riemann, *Grundriß der Musikwissenschaft*, p. 3.

[5] Einstein, 'Hugo Riemann zum 70. Geburtstag', p. 569.

[6] On 'bottom-to-top aesthetics' see Gustav Theodor Fechner, *Vorschule der Aesthetik*, 2nd edn (Leipzig: Breitkopf und Härtel, 1897), pp. 1–7. Riemann adopts the label from 'Der gegenwärtige Stand der musikalischen Aesthetik' (1878) on, in *Präludien und Studien* (reprint Hildesheim: Georg Olms, 1967), vol. 2, p. 50. However, he later claims that his approach had always been 'top-to-bottom'; see 'Ideen zu einer "Lehre von den Tonvorstellungen"', *Jahrbuch der Musikbibliothek Peters* (1914/15), p. 1. Peter Rummenhöller comments on this apparent paradox in *Musiktheoretisches Denken im 19. Jahrhundert* (Regensburg: Gustav Bosse, 1967), pp. 103–4. See also Hartmut Grimm, '"Ästhetik von unten": Hugo Riemanns Konzept der Musikästhetik', in Mehner and Böhme-Mehner, eds., *Hugo Riemann*, pp. 117–30.

This bottom-to-top approach also informed his aesthetics of the musical work, which tended to view musical forms as entities built up from the basic parts to the whole. In his model, the structure of the musical work thus unfolds before the listener, who cannot grasp the totality until it is completed before his or her ears.[7] As Riemann claimed in his three lectures on aesthetics, *Wie hören wir Musik? (How Do We Hear Music?)* of 1888, listening to musical structures bears great resemblance to viewing a work of architecture, in that both are to be contemplated as aesthetic totalities. However, the means of contemplation is different for music:

The visitor to Cologne Cathedral, however, who is not himself an architect, has one great advantage over any listener to the Ninth Symphony who is not a musician. The former stands in front of the cathedral and can spend as long as he likes absorbing in his imagination first the overall structure and then, gradually, more and more detail, first grasping the large-scale symmetries and passing from these to the smaller scale. Not so the listener. The music does not wait as it enters his ear, and if he does not succeed immediately in grasping it, he has lost the chance of understanding it better by comparing one passage with the next. Everything therefore depends on clearly grasping the most minute figures and their correct relationship to each other, in fact on understanding the smallest points of symmetry.[8]

In this way, Riemann's musical thought was centrally concerned with the aesthetic perception of the work under the category of a structural 'musical hearing'. This form of hearing is presented as a logical activity – and a strenuous one at that, which requires the full concentration of the listener. At the same time, the comparison with Cologne Cathedral – a gigantic medieval Gothic structure that remained incomplete until 1880 – is chosen carefully, resonating as it did in the later nineteenth century with a wealth of historical and political concerns, which appears to lend a distinct cultural dimension to Riemann's concept of musical hearing.

---

[7] See, for instance, the entry on 'Formen, musikalische' in Riemann, *Musiklexikon*, 5th edn (Leipzig: Max Hesse, 1900), pp. 332–4.

[8] Riemann, *Wie hören wir Musik?: Grundlinien der Musik-Ästhetik*, 6th edn (Berlin: Max Hesse, 1923), pp. 43–4, trans. in Bojan Bujić, *Music in European Thought 1851–1912* (Cambridge: Cambridge University Press, 1988), p. 357. 'Der Beschauer des Kölner Doms, der nicht selbst Musiker ist, befindet sich nun aber in einem gewaltigen Vorteil gegenüber dem Hörer der neunten Symphonie, der nicht Musiker ist. Jener steht vor dem Dom, läßt sein Bild, so lange er will, auf seine Phantasie wirken und versteht zunächst den Totalaufbau und allmählich mehr und mehr das Detail; er begreift zunächst die Symmetrien im großen und dringt von diesen allmählich zu den kleineren vor. Anders der Musikhörer. Flüchtig eilt das Tonbild an seinem Ohr vorüber, und wenn es ihm nicht sofort gelang, es festzuhalten, so ist die Möglichkeit, durch Vergleichung mit ihm Nachfolgendem es besser zu verstehen, verloren. Alles hängt also vom scharfen Auffassen der kleinsten Gebilde und ihrer richtigen Beziehung aufeinander, also von Verständnis der kleinsten Symmetrien ab.'

I

In the celebratory issue of *Zeitschrift für Musikwissenschaft* it was tactfully ignored that despite his towering stature within the discipline, Riemann never received a full tenured professorship, an *Ordinariat*.[9] After decades of financial insecurity in various minor posts, crisscrossing the country, from Bielefeld, Leipzig, Bromberg (Bydgoszcz), and Hamburg to Sondershausen and Wiesbaden, Riemann finally settled in Leipzig in 1895.[10] Even though he had received a number of international honours – from St Cecilia's Academy in Rome (1887), the Royal Academy in Florence (1894), the University of Edinburgh (1899), and the Royal Musical Association in London (1904) – his recognition inside Germany grew only slowly. In 1901 he was appointed extraordinary professor at Leipzig; the arrangement was formalised in 1905. In 1908, he additionally became the founder and director of the musicological institute. The University of Leipzig gave him an honorary professorship in 1911. Finally, in 1914, he became director of a newly founded semi-autonomous institute for musicological research.

Paradoxically, perhaps, it is conceivable that the impact and proliferation of Riemann's work was fostered by the circumstance of his not having the security of a tenured post. As Michael Arntz has recently suggested, Riemann's incessant publishing activity was mainly due to the lack of a regular income and the dire necessity to earn money to support his family. Since his days in Hamburg (1881–90), he therefore made a habit of working from four o'clock in the morning to ten at night – every day, save Christmas Day.[11] Among his prolific output, a range of short 'catechisms' and compendia on all aspects of musical activity enjoyed particular popularity, and ensured that his views on music spread fast, even beyond the narrow confines of academia.

---

[9] Biographical accounts of Riemann can be found in Willibald Gurlitt, 'Hugo Riemann (1849–1919)', *Veröffentlichungen der Akademie der Wissenschaften und der Literatur, Mainz: Abhandlungen der geistes- und sozialwissenschaftlichen Klasse* 25 (1950), pp. 1865–1901; Carl Mennicke, 'Eine biographische Skizze nebst einem Verzeichnis seiner Werke', *Riemann-Festschrift* (Leipzig: Max Hesse, 1909), pp. vii–xxiv; Michael Arntz, *Hugo Riemann (1849–1919): Leben, Werk und Wirkung* (Cologne: Concerto-Verlag, 1999), pp. 41–175, and '"Nehmen Sie Riemann ernst?": Zur Bedeutung Hugo Riemanns für die Emanzipation der Musik', in Mehner and Böhme-Mehner, eds., *Hugo Riemann*, pp. 9–16.

[10] It seems that Riemann was briefly considered for a professorship at Bonn as early as 1876 (that is, before he completed his *Habilitationsschrift*, the qualification normally required for academic teaching in Germany). However, due to what were perceived by the committee as Wagnerian leanings and anti-Classical tendencies, Riemann was struck off the shortlist. See Willy Kahl, 'Der "obskure" Riemann: Ein Brief F. Chrysanders', in *Studien zur Musikgeschichte des Rheinlandes* (Cologne: Arno Verlag, 1956), pp. 54–6.

[11] Arntz, *Hugo Riemann*, p. 45.

Time and again, the outcome of Riemann's systematic musicological project was praised for the cogency and internal coherence with which the individual aspects referred to one another. Thus Alfred Einstein continued his eulogy:

The unity of his oeuvre is exceptional: the theorist is in the service of the historian, the historian provides materials from all areas, whether it be the closest or farthest. If one wants to follow him fully and understand him fully, one must also know him fully.[12]

In the context of Einstein's earlier observation, that Riemann had not begun as a historian but rather – following Adler's basic distinction – as a 'systematic' musicologist, this statement is intriguing. In fact, however, both statements reflect Riemann's development accurately. Riemann had intermittently pursued projects with a historical component, such as his inaugural dissertation (*Habilitationsschrift*), *Studien zur Geschichte der Notenschrift* (*Studies in the History of Notation*, 1878), but the bulk of his research was concerned with the establishment of a thoroughgoing foundation of the general aspects of music.

The music historian Philipp Spitta, who had examined this inaugural dissertation, urged Riemann in a letter of 1890 to 'return to music history'.[13] But in a way, Riemann had been working on a 'return to music history' all along: once the systematic part of his musical project had been completed, he felt he had established once and for all what music actually *is* and how it is heard. With his theoretical framework in place, he could tackle specific music-historical projects – and it is no coincidence that his major publications on aspects of music history date from the period after he had formulated most of his theoretical views. As the last two chapters will explore, it was in this conceptual frame that much, though not all, of his later music-historical research was carried out.

Given his systematising efforts, it is perhaps not surprising that Riemann showed considerably less enthusiasm for a biographically based approach to music history. Rather, he considered research into the lives of the composers little more than a preliminary stage towards a more rigorous examination of musical structures. At the same time, this move away from biography constituted for him a necessary step in the process of the professionalisation of the discipline. Thus, he explained in 1901, while much of the groundwork had been covered in the nineteenth century by non-musicians skilled in archival work,

---

[12] Einstein, 'Hugo Riemann zum 70. Geburtstag', p. 570. 'Die Einheitlichkeit seines Schaffens ist außerordentlich: der Theoretiker steht im Dienst des Historikers, der Historiker schafft dem Theoretiker Stoff aus allen, den nächsten und entlegensten Gegenden herbei. Man muß, will man ihm ganz folgen und ihn ganz verstehen, ihn auch ganz kennen.'

[13] See Arntz, *Hugo Riemann*, pp. 117–18.

such as philologists and lawyers, more specialised skills were required nowadays:

Of course, where biographical and bibliographical work stops and questions begin as to the history of art forms or the aesthetic appreciation of artistic achievement, the superiority of philologists and lawyers ends, and musicians begin to make their voices heard. Since music history started examining the development of artistic technique and art theory, as well as stylistic genres and artistic tendencies, and since it has tackled critical editions of older compositions on a larger scale, professional musicians have entered more and more into the front line of music historians. Since historical work cannot successfully be done on the side, musicology has developed into a new branch of the musical profession whose representatives are neither composers nor practising musicians, except perhaps in the second place, but rather musical scientists.[14]

Elsewhere, Riemann summarised his contribution to the field of music history as his effort to move interest away from 'the life stories of the great masters towards the development of tonal forms and stylistic features'.[15] As another eulogy in the 1919 jubilee issue pointed out, this was in aid of a 'theory of music-historical principles (without which a scientific music history is not possible)'.[16] It was this holistic appeal, the idea that all aspects of the study of music could be unified and related back to one principle, or a small set of principles – that is to say, the tantalising possibility that an underlying essence of music might be discovered and studied by rigorous scientific means – that lent Riemann's ideas such clout in the academy.

The jubilant contributors of the 1919 *Festschrift* celebrated the organicism of Riemann's system – Riemann's image of Cologne Cathedral, mentioned above, seems to be chosen in the spirit of Goethe's reflections

---

[14] Riemann, *Geschichte der Musik seit Beethoven (1800–1900)* (Leipzig and Stuttgart: W. Spemann, 1901), pp. 762–3. 'Freilich wo die biographische und bibliographische Arbeit aufhört und die Geschichte der Kunstformen, die ästhetische Würdigung der Kunstleistungen in Frage kommt, da hört die Überlegenheit des Philologen und Juristen auf und der Musiker kommt zu Worte. Seitdem die Musikgeschichte ernstlicher auf die Entwickelung der Kunsttechnik und Kunstlehre, auf Stilgattungen und Kunstströmungen einzugehen begonnen und kritische Neuausgaben älterer Tonwerke in größerem Maßstabe in Angriff genommen hat, sind deshalb die Fachmusiker mehr und mehr in die erste Reihe auch der Musikhistoriker getreten und es hat sich, da die historischen Arbeiten sich nicht wohl mit Erfolg nebenbei besorgen lassen, mehr und mehr die Musikwissenschaft zu einem neuen Zweige des Musikerberufs entwickelt, dessen Vertreter weder Komponisten noch ausübende Musiker, wenigstens beides höchstens nebenher, vielmehr in erster Linie Musikgelehrte sind.'

[15] Hugo Riemann, *Handbuch der Musikgeschichte* (Leipzig: Breitkopf und Härtel, 1913), vol. 2/3, p. iii.

[16] Willibald Gurlitt, 'Hugo Riemann und die Musikgeschichte', *Zeitschrift für Musikwissenschaft* 1 (July 1919), p. 586.

on Strasbourg Minster in *Von deutscher Baukunst*. A subsequent critical tradition, by contrast, has taken issue with what could well be considered the basic germ-cell of Riemann's musical thought, namely the doctrine of harmonic dualism – in short, the idea that minor triads are symmetrically opposed to major triads and work upside-down. This idea, which will be reviewed in Chapter 1, became the accepted doctrine in late nineteenth-century German music theory but is comprehensively dismissed in contemporary scholarship.[17] Riemann's high-flying aspirations towards a unified musicology seem to come down with a crash: if as central a component of Riemann's all-encompassing musical thought as harmonic dualism is seriously flawed, one would assume that the remainder of his systematic edifice, conceived in the spirit of organicism, would collapse like a house of cards.

Strangely, perhaps, this has not happened: key aspects of Riemann's theoretical work continue to be in everyday use. Particularly in Germany, as well as parts of Central and Eastern Europe, Riemann's theory of harmonic function is common currency, and in fact replaces the Roman-numeral taxonomy common in English-speaking countries. However, the version of the theory that is taught under the name of Riemann is in fact based on the textbooks by Maler and Grabner – whose theories are entirely devoid of harmonic dualism.[18] (This process of removing harmonic dualism from Riemann's theories bears some resemblances to the process of turning Schenker's theories into a working model by decontextualising them and stripping them of any undesirable metaphysical baggage.[19])

These 'monistic' versions of harmonic function are paralleled by a sizeable body of critical literature that has amassed around Riemann's writings. With very few exceptions, the critics are in agreement that harmonic dualism is not merely redundant to the theory of harmonic function but in fact contradicts its essential features. In the words of one recent commentator, exhibiting an uncommon degree of sympathy towards Riemann's harmonic dualism, 'harmonic dualism and harmonic function are independent ideas and emerged in Riemann's work

---

[17] Some recent music-theoretical approaches, notably the analytical work following Daniel Harrison and David Lewin, take their inspiration from harmonic dualism, but neither would claim to endorse the tenets of this theory to the full.

[18] See Wolf von Forster, 'Heutige Praktiken im Harmonielehreunterricht an Musikhochschulen und Konservatorien', in Martin Vogel, ed., *Beiträge zur Musiktheorie des neunzehnten Jahrhunderts* (Regensburg: Gustav Bosse, 1966), pp. 260–1.

[19] On Schenker's de-ideologisation, see for instance Nicholas Cook, 'Schenker's Theory of Music as Ethics', *Journal of Musicology* 7 (1989), pp. 415–39; and Robert Snarrenberg, 'Competing Myths: The American Abandonment of Schenker's Organicism', in Anthony Pople, ed., *Theory, Analysis and Meaning in Music* (Cambridge: Cambridge University Press, 1994), pp. 29–56.

as responses to different problems'.[20] Usually the rejection of harmonic dualism is final and complete. To put it in Scott Burnham's terms: the current reception of Riemann has essentialised what he got right – harmonic function – and has discarded what he got wrong – harmonic dualism.[21]

From a practical point of view there is little to be criticised about this 'divorce of convenience' – the monistic version of the theory of harmonic function does indeed work much better than Riemann's original. Riemann himself, on the other hand, was adamant that harmonic dualism was at the centre of his music-theoretical endeavour, and inextricably connected with his ideas of harmonic function:

I cannot quite understand how some men who are acquainted with my theory have been able to see something of a retreat from the territory of harmonic dualism in the introduction of the taxonomy of function (*T S D* etc.) ... I still stand in the same position as thirty years ago; the only difference is that I have finally liberated myself fully from the legitimation of the principles of harmony through acoustical phenomena and uncovered the true roots of harmonic dualism.[22]

The real question here for us is: why would Riemann be so insistent on his concept of harmonic dualism? The criticisms that prompted Riemann's response, and similar ones, have since been made again and again, and have shown, as will be discussed in the first two chapters, that there are some genuine problems.[23] Is it possible that a whole generation

---

[20] M. Kevin Mooney, 'The "Table of Relations" and Music Psychology in Hugo Riemann's Harmonic Theory', PhD dissertation (Columbia University, 1996), p. 12.

[21] Scott Burnham, 'Musical and Intellectual Values: Interpreting the History of Tonal Theory', *Current Musicology* 53 (1993), p. 79.

[22] The symbols *T, S, D* refer to Riemann's concepts of tonic, subdominant and dominant respectively. They will be discussed in some detail in the following chapters. Hugo Riemann, 'Das Problem des harmonischen Dualismus', *Neue Zeitschrift für Musik* 51 (1905), pp. 69–70. 'Nicht ganz verständlich ist mir, wie mehrere meiner Theorie näher stehende Männer in der Einführung der Funktionsbezeichnung (*T S D* etc.) etwas wie einen Rückzug vom Boden des harmonischen Dualismus haben erblicken können ... Ich stehe heute noch auf demselben Standpunkte wie vor 30 Jahren; nur habe ich mich endlich ganz von der Begründung der Prinzipien der Harmonie durch die akustischen Phänomene freigemacht und die eigentlichen Wurzeln des Dualismus freigelegt.'

[23] Carl Dahlhaus rejects harmonic dualism in a number of articles on Hugo Riemann, which will be revisited particularly in Chapters 1 and 2. Even Elmar Seidel, who is usually Riemann's stout supporter, has to concede after an extended apologia for Riemann's theory of harmony, in 'Die Harmonielehre Hugo Riemanns', in Martin Vogel, ed., *Studien zur Musiktheorie des neunzehnten Jahrhunderts* (Regensburg: Gustav Bosse, 1966), pp. 91–2, that harmonic dualism is unnecessary and should have been discarded from the theoretical body. Recently, Henry Klumpenhouwer has revisited the Belinfante/ Dahlhaus criticism and has suggested an alternative interpretation that reconciles Riemann's harmonic dualism with his theory of function. See his 'Structural Relations between Riemann's Function Theory and his Dualism', unpublished manuscript. I am grateful to Professor Klumpenhouwer for making this paper available to me.

of scholars in imperial Germany from the late nineteenth century to the First World War – some of them no less than the founding fathers of the discipline – were so fundamentally deceived that they believed in an idea that was not only counter-intuitive but also patently and demonstrably wrong?

This vast discrepancy between the position of Riemann's musical thought in his own age and ours poses a problem. This is not simply a problem of music theory that would be hermetically sealed off in its own discursive space. On the contrary, since harmonic dualism is at the conceptual heart of Hugo Riemann's all-embracing musicological enquiry, its significance spills over into numerous other areas of musicological endeavour. To reformulate our question above: what would have been at stake for Riemann in giving up his doctrine of harmonic dualism, given that we know his system of harmonic function would not have suffered further damage? The answer to this question lies not in narrow music-theoretical concerns but rather leads us towards the wider-ranging consequences of his all-embracing musical thought.

Given that much of Riemann's musical thought was guided by the question *How do we hear music?* – to quote the title of his lectures on aesthetics again, the matter would seem to be further complicated: we can say with some degree of certainty that we do not hear minor triads upside-down, as harmonic dualism posited. Nor should we imagine that many nineteenth-century listeners would have done so. Even Riemann proceeds surprisingly gingerly on the question of how minor chords should actually be heard – a discussion of harmonic dualism is conspicuously absent from *Wie hören wir Musik?* However, in connection with issues of musical hearing, the problem of harmonic dualism can be relocated in the social construction of musical listening. The central question for Riemann's harmonic dualism, as we shall see, was not so much about how we *do* hear music. Rather, as Chapter 3 will examine, he exhibited a utopian concern with how we *ought* to hear music, and conversely, he argues that musical compositions ought to comply with harmonic dualism, even though the existing repertoire does not do so, or does so only partly. On this level, Riemann's musical thought touches aspects that merge epistemological and cognitive concerns with aesthetic ones: his musical thought becomes an aesthetic yardstick for past composers and an ethical guideline for composers of the present and the future.

This implicit 'ought' – in other words, the relentless normativity of Riemann's musical thought – is simply the flipside of his systematic and essentialising approach to music. These concerns combine in a notion of self-assumed responsibility of the principles of music theory (in its aesthetic and practical aspects) towards musical composition, as explored in Chapter 2. The constraints that his musical thought can have on musical

production are brought to the fore in a rare criticism of Riemann at the beginning of the twentieth century:

> He intensely studied older works, took measurements from left to right, from top to bottom, distilled the products in all sorts of aesthetic test tubes, separated, calculated, compared, divided, subtracted, cubed, cohobated, until he had happily found all the *ur*-elements of music. Now from this he construed rules, climbed on top of the mountain like Moses and began: 'Thou shalt –' But the first attempt had already missed the goal. Riemann forgot that one must never ask: 'What ought the artist to do?' but rather: 'What does he intend to do?' and 'Does he possess the artistic power to actualise this intent?' Riemann also forgot that norms in art are pointless, since they cannot be enforced.[24]

For Riemann, his rigorous musical thought might have formulated normative rules for all music, which he hoped to use as an aesthetic yardstick. The critic here, by contrast, considers it a stick with which to beat composers. The criticism points to a clear tension, a power struggle between, on the one hand, Riemann's musical thought – and by extension, the academic institution of musicology – and on the other, practising composers. No matter which position we side with, the example shows clearly the effects of Riemann's effort to combine normative rules of music theory with documents from the history of music, to arrive at the *ur*-components of music. The criticism goes right to the heart of the matter: what was at stake was no less than the definition of music, and the responsibility that academic musicology took in this matter, whether the composer agreed with it or not.

II

The famous tale of the public break between Riemann and his master pupil Max Reger in 1907 clearly belongs here, and should be briefly recapitulated, as it can serve to introduce some of the issues that will occupy us throughout the book. As a seventeen-year-old, Reger had begun

---

[24] Ferdinand Scherber, 'Degeneration und Regeneration', *Neue Musikzeitung* 29 (1908), p. 235. Reprinted in Susanne Shigihara, ed., *'Die Konfusion in der Musik': Felix Draesekes Kampfschrift von 1906 und die Folgen* (Bonn: Gudrun Schröder, 1990), p. 364. 'Er studierte mit heißem Bemühen ältere Werke, nahm ihnen Maß von links nach rechts, von oben nach unten, destillierte die Produkte in allen ästhetischen Retorten, schied, rechnete, verglich, dividierte, subtrahierte, kubierte, kohobierte, bis er die Urformen fröhlich beisammen hatte. Nun konstruierte er Regeln daraus, stieg auf den Berg wie Moses und begann: "Du sollst –". Doch der erste Schlag war schon daneben gehauen. Riemann vergaß, daß man nie fragen darf: Was soll der Künstler? sondern: Was will er? und: Hat er die künstlerische Kraft, seinen Willen zu verwirklichen? Riemann vergaß auch, daß Normen in der Kunst keinen Sinn haben, weil sie nicht durchsetzbar sind.' (Scherber's critique of Riemann parodies Goethe's *Faust*.)

composition lessons with Riemann in 1890.[25] Even before his arrival at the Riemanns' household, Reger knew Riemann's theories inside out; it is probably not an exaggeration to claim that Riemann was very much a father figure for the adolescent composer. But in return, Reger's brilliance also had a strong effect on his teacher: Riemann believed he had found a composer of outstanding talent who would promote his ideas of music and continue to put them into practice.

While Riemann's family was evidently greatly relieved when Reger left their household in 1895 in the aftermath of an argument with Riemann's wife Elisabeth, Riemann himself continued to support and admire his protégé. Even ten years later, he still enthused about his former pupil, though with the caveat, common in Riemann's writing, of not transgressing the boundaries set out by his musical thought. Thus he wrote in the sixth edition of his *Musiklexikon* in 1905, in an entry on Reger that still sounds very much like a personal address to his former student:

> The power of his imagination is so rich that one can only wish him to be guided by conscious self-restriction in the use of artistic means, and not by the deliberate attempt to outstrip his predecessors. This is in order that he be made the master who continues the series of the great composers.[26]

It gradually turned out that Riemann's hopes were not to be realised. It is difficult to date the beginnings of the rift between Riemann and his pupil, but it may well have preceded the public break of 1907, which occurred apropos a debate about the state of musical composition. Riemann had written a devastating critique of contemporary music entitled 'Degeneration und Regeneration in der Musik', and expressed genuine surprise when he found that Reger – whose name had not been mentioned by Riemann in that article at all – publicly denounced his former teacher and sided with the 'degenerate' composers. That was definitely the end of any relationship between Riemann and Reger. Compare the previous entry with that published in the next edition of the *Musiklexikon*, two years after the public éclat:

---

[25] The theoretical relationship between Riemann and Reger has been explored by Gerhard Sievers, *Die Grundlagen Hugo Riemanns bei Max Reger*, Dr. phil. dissertation (University of Hamburg, 1949), and 'Max Regers Kompositionen in ihrem Verhältnis zu der Theorie Hugo Riemanns', *Die Musikforschung* 3 (1950), pp. 212–23, and more recently by Petra Zimmermann, '"Erlaubt sich der Komponist einen üblen Scherz?": Fragen an Max Regers Klavierlied *Ein Drängen* (Op. 97, Nr. 3)', *Jahrbuch des Staatlichen Instituts für Musikforschung Preußischer Kulturbesitz* 1999, pp. 137–52.

[26] Riemann, *Musiklexikon* 6th edn (Leipzig: Max Hesse, 1905), p. 1073. 'Seine Erfindungskraft ist so reich, daß nur bewußte Beschränkung im Gebrauche der Kunstmittel, nicht aber absichtliche Überbietung seiner Vorgänger ihm als leitendes Schaffensprinzip zu wünschen ist, um aus ihm den Meister zu machen, der die Reihe der Großen fortsetzt.'

Example 1a Opening of Max Reger's 'Ein Drängen', Op. 97, no. 3.

As early as his first unpublished compositions, Reger already displayed a tendency to extreme complexity and prolixity of the technical apparatus so that his artistic development would have had to be one going in the opposite direction as that of, say, Wagner – one in which his imagination is firmly straddled so as progressively to purify it. Instead, he allowed himself to be influenced by tendencies *vis-à-vis* which contemporary criticism has lost all respect, and consciously heaps one ultimate foolhardy harmonic progression and arbitrary modulation upon the next. He does that in such a fashion as to make it impossible for listeners to follow his music empathetically . . . All too often the deliberate negation of plain naturalness in his simpler pieces and songs appears repugnant. For the continuous waste of the strongest means of expression quickly dulls their effect, and finally even overabundance turns into annoying stereotype and mannerism.[27]

Finally, some four years later, Reger was the target of a further broadside. In an epilogue to his epic *Große Kompositionslehre*, Riemann severely reprimanded the composer for writing the song 'Ein Drängen', Op. 97, no. 3, in wrong and confused harmonies, some of which are reproduced here in Example 1a. Example 1b shows how Riemann 'corrected' these harmonies so that they make sense in a single key. These corrections reveal that the harmonies essentially outline an arpeggiated F# major triad, mostly preceded by applied diminished-seventh chords.

---

[27] Riemann, *Musiklexikon*, 7th edn (Leipzig: Max Hesse, 1909), p. 1151. 'R[eger] zeigt bereits in seinen (nicht veröffentlichten) ersten Kompositionen Neigung zur äußersten Komplikation und zur Überladung des technischen Apparates, so daß seine Entwicklung notwendigerweise eine e. z. B. der Wagners gegensätzliche hätte werden müssen, eine durch strenge Zügelung seine Phantasie fortschreitende Abklärung. Statt dessen hat er sich durch Strömungen, denen gegenüber die zeitgenössische Kritik alle Haltung verloren hat, in gegenteiliger Richtung beeinflussen lassen und häuft bewußt die letzten harmonischen Wagnisse und modulatorischen Willkürlichkeiten in einer Weise, welche dem Hörer das Miterleben zur Unmöglichkeit macht . . . Dagegen wirkt in kleinen einfachen Stücken und Liedern das absichtliche Verneinen der schlichten Natürlichkeit allzu oft geradezu abstoßend. Dabei stumpft die fortgesetzte Verschwendung der stärksten Ausdrucksmittel deren Wirkung schnell ab und erscheint schließlich doch auch der Überreichtum als lästige stereotype Manier.'

Example 1b Reger's song in Riemann's 'corrected' version, from
Große Kompositionslehre, vol. 3.

   The underlying tonal sense in the sounding piece is very clear, but
the enharmonic notation obfuscates the harmonic relations in notation.
Riemann took Reger severely to task for this lack of clarity.

Even a dilettante who has not learned anything would be protected by his
musical instincts from writing such a heap of wrongly spelled notes... However,
if Reger writes like this... one has to ask: what does this mean? Is the composer
making a bad joke? Is he trying to mystify, to hide artificially what he's actually
doing? Or is he pretending to be a dilettante? Or does that mean the renunciation
of our way of thinking and reading music?[28]

In this extraordinary moment of unleashed rage, Riemann of course
suspected the answer to his barrage of questions: his real fear must
have been that the final one be answered in the affirmative.
   For many readers at the time, it may have seemed churlish that
Riemann would conclude a three-volume composition treatise, in many
ways the monumental summation of the practical aspects of his musical thought, on this bitter note, but for Riemann there was too much
at stake: Reger's disorderly music threatened his understanding of the
'*ur*-elements of music', his theoretical and aesthetic principles and
finally the continuous course of music history. Ultimately, Riemann's
notion of responsibility demanded that where musical composition and
musicological knowledge were at odds with each other, musicology had
to keep the upper hand. In other words, Reger's dangerous example
had to be exorcised.

---

[28] Riemann, *Große Kompositionslehre* (Stuttgart: W. Spemann, 1913), vol. 3, p. 236. 'Selbst
einen Dilettanten, der nichts gelernt hat, würde sein harmonischer Instinkt vor einer
solchen Häufung falsch geschriebener Noten bewahren... Wenn aber ein Reger so
schreibt,... so muß man doch fragen, was soll das heißen? Erlaubt sich der Komponist
einen üblen Scherz? Will er mystifizieren, künstlich verbergen, was er eigentlich macht,
oder heuchelt er Dilettantismus? Oder bedeutet das die Absage an unsere Art, Musik
zu denken und zu lesen?'

The example of Riemann's treatment of Reger is perhaps the most complete application of virtually all aspects of his musical thought – theoretical, aesthetic and historical – into critical practice, and can give us an initial idea of the consequences of the purported task of musicology – and its power struggle with musical composition. It also suggests that, despite Riemann's universalising and scientific aspirations, his musical thought was on one level thoroughly determined by the music of his own time, which he in turn tried to control.

In the final analysis, this notion of responsibility, and Riemann's musical 'ought', will highlight the tensions in the intersections between music theory and music history, between harmonic potential and compositional permissibility, indeed between nature and nation, in his attempts to channel the wider cultural significance of music. The investigation of the ways in which this responsibility manifests itself in the guise of harmonic dualism will gradually reveal the interactions between apparently narrowly focused music-theoretical issues on the one hand, and increasingly broad cultural concerns on the other. At the same time, it is little surprising that Riemann constantly felt beleaguered by various kinds of threats to the validity of his musical thought.

In this sense, we can indeed follow Einstein's advice that in order to 'understand him fully, one must also know him fully' in his theoretical and historical aspects. From its most fundamental technical aspects, encapsulated by the doctrine of harmonic dualism, to its broadest consequences – the looming end of music history – we can then follow Riemann's institutionally enshrined vision of what music was – or rather, what it ought to have been – in imperial Germany from the late nineteenth century to the First World War, in the birth hour of academic musicology.

1

Hugo Riemann's moonshine experiment

During a silent night in 1875, the young musicologist Hugo Riemann struck a key on his grand piano. He was listening for undertones, which he believed to exist in the sound wave.[1] His nocturnal experiment seemed successful – his aural experience confirmed his experimental hypothesis. These undertones, he would explain later, relate to one sounded tone exactly in the manner of the harmonic or overtone series but extending in the opposite direction. As Example 1.1 shows, where the overtone series extends above a given note (in this case, C two octaves below middle C), the undertone series extends below it (in this case, C two octaves above middle C), in the same integer ratios, to form its exact complement. In hearing these undertones, Riemann believed he had found the natural basis for the minor triad.

Since he discovered the works of the physicist-cum-music theorist Arthur von Oettingen in 1869, the young researcher had felt an affinity to the music-theoretical approach that became known as harmonic dualism, which explained the minor triad as the polar opposite of the major triad. Starting from the observation that both major and minor triads contain a perfect fifth and a major third, the dualists explained the major triad upwards from the bottom, and the minor down from the top. In this way, the minor triad is conceptualised as the exact inversion of the major. The F minor triad in Example 1.1 would therefore be named after its top note C; Riemann would call this triad 'under C', written °c.

Riemann's approach was more extreme than that of other dualists in that he built a complete musical system on the basis of the acoustical undertones that he had identified in his experiment. When Riemann's contention that the undertones are audible was not confirmed by others, he fiercely defended his position:

---

[1] The relevant entries from the *Musiklexikon* on the concept of 'undertone series' and other specific terms of Riemann's theoretical apparatus can be found in the glossary.

15

Example 1.1 Overtone and undertone series with pertinent triads: while the major triad is justified by the overtone series, the upside-down undertone series aims to legitimise the minor triad in equivalent terms.

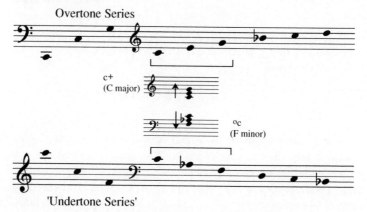

Overtone Series

c+
(C major)

°c
(F minor)

'Undertone Series'

However this may be, and if all the authorities in the world appeared and said: 'We cannot hear anything', I would still have to say: 'I can hear something, something very distinct.'[2]

Several authorities did in fact appear in due time and reported that they could not replicate Riemann's experiment. Employing a strategy familiar from debates in the natural sciences, Riemann countered by suggesting that the problem did not lie with the observation itself but merely with details in the experimental design.[3] For the precise replication of his experiment, he even recommended his brand of piano – made by Ernst Irmler.[4]

Riemann considered himself a serious natural scientist, or rather the founder of an empirical music aesthetics. By modern scientific standards, however, Riemann's experiment cannot be taken seriously on any account.[5] Dismissed as a scientific contribution, Riemann's moonshine experiment lives on as an anecdote, which has been told and retold

---

[2] Hugo Riemann, *Musikalische Syntaxis* (Leipzig: Breitkopf und Härtel, 1877; reprint Niederwalluf: Dr. Martin Sändig, 1971), p. 121. 'Wie dem auch sei und wenn alle Autoritäten der Welt auftreten und sagen "wir hören nichts", so muss ich ihnen doch sagen: "ich höre etwas und zwar etwas sehr deutliches".'

[3] This strategy is commonly found in post-Newtonian experimental science. The historian of science Simon Schaffer, for instance, explores how Newton's optical theory hinged on the make of the prism. See his 'Glass Works', in I. Bernhard Cohen and Richard S. Westfall, eds., *Newton: Texts, Backgrounds, Commentaries* (New York: Norton, 1995), pp. 202–17.

[4] Riemann, *Musikalische Syntaxis*, p. 121.

[5] The only sympathetic treatment of this episode can be found in Hans Peter Reinecke, 'Hugo Riemanns Beobachtung von "Divisionstönen" und die neueren Anschauungen

16

countless times in music theory classes. The almost endearing qualities of this old chestnut are punctuated by Riemann's scientific zeal to prove and defend what was evidently a lost cause. The moral of the anecdote in the music theory classroom is that today we know better: Riemann's observation of audible undertones has been refuted; acoustical undertones simply do not exist in the sound wave. Along with this scientific certainty, Riemann's harmonic dualism is completely discredited in current thought.

However, it is easy to forget that outside the theory classroom the anecdote has a different ending: Riemann's theory of harmony, which, as he insisted, was founded on this notion of harmonic dualism, went on to be the institutionally accepted doctrine in German musicology well into the twentieth century. His theory of harmonic function was an international success, and was translated into several European languages within a decade of its inception: his chief harmony tutor, *Vereinfachte Harmonielehre* (*Harmony Simplified*) of 1893, which went into its second edition in 1903, was also issued in English (1896), Russian (1896, second edition 1901), and French (1899); the third edition of his *Handbuch der Harmonielehre* (*Handbook of Harmony*) of 1898 was translated into French (1902) and Italian (1906). It would seem surprising – if not indeed a glaring paradox of history – that in spite of this evidently false notion of harmonic dualism, which he asserted was at the heart of his writings on harmony, Riemann was to become the most important German musicologist of his age.

It almost seems as if the initial anecdote, which continues to haunt the history of music theory, resonates with a sense of embarrassment that the establishment could be deceived so fundamentally. The image of Riemann hearing undertones has become a derisory emblem of theoretical hermeticism, coupled with a level of wrong-headedness that is so much beyond our comprehension that ridiculing the approach seems to be the only way to cope with the sheer absurdity of the concept of harmonic dualism. As one twentieth-century commentator puts it: 'One turns a man on his head and out comes a woman – *voilà!*'[6]

This said, it would be wrong to believe that critical voices did not exist during Riemann's lifetime. Witness the following criticism dating

---

zur Tonhöhenwahrnehmung', in Wilfried Brennecke and Hans Haase, eds., *Hans Albrecht in Memoriam* (Kassel: Bärenreiter, 1962), pp. 232–41. Reinecke points out that what Riemann believed to be undertones were in fact combination tones, but concedes – as a consolation prize, as it were – that Riemann's ability to hear these with the 'naked ear' means that his perceptive powers must have been extraordinary.

[6] R. Stein, cited in Martin Vogel, 'Arthur v. Oettingen und der harmonische Dualismus', in *Beiträge zur Musiktheorie des neunzehnten Jahrhunderts*, ed. Martin Vogel (Regensburg: Gustav Bosse, 1966), p. 132. 'Man stelle einen Mann auf den Kopf, so ist es ein Weib. Voilà.'

from 1878, the year after the publication of Riemann's first treatise on harmony, *Musikalische Syntaxis*:

One is trying to force Nature to sound undertones, which cannot exist according to the laws of mechanics, and the most recent dualist Dr Hugo Riemann tells us that he and nobody else, save perhaps for Aristotle two thousand years ago, has heard these undertones, which alone are supposed to explain the consonance of the minor triad.[7]

Comments such as this one correspond to the currently prevalent view of harmonic dualism and testify that even in Riemann's own time, the dualistic approach was not without problems.[8] However, we must take care not to overemphasise the significance of such statements: they would seem to ring louder because we believe we can hear the voice of truth in them. Or, to put it in historical terms, their argumentative strength is only validated retrospectively, from our present position. We are far more susceptible to voices rejecting harmonic dualism than those upholding it because they reconfirm what we ourselves believe or would like to hear. The balance is tilted against dualism. However, as Riemann's stature in nineteenth-century musicology suggests, his own age judged differently.[9] In the same spirit, one reads again and again statements such as this one by a reviewer who wrote in 1896: 'One must be interested in what he writes, whether one agrees with his views or not.'[10] In other words, Riemann had become a musicological institution.

This is where our investigation begins. We should ask in this 'archaeological dig' how harmonic dualism became possible, and what

---

[7] Karl von Schafhäutl, 'Moll und Dur', in *Allgemeine Musikalische Zeitung* 13 (1878), col. 90. 'Man [d.i. die Dualisten] will die Natur dazu zwingen, Untertöne hören zu lassen, die nach mechanischen Gesetzen nicht existiren können, und der neueste Dualist Dr Hugo Riemann erzählt uns, dass er und sonst Niemand, als vielleicht Aristoteles allein vor 2000 Jahren, diese Untertöne, welche allein die Mollconsonanz erklären können, gehört habe.' (Schafhäutl is here referring to the concluding remark in Riemann's *Musikalische Syntaxis*.)

[8] A case in point would be Georg Capellen, who attacked Riemann's harmonic dualism in an extended, highly polemical, serialised article, 'Die Unmöglichkeit und Überflüssigkeit der dualistischen Molltheorie Riemann's', *Neue Zeitschrift für Musik* 68 (1901), pp. 529–31, 541–3, 553–5, 569–72, 585–7, 601–3, 617–19. Riemann's riposte, 'Das Problem des harmonischen Dualismus', published in the same journal four years later, makes reference to Capellen, but carefully avoids all mention of the article. This tactic of silencing one's opponents by ignoring them can also be observed in a similar polemic with Bernhard Ziehn. See Michael Arntz, *Hugo Riemann (1849–1919): Leben, Werk und Wirkung* (Cologne: Concerto-Verlag, 1999), pp. 260–5.

[9] Arntz, *Hugo Riemann*, pp. 179–300, examines the gradual establishment of Riemann's writings in the German institutions in some detail.

[10] Otto Taubmann, review of Riemann's *Präludien und Studien*, *Allgemeine Musikzeitung* 23 (1896), pp. 671–2. See also Arntz, *Hugo Riemann*, p. 268.

brought it to the fore, by considering the factors that lent the idea appeal and persuasive power. The guiding questions can be formulated quite simply: how could the concept of harmonic dualism, which seems so patently wrong to us, have been patently right in the later nineteenth century? What made this ostensibly absurd idea so convincing in Riemann's own age?

One post-war musicologist, Martin Vogel, has attempted an explanation by suggesting that all 'monists' of the period – that is, music theorists who explained major and minor triads in the conventional way, bottom-up – were intellectual lightweights.[11] However, the idea that dualism came to the fore by default, so to speak, confuses cause and effect: even if the matter could be solved by simple reference to the intellectual prowess of the individual theorists, it would still beg the question of why the more intelligent theorists at the time all favoured harmonic dualism. This question, inevitably, moves the argument away from individual minds, and towards the modalities of the discourse about harmonic dualism. On this level of enquiry, questions of legitimation and institutional authority come to the fore. For while the objections to harmonic dualism during Riemann's lifetime were in principle as obvious as they are now, his own high-ranking position within the musicological establishment suggests that the discursively encoded epistemologies at the time favoured the idea of harmonic dualism. The central question must therefore be: what institutional factors privileged the dualistic approach in nineteenth-century Germany? What was it that put harmonic dualism 'in the right'?

I

In the mid-nineteenth century, at the beginning of Riemann's career, the question of what music theory had to do to be 'in the right' was quite easy to answer: it had to be scientific.[12] Riemann clearly recognised this need: not only can we gauge this by his experiment where he claimed to be able to hear the undertones, but also because he was explicit about the need to establish music theory on a scientific basis. In a letter Riemann wrote to the idol of his youth, Franz Liszt, in 1879, he expressed his creed:

---

[11] Vogel, 'Arthur v. Oettingen und der harmonische Dualismus', p. 131.

[12] David Cahan, 'Helmholtz and the Civilizing Power of Science', in *Hermann von Helmholtz and the Foundations of Nineteenth-Century Science* (Berkeley and Los Angeles: University of California Press, 1993), p. 582. I also take the expression 'in the right' from there, although the more Foucauldian sense in which I use it here takes its cue from Georges Canguilhem.

Music theory belongs among the natural sciences, in the sense that art is nature; music theory would have a right to exist even if it only fulfilled the single purpose of proving the immanent law-abiding order of artistic creation.[13]

Riemann's aesthetic views might raise some eyebrows in this unreflected equation of art and nature. However, such scientific approaches to aesthetics and mimesis were in no way out of line with the general trends of later nineteenth-century aesthetic thought.[14] In particular, Theodor Fechner's psycho-physical aesthetics proved popular in the circles around Riemann – his work also provides the basis for the faith in the symmetrical principles on which harmonic dualism is based.[15] What is more, Riemann recognised that in order for music theory to be taken seriously, if it wanted to say anything authoritative about music at all, it had to partake of the prestige that the natural sciences enjoyed.

However, at the same time, the natural sciences were also at the core of Riemann's worry, for the 'immanent law-abiding order of artistic creation' that he found at the core of his enquiry had come under threat from precisely that direction. No less a figure than Hermann von Helmholtz, the most famous German physicist and physiologist of his time, had also written his own work of music theory – *Die Lehre von den Tonempfindungen* (*On the Sensations of Tone*) of 1863 – which approached harmony from the perspective of scientific principles. On the basis of physical measurements, taking into account acoustical phenomena such as the clashes between upper harmonics and the beatings of summation tones, Helmholtz had pronounced minor harmonies 'obscurely harmonious', 'ambiguous' and acoustically impure, and concluded that they must count as inferior to major harmonies.[16]

---

[13] La Mara (pseud. Maria Lipsius), *Briefe hervorragender Zeitgenossen an Franz Liszt* (Leipzig: Breitkopf und Härtel, 1904), vol. 3, p. 341. 'In diesem Sinne gehört die Musiktheorie unter die Naturwissenschaften, soweit nämlich die Kunst Natur ist; sie würde eine Existenzberechtigung haben, auch wenn sie nur den einen Zweck verfolgte, die immanente Gesetzmäßigkeit des künstlerischen Schaffens nachzuweisen.' See also Willibald Gurlitt, 'Hugo Riemann (1849–1919)' in *Veröffentlichungen der Akademie der Wissenschaften und der Literatur, Mainz: Abhandlungen der geistes- und sozialwissenschaftlichen Klasse* 25 (1950), p. 1875.

[14] See for instance, Paul Moos's retrospective survey of music aesthetics, first published in 1901, *Philosophie der Musik*, 2nd edn (reprint Hildesheim: Georg Olms, 1975), pp. 526–47, and Bojan Bujić, ed., *Music in European Thought 1851–1912* (Cambridge: Cambridge University Press, 1988), pp. 275–304.

[15] Gustav Theodor Fechner, Elemente der Psychophysik, 2 vols. (Leipzig: Breitkopf und Härtel, 1860), and *Vorschule der Aesthetik*, 2nd edn (Leipzig: Breitkopf und Härtel, 1897), pp. 62–5. On Fechner's psycho-physical parallelism, see Katherine Arens, *Structures of Knowing: Psychologies of the Nineteenth Century* (Dordrecht: Klüver, 1989), pp. 107–14.

[16] Hermann von Helmholtz, *On the Sensations of Tone*, trans. Alexander J. Ellis (London, 1885; reprint New York: Dover, 1954), pp. 299–300.

Helmholtz was by no means the first to declare the minor harmony a lesser or impure version of the major harmony, but because of his authority as a scientist of rank, his judgement appeared indisputable. He wrote:

This assertion that the minor system is much less consistent than the major will be combated by many modern musicians, just as they have contested the assertion already made by me, and by other physicists before me, that minor triads are generally inferior in harmoniousness to major triads. There are many eager assurances of the contrary in recent books on the theory of harmony.[17]

Considering Helmholtz's work, in particular the last sentence quoted, we can begin to understand the dilemma of nineteenth-century music theory: the aesthetic postulate that major and minor should occupy an equivalent position in Western music is sharply contradicted by the experimental findings of the likes of Helmholtz. Helmholtz regretted this mismatch, but his scientific facts appeared unequivocal. In fact, he added a discussion reappraising the minor mode in light of its acoustical imperfections, which sounds somewhat like a consolation prize:

But I am by no means of the opinion that this character depreciates the minor system. The major mode is ... quite unsuited to indistinct, obscure, unformed frames of mind, or for the expression of the dismal, the dreary, the enigmatic, the mysterious, the rude, and whatever offends against artistic beauty; – and it is precisely for these that we require the minor mode, with its veiled harmonious- ness, its changeable scale, its ready modulation, and less intelligible basis of construction. The major mode would be an unsuitable form for such purposes, and hence the minor mode has its own proper artistic justification as a separate system.[18]

But a 'justification as a separate system' is precisely what the minor mode did not obtain from Helmholtz. Just as the acoustical inferiority of the minor triad was explained – with a barrage of feminising adjectives – by its dependency on the acoustical *Klang* (sonority), which corresponds to the major triad, so the aesthetic effects of the minor mode, too, depend on what the major mode is capable of signifying. The minor mode is only of aesthetic use for that which is excluded by the major mode. Both acoustically and aesthetically, the minor system remains fundamentally no more than a failed major mode.

What is more, since the scientific prestige of Helmholtz's work auto- matically put him 'in the right', the only way to refute this judgement of science was to apply the same principles, to beat science with its own weapons. Riemann's experiment was designed to remedy this mismatch and to bring scientific observation in line with aesthetic postulates. To put it bluntly, if nature was not in a position to justify our aesthetic sense,

---

[17] Ibid., p. 301.   [18] Ibid., p. 302.

Example 1.2 Oettingen explains his principles of tonicity and phonicity by means of overtones.

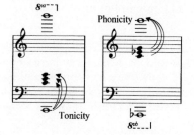

nature was wrong and had to be changed. Nature *ought* to work as music demands it, in order to satisfy Riemann's aesthetic requirements.

These aesthetic requirements were met by the idea of harmonic dualism, as it had been espoused by two other German nineteenth-century music theorists, Moritz Hauptmann and Arthur von Oettingen (who had in fact coined the term 'harmonic dualism').[19] However, both Hauptmann and Oettingen had taken a somewhat different approach from Riemann in the formulation of their theoretical ideas. To understand the considerable debate surrounding harmonic dualism, we have to examine briefly what those other theorists had to say on the matter of major and minor triads.

Oettingen, whose main field was physics, tackled Helmholtz head-on: he used the same kind of evidence, namely acoustical overtones, but drew radically different conclusions. He postulated corresponding degrees of chordal consonance for major and minor triads. Oettingen's argument was based on the observation, as the second part of Example 1.2 shows, that all three constituents of the minor triad did share certain overtones.[20] (Helmholtz had also noted this, but only in Oettingen's

---

[19] This story has been retold numerous times, beginning with Richard Münnich, 'Von [der] Entwicklung der Riemannschen Harmonielehre und ihrem Verhältnis zu Oettingen und Stumpf', in Carl Mennicke, ed., *Riemann-Festschrift* (Leipzig: Max Hesse, 1909), pp. 60–76. Modern discussions can be found in Suzannah Clark, 'From Nature to Logic in Schubert's Instrumental Music', PhD dissertation (Princeton University, 1997); Daniel Harrison, *Harmonic Function in Chromatic Music* (Chicago and London: University of Chicago Press, 1994); Dale A. Jorgenson, 'A Résumé of Harmonic Dualism', *Music and Letters* 44 (1963), pp. 31–42; Henry Klumpenhouwer, 'Dualistic Tonal Space and Transformation in Nineteenth-Century Musical Thought', in Thomas Christensen, ed., *The Cambridge History of Western Music Theory* (Cambridge: Cambridge University Press, 2002), pp. 456–76; David Kopp, 'A Comprehensive Theory of Chromatic Mediant Relations in Mid-Nineteenth-Century Music', PhD dissertation (Brandeis University, 1995), and William C. Mickelsen, *Hugo Riemann's Theory of Harmony and History of Music Theory, Book III* (Lincoln, Nebraska: University of Nebraska Press, 1977).

[20] Arthur von Oettingen, *Harmoniesystem in dualer Entwickelung* (Dorpat: W. Glässer, 1866), p. 32. This music example follows Harrison's very clear representation of Oettingen's

theory did this observation become an important point of his argument.) Oettingen went on to redefine the notion of consonance, declaring the minor triad consonant ('phonically consonant' – *phonisch konsonant* – as he called it) in so far as the lowest of these overtones corresponds harmonically to the sounding minor triad, in this example the G two octaves above.

On this basis, he then set out to reinterpret the major triad: as the first half of Example 1.2 shows, the three constituents of the major triad do also have an overtone in common. However, as it is not consonant with the triad itself, the major triad is defined as dissonant, at least according to Oettingen's 'phonic' criteria. Instead, the constituents of the major triad can in turn all be regarded as partials relating to one and the same fundamental, two octaves below the root – he therefore declared the major triad 'tonically consonant', or *tonisch konsonant*. An equivalent fundamental also exists in the minor example – in this case A♭. However, this fundamental is dissonant with the minor triad above it; the minor triad is therefore considered, correspondingly, to be 'tonically dissonant'.

The dissonant A♭ below the C minor triad corresponds inversely to the dissonant B above the C major triad, just as the C below the C major triad corresponds inversely to the G above the C minor triad. Based on the precise geometrical symmetry of these models, Oettingen concluded that major and minor triads are equivalent insofar as the major triad was phonically dissonant, but tonically consonant, while the minor triad was phonically consonant and tonically dissonant.[21]

Hauptmann, by contrast, whose work preceded that of Helmholtz by a decade, attempted to overcome the hurdle set by natural science by staying clear of argumentation along the lines of acoustics altogether. In the preface of his book *Die Natur der Harmonik und Metrik* (1853), he stated: 'Neither the truth nor the falsehood of the acoustical presuppositions has any further influence upon this theory itself; although in view of the untruth and half-truth of these presuppositions this can only redound to the advantage of the theory.'[22] Instead, Hauptmann sought to discover one single source, one natural principle, with which to explain harmony and metre in its entirety. For this reason, he turned to

---

principles; see Harrison, *Harmonic Function in Chromatic Music*, pp. 244–5. For a recent discussion of Oettingen's music-theoretical views, see Suzannah Clark, 'Seduced by Notation: Oettingen's Topography of the Major-minor System', in Suzannah Clark and Alexander Rehding, eds., *Music Theory and Natural Order from the Renaissance to the Early Twentieth Century* (Cambridge: Cambridge University Press, 2001), pp. 161–80.

[21] Oettingen, *Harmoniesystem in dualer Entwickelung*, p. 45.

[22] Moritz Hauptmann, *Die Natur der Harmonik und Metrik: Zur Theorie der Musik* (Leipzig: Breitkopf und Härtel, 1853); trans. and ed. William E. Heathcote as *The Nature of Harmony and Metre* (reprint New York: Da Capo Press, 1991), p. xxxviii (translation modified).

Example 1.3 Hauptmann's dialectical explanation of the major triad

(I) - (III)
C - e - G
(I)   -   (II)

constructing his theory on the basis of triples of dialectics and quasi-Hegelian idealism, which, for him, were 'second nature'.[23]

The major triad was for Hauptmann the embodiment of the three dialectical moments in the simultaneously sounding elements. Hauptmann postulated that there were only three 'directly intelligible intervals', the octave, the fifth and the (major) third.[24] All other intervals, he contended, were compounds of these three (the minor third, for instance, being the difference between the fifth and the major third). He represented the triad, in Example 1.3, as the product of these intervals in three dialectical steps: the octave (which here appears, at stage (I), as the unison) as the manifestation of unity and identity; the fifth (II), which Hauptmann heard with respect to (I) as a 'hollow' duality, and the synthetic third (III), which re-unites the opposed two components. At the same time, the double designation of (I) indicates that the principal tone of the chord, from which the intervals are reckoned up, is fixed in the pitch C.

Hauptmann regarded 'the minor triad as an inverted major triad',[25] and was quick to translate this symmetrical relationship into dialectical terms without much further explanation, as reproduced in Example 1.4a. In this form, which is the precise inversion of the dialectics of the major triad, the principal tone (C) is located in its fifth, as the double (I) underscores or, in his words, 'as Fifth determining Root and Third'.[26] Hauptmann did, however, present an alternative derivation of the minor triad in accordance with his later statement 'that all harmonic form shapes itself from below upwards',[27] which then, by necessity, results in something that is not the exact inversion of the major triad, as Example 1.4b shows. To preserve his initial axiom of the three directly intelligible intervals, Hauptmann had to assign a prominent role to the

[23] Hauptmann's theory is discussed in detail in Peter Rummenhöller, 'Moritz Hauptmann, der Begründer einer transzendental-dialektischen Musiktheorie', in Martin Vogel, ed., *Beiträge zur Musiktheorie im 19. Jahrhundert* (Regensburg: Gustav Bosse, 1966), pp. 11–36.

[24] Hauptmann, *Nature of Harmony and Metre*, p. 5. This is not the place to concern ourselves with the precise nature and validity of his arguments here, which would require a more detailed discussion of Hegelian and Fichtean dialectics in Germany. For detailed studies of Hauptmann see Peter Rummenhöller, *Moritz Hauptmann als Theoretiker: eine Studie zum erkenntniskritischen Theoriebegriff in der Musik* (Wiesbaden: Breitkopf und Härtel, 1963), and Dale A. Jorgenson, *Moritz Hauptmann of Leipzig* (Lewiston, NY: E. Mellen Press, 1986).

[25] Hauptmann, *Nature of Harmony and Metre*, p. 16.

[26] Ibid., p. 17.   [27] Ibid., p. 102.

Example 1.4a Hauptmann's dialectical explanation of the minor triad as the inverse of the major triad.

(I) - **(II)**
F - a♭ - C
    (I) - **(III)**

Example 1.4b Hauptmann's alternative explanation of the minor triad, bottom-up but no longer dialectical.

(I) - **(II)**
F - a♭ - C
(I) - **(III)**

major third between a♭ and C, whilst ignoring the minor third between F and a♭.[28] The emerging problem is obvious: how can one element of the triad, the C, represent two moments of the dialectic (II and III) at once? It is a dialectical impossibility to locate antithesis and synthesis in the same moment, as the former is supposed to be sublated by the latter. If the two are located in the same moment, the desired dialectical 'identity of identity and non-identity' is not attainable: the structure either becomes a simple contradiction or has had no true opposition in the first place.

Nevertheless, it was paramount for Hauptmann to present the minor triad theoretically as the opposition of the major triad; at the same time, however, he was at pains not to create the impression that the minor triad was actually generated downwards, as Riemann was to argue twenty years on.[29] To bolster the opposition between major and minor without suggesting that minor does in fact function top-down, Hauptmann introduced a metaphor, in which he tried to relate the character of the harmonic mode to its construction:

The minor triad thus being of passive nature, and having its starting-point above (not its most real starting-point, yet that which is determined as unity), and forming from it downwards, there is expressed in it, not upward driving force, but downward drawing weight, dependence in the literal, as well as in the figurative sense of the word. We therefore find in the minor chord the expression

---

[28] The use of small and capital letters, or of dashes above or below letters, in nineteenth-century German music theory signifies a tuning difference (usually of a syntonic comma). These slight differences play no part in this discussion here.

[29] In fact, Riemann regarded Hauptmann's theory as a major breakthrough in the formation of harmonic dualism. Brushing all of Hauptmann's qualms aside, Riemann confidently exclaimed in 'Die Natur der Harmonik', *Waldersees Sammlung musikalischer Vorträge* 4 (1882), p. 181, that Hauptmann's idea 'to regard the minor triad as a major triad put on its head, developed negatively', was 'sensational'. Later on, Riemann's enthusiasm for Hauptmann cooled down considerably; see Peter Rummenhöller, *Musiktheoretisches Denken im 19. Jahrhundert* (Regensburg: Gustav Bosse, 1967), p. 80, n. 11.

for mourning, the hanging boughs of the weeping willow as contrasted with the aspiring arbor vitae.[30]

The choice of metaphor can be read to reflect poignantly Hauptmann's problem: the boughs of the weeping willow hang down, while its root – biologically as well as musically – is still at the bottom, firmly attached to the soil. In the metaphorical realm, Hauptmann was in a position to solve the problem of the minor 'root'. (To be sure, the English term is more suggestive in this respect than its more perfunctory German equivalent, *Grundton*). At the same time, it can hardly be denied that Hauptmann was trying to square the circle. His weeping willow metaphor was consequently adopted happily by later dualists while the ironic ambiguity of the image became – literally and figuratively – uprooted.

II

Given this short overview of Riemann's immediate predecessors, to whose work he made reference repeatedly, it would seem that the contiguous relation between Hauptmann, Oettingen, and Riemann, and their involvement with the same problems, would make for a clear-cut group of nineteenth-century harmonic dualists. However, there is considerable disagreement as to who to count as a dualist – or, indeed, how to define harmonic dualism (which is often a function of the previous question).

There are usually two levels at which harmonic dualism is defined: first, in terms of the conceptual approach to harmony taken, that is, as the 'means of explaining the minor triad in a reverse sense from the explanation of the major triad'.[31] Under this definition, it becomes possible to count a wide range of thinkers as harmonic dualists, who had nothing directly to do with the circles around Riemann, even unlikely figures as Johann Wolfgang von Goethe. Goethe made his 'dualistic' point succinctly by means of a syllogism:

1. Musical practice recognises major and minor as equivalent.
2. The overtone series questions the equality of modes.
3. Therefore the overtone series is insufficient as an explanation for both modes.

---

[30] Hauptmann, *Nature of Harmony and Metre*, p. 17. In the original German this remarkable passage goes: 'In dieser passiven Natur und indem der Molldreiklang, zwar nicht seinen realen, aber seinen zur Einheit bestimmten Ausgangspunkt in der Höhe hat und sich an diesem nach der Tiefe bildet, ist in ihm nicht aufwärts treibende Kraft, sondern herabziehende Schwere, Abhängigkeit, im wörtlichen wie im figürlichen Sinne des Ausdruckes ausgesprochen. Wie in den sinkenden Zweigen der Trauerweide, gegen den strebenden Lebensbaum, finden wir darum auch im Mollaccorde den Ausdruck der Trauer wieder.'

[31] This definition is taken from Jorgenson, 'A Résumé of Harmonic Dualism', p. 31.

Goethe was quite content to conclude that 'Man *belongs* to Nature and he *is* Nature' and to leave the discussion at that.[32] However, in comparison with the approaches to dualism encountered previously, it is notable that Goethe made no attempt to give any detail as to the 'means of explaining' the two triads as opposites – in fact, unlike the circle around Riemann, Goethe's syllogism shows that he had no interest in acoustical arguments at all. At this level of definition, harmonic dualism is therefore perhaps better grasped in terms of the aesthetic postulate that the major and minor modes are equivalent and should consequently be treated as such by theory. The 'means' of explanation is thus better understood as the necessity to argue against the Helmholtzian paradigm, that the minor mode is not a derivative or an inflection of the major mode. As Goethe expressed in a bon mot, 'a Scandinavian theorist could say just as well that the major third was used in place of the minor'.[33] In other words, only if we presuppose the universal validity of acoustical measurements as the basis of musical consonance does it follow that the major triad is somehow 'natural' and less problematic than the minor.

While our first definition of harmonic dualism, on the basis of aesthetic desiderata, is wide-ranging, other critics have tried to define harmonic dualism on the level of methodology. In this second approach those aspects that distinguish the views held by thinkers such as Goethe from those of Riemann, as pointed out above, are considered crucial. In other words, the essence of harmonic dualism is here defined as positing a polarity between major and minor triads, and a methodology that orientates itself by the natural sciences.[34] As a consequence, the group of harmonic dualists becomes very small indeed – to the extent that, in the eyes of some critics, even Hauptmann cannot be counted as a proper harmonic dualist, and should thus not be grouped together with Riemann.[35]

---

[32] Jorgenson, 'A Résumé of Harmonic Dualism', p. 37. For recent commentaries on Goethe's views of music theory, see Dieter Borchmeyer, 'Anwalt der kleinen Terz: Goethe und die Musik', in Thomas Daniel Schlee, ed., *Beethoven, Goethe und Europa: Almanach zum Internationalen Beethovenfest Bonn 1999* (Laaber: Laaber-Verlag, 1999), pp. 41–62; and Thomas Daniel Schlee, 'Zelter hatte doch recht: Parerga zur großen Terz', in ibid., pp. 63–8.

[33] Jorgenson, 'A Résumé of Harmonic Dualism', p. 37.

[34] This definition is put forward, for instance, by Peter Rummenhöller. See his 'Moritz Hauptmann, der Begründer einer transzendental-dialektischen Musiktheorie', pp. 28–31.

[35] It is obvious that such revisionist attempts often go hand in hand with the desire to cleanse particular theorists from the taint of harmonic dualism and rehabilitate them as serious theorists. See Rummenhöller, 'Moritz Hauptmann, der Begründer einer transzendental-dialektischen Musiktheorie'. In a similar vein, Martin Vogel has attempted to separate Oettingen from Riemann, see 'Arthur v. Oettingen und der harmonische Dualismus', p. 107.

It is, however, possible to arrive at a definition of harmonic dualism from a third perspective, which combines aspects from both definitions and links them on the basis of a historical argument. As we have seen above, harmonic dualism, taken at its basic level, is the postulate of theoretical equivalence between the major and minor systems. There is little controversy about this point. Rather, the controversy of harmonic dualism is concerned with its attempt to explain and ground this equivalence. The 'means' that was underlined in the first definition of harmonic dualism becomes crucial with respect to this controversy: it was apparently no problem for a theorist such as Goethe, or the sixteenth-century Gioseffo Zarlino – whom Riemann regarded as the founder of the dualistic tradition – to argue for an equivalent formation of the minor triad. It seems that it is only in the aftermath of Riemann's experiment that harmonic dualism became a problem.

If this is so, one must ask whether it is indeed possible to speak of a dualistic tradition extending further back than the mid-nineteenth century, as the proponents of the first definition – and Riemann himself – would do. As a prominent twentieth-century critic, Carl Dahlhaus implicitly turns to this issue when he devotes an article to the question 'Was Zarlino a dualist?' – and, predictably perhaps, answers it in the negative.[36] Dahlhaus shows how Riemann mistranslated and quoted out of context in order to make Zarlino's theory fit his own ideas and in this way to fashion him into an early proponent of harmonic dualism. However, Dahlhaus goes too far in his zeal to exorcise Zarlino from Riemann's dualistic spell.[37] Although it is true that Zarlino had not read minor triads top-down the way Riemann did, he nevertheless considered the relationship between the two formations that came to be called 'minor and major triads' as symmetrically related:

While the extremes of the fifth are invariable and always in the same ratio... the extremes of the thirds are placed differently within the fifth. I do not mean that such thirds differ in proportion but in location. For... when the major third is below, the harmony is gay, and when it is above, the harmony is sad.[38]

---

[36] Carl Dahlhaus, 'War Zarlino Dualist?', *Die Musikforschung* 10 (1957), pp. 286–90.

[37] Dahlhaus's argument rests on the mathematical basis of Zarlino's harmony, as a rational proportion of no musical or sensual impact, perhaps to counter Riemann's approach to the triad as a musical and conceptual entity. It is interesting to note, however, that in Chapter 31 Zarlino was discussing 'perfect proper harmony', which is defined in Part II, Chapter 12 as a perfect consonance mediated by an inner-part imperfect consonance. The terminology would seem to suggest that this 'perfect' three-part harmony is superior to the 'imperfect' two-part harmony, while the mathematical ratios, conversely, become more complex – or less 'perfect' – in three-part harmony.

[38] Gioseffo Zarlino, *Le istitutioni harmoniche* (Venice, 1573), p. 211; English trans. by Claude V. Palisca and Giulio A. Marco as *The Art of Counterpoint* (New Haven, Conn.: Yale University Press, 1968), pp. 69–70. 'Ma perche gli estremi della Quinta sono invariabili

Ironically, this statement describes precisely the way in which Dahlhaus explains harmonic dualism, namely that 'in major the major third is incorporated at the bottom, in minor at the top, into the fifth'.[39] Dahlhaus argues, however, that Zarlino's last sentence in the above excerpt, on which Riemann's appropriation of Zarlino as a dualist hinges, is of no theoretical consequence. What Zarlino meant to say, Dahlhaus infers, was rather that it is 'not the different positions of the *major* third [that] effects the character difference of the triads, but the difference of the *bottom* third (major or minor)'.[40] However, this 'monistic' reading of Zarlino is clearly as tendentious as Riemann's, for Zarlino did not in fact single out the *bottom* interval at all in this context.[41]

A musical example from Zarlino's *Istitutioni harmoniche*, although it appears in a context unrelated to this particular argument, illustrates how his point might be better understood. Zarlino includes a canon in his work, realised in Example 1.5, which alternates major and minor triads at the beginning of every odd-numbered bar.[42] The polyphonic texture makes it obvious that neither Riemann's dualism, conceptualising minor triads from top to bottom, nor Dahlhaus's 'monism', conceptualising minor triads from bottom to top, are appropriate readings of Zarlino. As Zarlino described above, here it is indeed the position of the major third – to which the minor third is added above or below – that makes all the difference. There are, in other words, viable alternatives to

---

& sempre si pongono contenuti sotto una istessa proportione . . . però gli estremi delle Terze si pongono differenti tra essa Quinta. Non dico però differenti di proportione; ma dico differe[n]ti di luogo; percioche . . . qua[n]do si pone la Terza maggiore nella parte grave, l'Harmonia si fà allegra; & qua[n]do si pone nell'acuto si fà mesta.' Daniel Harrison, too, re-examines Zarlino's alleged dualism in *Harmonic Function in Chromatic Music*, pp. 259–61, and notes that there is one correspondence with Riemann, namely the importance given to the interval of the major third while the minor third is not mentioned as a constituting factor in the minor harmony. Riemann used this quotation in his *Geschichte der Musiktheorie*, 2nd edn (Berlin: Max Hesse, 1921; reprint Hildesheim: Olms, 1990), p. 393.

[39] Dahlhaus, 'War Zarlino Dualist?', p. 287. The rest of Dahlhaus's definition, strangely, refers to Oettingen's dualism, not to Riemann's.

[40] Ibid., p. 290. Emphasis in original.

[41] What Zarlino in fact wrote is more ambiguous: 'Whereas in the first group the major third is often placed beneath the minor, in the second the opposite is true' (*Art of Counterpoint*, p. 21). To be accurate, Zarlino drew on at least three ways of explaining major and minor formations. Besides the one quoted above, he argued that the major third and major sixth are 'lively and cheerful' intervals, while the minor third and minor sixth 'although sweet and smooth, tend to be sad and languid' (p. 21). Further, the major mode is divided harmonically, according to string divisions, while the minor mode is arithmetically divided, the consonances are arranged 'contrary to the nature of the sonorous number' (p. 22).

[42] I first found this canon mentioned in Alan Gosman's 'Rameau and Zarlino: Polemics in the *Traité de l'harmonie*', *Music Theory Spectrum* 22 (2000), pp. 46–7, where it appears in a different context.

Example 1.5 Zarlino's double canon *per inversionem*, from *Istitutioni harmoniche*, vol. 3. The boxes highlight the alternation of the minor third above or below the major third.

Bars 3   5   7   9

Riemann's dualism and Dahlhaus's monism. The implicit assumption on both Riemann's and Dahlhaus's parts, that Zarlino must be either a dualist or a monist, is pure music-theoretical ideology.

In this sense, the very question of whether Zarlino – or any other pre-nineteenth-century music theorist, for that matter – was a dualist actually misses the point. It is, as the sociologist Ernest Gellner

knew, perhaps the one established law in the History of Ideas that 'whatever has been said, has also been said by someone else on an earlier occasion'.[43] So the reply to Dahlhaus's question should be: Zarlino's music theory may indeed have adumbrated some features that became important to Riemann later.[44] Given that all ideas 'are in effect everpresent' – following Gellner's law – the central question is not how Zarlino's theory pre-empted Riemann's but rather how the concept of harmonic dualism should have become a powerful and convincing approach in the nineteenth century.

Nineteenth-century harmonic dualism, then, is qualitatively different from any other outlook on music that seeks to present the minor system as equivalent to the major system: it only became a problematic concept in a particular cultural, intellectual and social constellation. From now on we shall only speak of harmonic dualism with reference to its nineteenth-century proponents. With the exception of Vincent d'Indy (who has occasionally been accused of simply copying Riemann's ideas), this group is exclusively German. Harmonic dualism is marked by self-awareness and by a special effort to find an invincible epistemology. It is no coincidence that the term should have been coined in the nineteenth century, for the very idea of dualism only makes sense in the context of its counterpart, the views of acousticians of Helmholtz's calibre.[45] Prior to this view of music, and the conflicts arising from it, there was no need for a separate tradition of music theory. Harmonic dualism, we could redefine, is the attempt to declare the major and minor modes as natural, in conflict with the scientifically accepted concept of nature at the time. In other words, the problems of dualism lay outside the musicological discourse; they were caused by the standards set by natural science, to which music theory aspired, as Riemann explained in his letter to Liszt quoted above. We can now see from this angle that Hauptmann, who so ferociously reacted against arguments that draw on physical acoustics, was no exception from this: he was by the same token deeply entangled in the debate.

III

What has changed since the nineteenth century? Why did harmonic dualism go out of fashion in the early twentieth century, and become considered 'wrong'? In principle, nothing has changed regarding the gap between aesthetic desiderata and acoustical data. And yet, hardly

---

[43] Ernest Gellner, *Relativism and the Social Sciences* (Cambridge: Cambridge University Press, 1985), p. 9.

[44] See Daniel Harrison, *Harmonic Function in Chromatic Music*, pp. 259–61.

[45] To my knowledge, the sole notable exception to this is Rameau's treatise *Génération harmonique* (Paris, 1737), which will be discussed in Chapter 3.

any living theorist would consider harmonic dualism a viable solution to this problem. The difference is simply that while for Riemann the issue of closing this gap was at the very heart of his music-theoretical endeavour, we have become used to ignoring the problem. While the clashes between overtones and beatings of summation tones are still the same as in Helmholtz's day, we have taken the other avenue, and – with few exceptions[46] – tend to disregard acoustical science altogether when talking about major and minor harmonies. With this music-theoretical paradigm shift, however, harmonic dualism became redundant; it became an attempt to answer a question that no longer interests us.

The conclusion that harmonic dualism is historically redundant is markedly different from the initial derisory anecdote of Riemann's moonshine experiment, which held that his failed undertone hypothesis rendered the whole dualistic view untenable. Of course, the aural observations Riemann made during that fateful night were undeniably false, but to what extent does this circumstance actually invalidate his theoretical claims? Given that acoustical data are of virtually no importance to tonal theory in the current age, it would seem strange to dismiss one music theory on the basis of criteria that are not applied to others. (The twentieth-century adaptations of Riemann's theory of harmonic function, most of which operate without the acoustical underlay of dualism, seem to confirm that this is a distinct possibility.[47])

Contrariwise, it might be objected that Riemann brought all this upon himself in this silent night, by setting such 'scientific' standards for himself in the first place. However, at the risk of spoiling the anecdote once and for all by dissecting the punchline in even greater detail, the joke – and along with it the notion of the 'wrongness' of Riemann's theory – thrives on a peculiar twist in the paradigm shift. For while musicology, or rather its epistemological aspect, has moved away from a paradigm based on acoustical science, the acquisition of knowledge in most other areas of society has remained firmly anchored in an unwavering faith in science. It is this double-layered epistemology that makes the joke of the Riemann anecdote and, crucially, stops us from contemplating the issues any further. Once we start rethinking it, however, the certainty with which harmonic dualism is habitually rejected as absolutely 'wrong' would have to give way to a more considered verdict.

What the anecdote does not betray (as it would certainly spoil the punchline) is that Riemann's claim that undertones were audible was

---

[46] Martin Vogel is perhaps the only twentieth-century theorist who proposes an acoustically based kind of harmonic dualism on the basis of Oettingen's theory.

[47] For a survey and study of these post-Riemannian systems of harmonic function, see Renate Imig, *Systeme der Funktionsbezeichnung seit Hugo Riemann* (Düsseldorf: Verlag der Gesellschaft zur Förderung der systematischen Musikwissenschaft, 1971).

only one stage in a number of different attempts to find a foundation in which to ground his dualistic ideas. The precise nature of Riemann's harmonic dualism (and the undertone series) changed throughout his career and was redefined no fewer than four times. First he posited – as a 'small hypothesis' at the outset of his doctoral dissertation – that undertones are generated in the ear, that is to say that the cilia on the basilar membrane swing in places corresponding to simple fractions of the sounding tone which are picked up by auditory nerves.[48] This audacious assertion did not fare well: Riemann's thesis was rejected at the University of Leipzig – the 'small hypothesis' was perhaps a big stumbling block for its acceptance. At the same time, it was probably no great coincidence that Göttingen's famous philosopher Hermann Lotze accepted his thesis. In the commentary on Riemann's dissertation Lotze remarked with good humour:

It is a pity that he (Riemann) has the same trust not only in the pretty experiments of the natural scientist (Helmholtz) but also in the latter's audacious conjectures and his arbitrary psychological assumptions. The actual psychological element of his work is therefore least satisfactory and independent. He even makes rather wasteful use of 'brain oscillations'.[49]

Although Lotze remained sceptical of Riemann's explanations (it would appear from his comments that he did not believe a word of it), he nonetheless let his student pass. For it seems that Riemann's dualistic arguments did strike a sympathetic chord with Lotze in spite of their highly speculative nature. As I shall examine in greater detail in Chapter 3, it was perfectly possible in Lotze's philosophy to build on phenomena that 'ought to' exist but did not.

Riemann's experiment at the grand piano falls into his second phase of harmonic dualism, where he relocated the undertones from the basilar membrane to the sound wave itself; he believed he could hear the undertones objectively.[50] Not dissimilarly from Rameau in *Génération*

---

[48] Riemann, *Über das musikalische Hören*, Dr. phil. dissertation (Göttingen University, 1873), publ. as *Musikalische Logik* (Leipzig: C. F. Kahnt, 1874), p. 6.

[49] Cited in Jacques Handschin, *Der Toncharakter*, intro. Rudolf Stephan (reprint Darmstadt: Wissenschaftliche Buchgesellschaft, 1995), p. 129. 'Zu bedauern ist einigermassen, dass er (Riemann) nicht nur den schönen Experimenten dieses Naturforschers (Helmholtz), sondern auch seinen kühnen Konjekturen und den willkürlichen psychologischen Annahmen desselben ganz gleiches Vertrauen schenkt; das eigentlich psychologische Element seiner Arbeit ist daher am wenigsten befriedigend und selbständig; wird doch sogar von Hirnschwingungen ziemlicher Verbrauch gemacht' (Additions in parentheses by Handschin). Also see Riemann, *Handbuch der Akustik (Musikwissenschaft)* 3rd edn (Berlin: Max Hesse, 1921), p. 93n.; and Gurlitt, 'Hugo Riemann (1849–1919)', pp. 1872–3.

[50] The article, 'Die objective Existenz der Untertöne in der Schallwelle', *Allgemeine deutsche Musikzeitung* 2 (1875), pp. 205–6, 213–15, has an intriguing reception history. The chief summaries of Riemann's works on harmony (by Elmar Seidel, William Mickelsen and Daniel Harrison) refer to it in passing; there is no indication, however, that Seidel has

harmonique a century and a half before him, Riemann believed that 'strings that are not stopped with a mute and which correspond to the undertones of a sounded tone not only vibrate in parts but also in total'.[51] Riemann brushed aside the objection that these total vibrations still remain inaudible simply by claiming that they were only very soft.

After 1891 Riemann changed his argument to a demonstration that the undertones were necessarily inaudible due to acoustical interference between sound waves.[52] This argument provided him with a comfortable position, since he could still claim the nominal existence of the undertones without having to prove their audibility. Finally, after 1905, Riemann agreed to do away with arguments based on undertones altogether, provided that overtones were not used either in the arguments of music theory.[53] With this last stage, where acoustical undertones were no longer necessary as a conceptual crutch,[54] Riemann's theory verged on a new paradigm: the age of psychology was about to supersede the age of acoustics.

IV

One of the puzzling consequences of the position of music theory in modernity – particularly the nineteenth century – is that whilst its principal function is bound up with the legitimacy of musical structures and works, it itself also requires legitimation for the principles it posits. It is notable that the most popular categories of legitimation are those that locate themselves outside the human element.[55] In this way, the limits that music theory imposes on music are alleged not to be capricious but

in fact consulted the article ('Die Harmonielehre Hugo Riemanns', p. 52n.). Mickelsen, *Hugo Riemann's Theory of Harmony and History of Music Theory, Book III* (Lincoln: Nebraska University Press, 1977), pp. 33–5, admits to not having read it but nevertheless proceeds to reconstruct its contents. Harrison, at the end of this line, then only refers to Mickelsen's hypothetical reconstruction, in *Harmonic Function in Chromatic Music*, p. 256.

[51] Riemann, *Musikalische Syntaxis*, p. xiii.

[52] Riemann, *Handbuch der Akustik*, pp. 78–81. See also Chapter 3 below.

[53] Riemann, 'Das Problem des Dualismus', p. 26. An earlier version of this psychology-based argument is presented in the article 'Die Natur der Harmonik'. A tentative step towards relinquishing arguments using undertones can be found in *Handbuch der Akustik*, pp. 93–6.

[54] Just to be sure, however, an explanation that made reference to the acoustical wave was retained by Riemann even in 'Das Problem des harmonischen Dualismus'. See Chapter 3, n. 105 below.

[55] For further information on this vast topic, see Nicholas Cook, 'Epistemologies of Music Theory', in Thomas Christensen, ed., *The Cambridge History of Western Music Theory* (Cambridge: Cambridge University Press, 2002), pp. 78–105; Suzannah Clark and Alexander Rehding, eds., *Music Theory and Natural Order from the Renaissance to the Early*

immutable and incorruptible – or, put more concretely, the limitations are presented as natural, rational or dictated by history. Music theory tries to anchor itself in the extra-musical in this way. Its claims of (and to) legitimacy are thus not perceived as arbitrary but as obeying a higher imperative.

It would be fallacious to assume that music theorists pick and mix these foundations at will. These constructs are not usually adopted self-consciously but are rather dictated by the epistemologies that are institutionally sanctioned at the time of their conception, and in this way they assign music a position within society. This approach questions not only what the legitimising categories of a music theory are but also how they are (re)constructed by the music theory under scrutiny and how they function within it. The questions asked are no longer: 'What does a given theory do, and is what it does correct?', but: 'Why does this theory want its users to think about tonal harmony in this way and not in any other way?'[56] As soon as we accept that the 'wrongness' of harmonic dualism is not an intrinsic quality of the theory but is brought about by a change of paradigm, these continual changes, the perpetual reformulation of the foundational elements of Riemann's theories, the undertone hypothesis can in fact be a very useful tool, aiding us in understanding what made Riemann's theories of harmony the success story that they were in the later nineteenth century.

If we now return from this new position to Riemann sitting at his grand piano that silent night in 1875, the moonshine experiment takes on a different significance. While Hauptmann and Oettingen may be seen to epitomise the two main strands of German *Wissenschaft* in the nineteenth century – the speculative philosopher in the shadow of Hegel on the one hand, and the rigorous natural scientist on the other – Riemann synthesised features from both of them. In this sense, when Riemann heard fictitious undertones ringing through the night, as we shall see over the next four chapters, what he was in fact doing was to accomplish the peculiar wedding of speculative philosophy and 'hard' natural science that characterised the epistemology of Wilhelmine Germany.

Twentieth Century (Cambridge: Cambridge University Press, 2001); Carl Dahlhaus, *Die Musiktheorie im 18. und 19. Jahrhundert; Erster Teil: Grundzüge einer Systematik* (Darmstadt: Wissenschaftliche Buchgesellschaft, 1984), pp. 34–63; and Rudolf Heinz, *Geschichtsbegriff und Wissenschaftscharakter in der Musikwissenschaft in der zweiten Hälfte des 19. Jahrhunderts* (Regensburg: Gustav Bosse, 1968).

[56] Scott Burnham poses related questions in 'Musical and Intellectual Values: Interpreting the History of Music Theory', *Current Musicology* 53 (1993), p. 79.

2

The responsibilities of nineteenth-century music theory

While re-examining the charge of 'wrongness' against Riemann's harmonic dualism in the previous chapter, I completely omitted from consideration one aspect of music theory that is usually considered crucial, namely the relation of music theory to its musical object. The prevailing view for many contemporary music theorists and analysts is that the decisive criterion is an instrumentalist one: on the most basic level, a music theory is considered 'right' if it can tell us something about musical practice, or about a musical composition, that in turn enhances the listening experience. In many ways, this relationship between music theory and music appears so commonsensical – certainly after the establishment of analytical practice as a field of enquiry in the nineteenth century – that it is hard to imagine how this could ever have been substantially different.[1] Harmonic dualism, it would seem, has little chance of ever being 'right' in this instrumentalist sense: as has been pointed out almost without fail, music simply does not work upside down – or, as the saying goes, we do not hear it that way.[2]

Such concerns were of little interest to Riemann. Given the comparatively small output of musical analyses among his vast body of music-theoretical writings, it would appear that applying his principles was not a top priority. Moreover, it is striking that aspects of the kind of oppositional symmetry on which harmonic dualism builds play virtually no part in his analytical observations. Witness, for instance, the opening of Beethoven's 'Waldstein' sonata, as reproduced in Example 2.1. Even the most cursory engagement with his analysis can give us some initial insights into the relationship between theory and analysis in Riemann's work.

---

[1] For an excellent introduction to analytical and theoretical practice see Ian Bent, *Music Analysis in the Nineteenth Century*, 2 vols. (Cambridge: Cambridge University Press, 1995).

[2] Even though David Lewin advocates a top-to-bottom listening strategy in some instances, in his article 'A Formal Theory of Generalized Tonal Functions', *Journal of Music Theory* 26 (1982), pp. 23–100, he is ultimately not supporting the tenets of harmonic dualism, as he listens to major and minor triads top-to-bottom alike.

Example 2.1 Excerpt from Riemann's analysis of Beethoven's 'Waldstein' Sonata, from *L. van Beethovens sämtliche Klavier-Solosonaten*, vol. 3. The analysis suggests that the thirteen opening bars should be heard as an eight-bar period.

This analysis is noteworthy as much for the things it observes as for the things it neglects. The wide harmonic range in that passage – encompassing at its extremes D major and Bb major harmonies – and the opposition of harmonic functions could be a striking demonstration of an essentially dualistic view of harmony: the tonal space is first explored towards the dominant side, by incorporating the secondary dominant, the D major seventh chord, which is labelled $\mathcal{D}$ by Riemann. Then the second four bars expand the subdominant side, stretching symmetrically to Bb major, the subdominant of the subdominant – which, analogously, Riemann normally labelled $\overset{S}{S}$ but which is here spelled out: the parentheses around the symbols *S* and *D* indicate that those functions are subject to the following *S*, which is sounded in the seventh bar.

However, Riemann chose not to make this symmetrical potential into a feature of his analysis. Unlike his colleagues Oettingen and Ziehn, Riemann did not make extensive use of the symmetrical potential of his dualistic approach.[3] Rather, Riemann decided not only to break down the functional balance between the two four-bar phrases, but also to

---

[3] In his doctoral dissertation, *Über das musikalische Hören* (Göttingen, 1873) published as *Musikalische Logik* (Leipzig: C. F. Kahnt, 1874), p. 47, Riemann pointed out: 'It is, incidentally, not my intention to stand up for a rehabilitation of the pure minor mode in an extreme way, as does A. v. Oettingen, so as to propagate for pieces to be written in pure minor, just as they have occasionally been written in pure major.' It is daunting to think what Oettingen would have made of the inversional fugal subjects that Riemann analysed rather soberly in his *Handbuch der Fugenkomposition*, 8th edn (Berlin: Max Hesse, n.d.). Although not explicitly a harmonic dualist, Bernhard Ziehn developed a special interest in such inversional fugues.

Example 2.2 Riemann's ideal eight-bar period, from *Grundriß der Musikwissenschaft*. The Arabic numerals in parentheses indicate the 'ideal' bar numbers, while the Roman numerals indicate relative metric weight.

erase the most obvious traces of symmetry. Bar 5 is clearly a repeat of the opening, transposed down a whole tone; yet Riemann's labels instead make no note of this equivalence: he determined the first chord as tonic *T*, and the equivalent chord at bar 5 as a subdominant *S* – dependent in turn to the subdominant harmony in bar 7. In other words, his analysis implies that any symmetrical order is subsidiary to other concerns – in this case, as I shall explore in more detail in the next chapter, to his concern with full cadential statements and eight-unit periods.

Effectively, the analysis turns the opening of the 'Waldstein' sonata into what Riemann calls a 'two-sided cadence', a succession of the harmonic functions of *T – S – D – T*, which is spread out over an ideal eight-bar unit – not an easy task, given that the opening actually consists of thirteen bars.

Example 2.2 shows Riemann's 'idealised' eight-bar metric structure, which is subdivided into four bars of antecedent and four of consequent, then into two-bar groups, and finally single-bar units. (As the example shows, for Riemann, a bar unit is always anacrustic and cuts across the barline.) The Roman numerals above each bar in Example 2.2 indicate the relative metric weight (that is, the 'heaviness' of each downbeat within the period); while a Roman number is missing for the final downbeat in this example, this bar receives the greatest metric weight in Riemann's system. The Roman numerals Riemann uses in this example are simply an explanatory device and do not normally occur in his analytical observations; elsewhere he simply uses the Arabic numerals, which are marked in parentheses under every other barline in Example 2.2. These Arabic numerals also convey the relative metric weight of the bar unit by assigning 'ideal' ordinal bar numbers.

How this is done in practice can be seen back in Example 2.1. Thus, the third bar is marked (2): it represents the second bar of the idealised eight-bar model. The 'ideal' bar 4 is not heard until what is written as the seventh bar: Riemann took two written bars as the basic unit, which become one 'ideal' bar of his eight-bar model. The 'ideal' bar 6, however, comes earlier than expected. In this way, Riemann manages to present the thirteen-bar opening as if it were an eight-bar period. Only in suggesting these ordering mechanisms, we could preliminarily

conclude, could Riemann arrive at a structure that is congruent with his ideas about cadential order.

The effects of harmonic dualism as an analytical end in its own right seem to play a small part in Riemann's discussion of the sonata. Nor, incidentally, does he take any notice of the chromatically descending motion in the bass, which is often seen as the principal feature of this passage. Altogether, it seems that Riemann is not interested in the special features of the opening. Rather – it would appear – he plays down the particularity of this opening in favour of its general features. While we have come to appreciate the first few bars of the 'Waldstein' sonata as a paradigm of Beethoven's harmonic boldness, Riemann's analysis of this passage is actually a demonstration of its ordinariness.

I

With these admittedly preliminary conclusions in mind, we would already have to modify the commonsensical instrumentalist approach to analysis: it seems that Riemann's analysis is not particularly suitable for enhancing our experience of the 'Waldstein' sonata in particular. Rather, the analysis is trying to make a more general point; it may well attempt to instruct us about musical form in a more general sense. Riemann expressed this view repeatedly from his very first essays onwards:

It is not the musical idea, in its logically strict formulation, that elevates us, but only its general form, its subsumption in imponderable depths and dimensions, which can only be perceived but not pronounced.[4]

In a way, the analysis of the 'Waldstein' sonata is fashioned to make the same point: the opening here is little more than a specimen of a more universal musical structure. As we shall see, this is a side effect of the important *historical* task that music analysis had to fulfil in Riemann's theoretical system.

To do this, we must consider Riemann's position in the context of the period of German music theory immediately preceding his work. Although we are still largely indebted to theoretical apparatuses from that time, their focuses were quite different from our own – and in many ways, Riemann's approach occupies a space between their concerns and our own.

---

[4] Hugo Riemann (pseudonym: Hugibert Ries), 'Aesthetische Essays über das Dreikunstwerk', *Neue Zeitschrift für Musik* 66 (1870), p. 198. 'nicht aber der logisch streng formulirte Gedanke erhebt uns, sondern erst seine Verallgemeinerung, sein Aufgehen in unabsehbare Weiten und Tiefen, die nur empfunden, nicht ausgesprochen werden können.' See also Michael Arntz, *Hugo Riemann (1849–1919): Leben, Werk und Wirkung* (Cologne: Concerto-Verlag, 1999), p. 148.

What must be noted in the first place is the important part music theory played in nineteenth-century Germany: if quantity can be taken as a coarse but broadly reliable indicator of importance, the sheer amount of music theory produced suggests that its role was more portentous than in any other European country. The wider importance of music theory in this cultural context can be gauged by taking a step back from Riemann and considering a competition that Franz Brendel's journal *Neue Zeitschrift für Musik* announced in 1859: to celebrate its fiftieth issue, Brendel invited treatises that would provide an 'explanatory elucidation and musical-theoretical argument accounting for the transformation and progress of harmony, as effected by the most recent artistic creations'.[5]

The two winning entries – by Weitzmann and Count Laurencin, as winner and runner-up, respectively – could not be more different. Laurencin, whose treatise was entered under the telling motto 'Free is the Spirit', asserted that conventional theory of harmony was but a faint echo of an ever-progressive musical practice. Such conventional theory of harmony that seeks to abstract universal rules from old masterworks (traditionally by Palestrina), he explained, is fundamentally wrong-headed. As each compositional style was in Laurencin's eyes inextricably bound up with the prevailing Hegelian *Zeitgeist*, such an ossified approach of abstract rules cannot yield correct results.[6] The rules that such 'retrospective' music theory deploys are not applicable to any composer other than the one that was chosen as a role model in the first place. Thus the rules of Palestrinian counterpoint no longer apply to the following generation of composers, let alone Bach and more recent composers.[7]

A music theory that takes account of the spirit of the age, contended Laurencin, must not be a rigid system of rules, but must allow for historical progress and continuous change in harmonic expression.[8] Following this method, he explained the advance of harmony from Beethoven and Schubert to Schumann, Chopin, Berlioz, and finally to the most recent compositions of Liszt and Wagner. In each case he used some harmonic anomaly, such as consonant six-four chords in *Lohengrin* or augmented

---

[5] Franz Brendel, 'Zur Eröffnung des 50. Bandes der Zeitschrift', *Neue Zeitschrift für Musik* 50 (1859), p. 1. Carl Weitzmann, 'Erklärende Erläuterung und musikalisch-theoretische Begründung der durch die neuesten Kunstschöpfungen bewirkten Umgestaltung und Weiterbildung der Harmonik' was published in *Neue Zeitschrift für Musik* 52 (1860), pp. 1–3, 9–12, 17–20, 29–31, 37–9, 45–6, 53–4, 65–6, 73–5; and Franz P. Graf Laurencin, 'Erklärende Erläuterung und musikalisch-theoretische Begründung der durch die neuesten Kunstschöpfungen bewirkten Umgestaltung und Weiterbildung der Harmonik' in *Neue Zeitschrift für Musik* 54 (1861), pp. 4–5, 9–14, 21–4, 29–34, 41–3, 53–5, 61–4.

[6] Laurencin, 'Erklärende Erläuterung', pp. 4–5.   [7] Ibid., p. 9.   [8] Ibid., p. 10.

triads in Liszt's *Faust Symphony*, to explain how forbidden features make perfect sense when considering the immanent – historical – logic of the individual composition.

Weitzmann's approach was fundamentally different: he proceeded in an entirely textbook-theoretical fashion. His method did not take history into account as an essential category, as did Laurencin, yet the historical progress that was to be explained also became apparent in Weitzmann's presentation. By incorporating theoretical traditions – for instance, Hauptmann's dialectical approach to triadic harmonies[9] – Weitzmann could show how the pedagogical tools of the tried and tested theories could still be used if their screws were tightened a little. Weitzmann demonstrated that certain features of contemporary composition such as augmented triads and diminished-seventh chords, which had posed big problems for music theory, could be explained by very clear voice-leading and suspension procedures. This way he aimed to prove that 'any consonant chord can follow any other consonant chord'.[10]

In many ways, these two theoretical approaches present the Scylla and Charybdis of nineteenth-century theories of harmony. Laurencin cannot ultimately refute the argument against which he battled polemically – that music theory is always a delayed reflection of past musical practice, and therefore out of step with the Hegelian Spirit. His theory is a little closer to the music it deals with, but still lags behind. Weitzmann, on the other hand, tried to be so permissive and all-embracing that by explaining everything, ultimately his theory explains nothing.

So why were Weitzmann and Laurencin the winning entries? The journal had explicitly reserved the right to reject the submissions if it felt that none of them lived up to its expectations, and to call for a new competition. But with a view to the express aim of the contest, the two entries had both succeeded in fulfilling the primary goal, namely to find a 'theoretical argument' for the 'justification of the progress which has been effected in the field of harmony through the works of Schumann, Berlioz, Wagner and Liszt and all those who have followed in the new movement'. This was in aid of gaining 'solid ground under the feet for the harmonic potential of music both already achieved and further to be reached'.[11] Both entries had indeed fulfilled this task.[12] The description

---

[9] Weitzmann, 'Erklärende Erläuterung', pp. 9–10.   [10] Ibid., p. 18.

[11] *Neue Zeitschrift für Musik* 50 (1859), p. 2.

[12] Weitzmann's case is particularly piquant, since he was also a member of the jury. Although he abstained from voting on his own submission, it is notable that he chose some well-placed examples from the works of the other adjudicators, Franz Liszt and Moritz Hauptmann. What he could not know was that Hauptmann would resign shortly before the selection process and that he would be replaced by Johann Christian Lobe. See *Neue Zeitschrift für Musik* 52 (1860), p. 2.

of the competition makes clear what the journal expected from the entrants: namely, legitimation of the 'progressive' Wagnerian orientation of its contributors. Elsewhere, the editor-in-chief Brendel offered a more specific explanation for this need for theory:

> The nature of contemporary art is characterised above all by the fact that it no longer builds upon the pre-given foundations in the old, naturalistic [i.e. unreflected] manner, but that, on the contrary, theory and critique have stepped between the anterior and the contemporary, that our art contains theory and critique as a prerequisite.[13]

Theory played an important role in the agenda of the *Neue Zeitschrift für Musik*, one that was inextricably bound up with its own notion of progress. Although Brendel was only speaking for his own 'New German School', the ramifications of this position are more widely applicable: the modernity of nineteenth-century music is inextricably bound up with its increasing reflexivity. And this reflexivity could be supplied by music theory. The difference between Laurencin and Weitzmann can best be understood by means of a distinction between 'implicit' and 'explicit' theories: the notion of an 'implicit' theory signifies a kind of compositional logic immanent in the musical work, which the theory seeks to unearth, while an 'explicit' theory refers to systematic theoretical constructs that provide a sense of general order but do not engage with the particularity of a work.[14]

It is conspicuous that the jurors of the *Neue Zeitschrift für Musik* did not make this distinction between 'implicit' and 'explicit' theories: both Laurencin, who regarded tonal harmony as a practice that manifested itself in a body of works, and Weitzmann, who conceptualised tonal harmony as an abstract body of rules, could apparently stand side by side and were both awarded prizes. The vast gulf separating the two approaches did not seem to matter to the jury, or was perhaps not even perceived to exist.

The equivocation between 'explicit' and 'implicit' theories opened up wide-ranging possibilities for nineteenth-century music theory – it

---

[13] Franz Brendel, *Geschichte der Musik in Italien, Deutschland und Frankreich*, 4th edn (Leipzig: Breitkopf und Härtel, 1867), p. 624. 'Das Wesen der gegenwärtigen Kunst besteht vor allem darin, daß die nicht mehr in alter naturalistischer Weise auf den gegebenen Grundlagen weiterbaut, im Gegenteil, daß Theorie und Kritik zwischen das Frühere und das Gegenwärtige getreten sind, daß unsere Kunst Theorie und Kritik in sich als Voraussetzung hat.' See Carl Dahlhaus, *Klassische und Romantische Musikästhetik* (Laaber: Laaber-Verlag, 1988), p. 267.

[14] These terms, originally developed in the context of Schoenberg's aesthetics, are taken from Carl Dahlhaus, 'Was heißt "Geschichte der Musiktheorie"?', in Frieder Zaminer, ed., *Ideen zu einer Geschichte der Musiktheorie* (Darmstadt: Wissenschaftliche Buchgesellschaft, 1985), p. 10.

allowed the theory of tonal harmony to exist independently from musical works. By linking a 'progressive' composition to very plain familiar harmonic procedures, theory not merely explains but at the same time creates a historical lineage. This historical connection is evident in Laurencin, who drew up a musical genealogy spanning the German composers from Bach to Wagner. In Weitzmann's case, this historical agenda, albeit unexplicated, was nevertheless present in the theory: by linking the basic elements of harmony textbooks with the practice of contemporary composers through very simple devices, he contrived a structural link with the theoretical model, whilst emphasising the advance of contemporary harmony from these basic models. These models, in turn, fulfil the function of a past practice from which progressive music had departed; they represent a simulacrum of harmonic structures that never actually existed in musical reality.

Above all, the discrepancy between the two winning entries of Brendel's competition shows to what an extent nineteenth-century music that regarded itself as progressive relied on music theory to legitimise and confirm its progressive status. This mechanism is commonly known from the machinations of nineteenth-century modernity. It must be remembered that modernity invokes the category of the 'new' not so much for its own sake, but rather as a function of its reflexivity.[15] Situated thus, music theory can be seen as one of the institutions on which the modernity of music rests.

In a sense, the readiness with which music theory was accommodated in the context of the *Neue Zeitschrift für Musik* to fulfil this historiographic task was itself based on a rather unique historical constellation – of which the equivocation of 'explicit' and 'implicit' theory is part and parcel. For barely half a century later, the two approaches had drifted apart and seemed irreconcilably opposed: the period of music history that is normally marked as the end of the period of harmonic tonality often had little time for 'explicit' theory, as it was perceived to obstruct (rather than confirm) the genuine historical progress of musical composition. This is nowhere marked more clearly than in one of Schoenberg's celebrated tirades:

To hell with all these theories, if they always serve only to block the evolution of art and if their positive achievement consists in nothing more than helping those who will compose badly anyway to learn it quickly.[16]

[15] See, among countless others, Jürgen Habermas, *The Philosophical Discourse of Modernity*, trans. Frederick G. Lawrence (Cambridge, Mass.: MIT Press, 1987); Matei Calinescu, *Five Faces of Modernity* (Durham, NC: Duke University Press, 1987), esp. pp. 41–6; and Anthony Giddens, *Modernity and Self-Identity* (Cambridge: Polity Press, 1991), esp. p. 20.

[16] See Arnold Schoenberg, *Theory of Harmony*, trans. Roy E. Carter (London: Faber and Faber, 1978), p. 9.

'Explicit' theories, explaining tonality as an autonomous system or a canon of rules prior to any particular composition, effectively mapped out that which was possible or permissible. It was this perceived restriction that Schoenberg reacted against. (What he ignored, ironically, was that these 'explicit' theories had not ceased to function as a historical yardstick: in a sense, Schoenberg's vociferous reaction against 'explicit' theory was nothing but a way of drawing attention to the fact that his music had progressed beyond such theories. In other words, the break with tradition that Schoenberg self-consciously carried out – and at times denied – in his compositions, was most evident in this emblematic break with theory.)

It would seem that while reactions against 'explicit' theory thrived in a climate of renewed emphasis on individual creativity and genius – as promoted by Schoenberg himself – 'implicit' theory was still admissible, as it did not compromise the priority of the composer over the theorist. In explaining the immanent 'musical logic' of a composition, 'implicit' theory justifies the composer as having been right all along. At the end of his *Harmonielehre*, after a discussion of his own works, Schoenberg clarified this admissibility and usability of 'implicit' theory in a much more conciliatory tone:

[A]s soon as a tone is misplaced the meaning changes, the logic and utility is lost, coherence seems destroyed. Laws apparently prevail here. What they are, I do not know. Perhaps I shall know in a few years. Perhaps someone after me will find them.[17]

Schoenberg's apparent nonchalance is deceptive: the temporal aspect in Schoenberg's statement of faith is crucial. 'Implicit' theory is admissible – even necessary – in this context, as it still serves as a justificatory mechanism in Schoenberg's aesthetics without having any prescriptive power over his composition. By necessity, then, 'implicit' theory invariably follows composition.[18] Consequently it cannot, to adopt Schoenberg's organicist rhetoric, hamper the 'evolution of art'.

'Implicit' theory, in other words, lacks the prescriptive element that 'explicit' theory possesses and that – in Schoenberg's eyes – renders it an

---

[17] Schoenberg, *Theory of Harmony*, p. 421. Schoenberg's double-edged position towards theory in the context of ideas about the genius-composer is further examined in Suzannah Clark and Alexander Rehding, 'Introduction', in *Music Theory and Natural Order from the Renaissance to the Early Twentieth Century* (Cambridge: Cambridge University Press, 2001), p. 12.

[18] Robert W. Wason, who comments on the Weitzmann/Laurencin contest in his 'Progressive Harmonic Theory in the Mid-Nineteenth Century', *Journal of Musicological Research* 8 (1988), p. 57, wonders how Laurencin could even have been considered for the prize, which would seem to indicate that his sympathies – and by extension those of post-war, Schenker-inspired American music theory at large – lie with the 'explicit' approach.

obstacle to progressive composition. In the context of the competition of the *Neue Zeitschrift für Musik*, still firmly situated in the age of tonal practice, this was of little consequence. However, on closer scrutiny, a detail in the description of the 1859 competition would point to the potential inherent in 'explicit' theory: the entries, it is determined, should make theoretical predictions as to the 'harmonic potential of music ... further to be reached'.[19] Reconsidering the preoccupation of modernity with history, hinted at above, it emerges that music theory was required not only to make historical connections linking the present with the past, but also to cast historical trajectories into the future. It must present a vision, or what sociologist Anthony Giddens calls an 'organised future'. This is no less true for the age of late modernity, of which Giddens speaks here, than for the nineteenth century, which saw history as an objective process. Giddens explains his position as follows:

Given the extreme reflexivity of late modernity, the future does not just consist of the expectation of events yet to come. 'Futures' are organised reflexively in the present in terms of the chronic flow of knowledge into the environments about which such knowledge was developed.[20]

In this respect, Laurencin's 'implicit' approach was doomed to fail. Laurencin's decision to uncover historical trends as immanent in musical creations, as manifestations of the mysterious Hegelian 'spirit', prevented him from making any predictions about works that are as yet unwritten. (To be sure, related criticisms have been levelled at Hegel himself.) Weitzmann's systematic approach, whose textbook style falls into the 'explicit' category of music theory, seems at first more successful, precisely because his theory does not rely on already written musical scores. Music theory can only fulfil this historical task charged by the jury of the *Neue Zeitschrift für Musik*, it seems, if it emancipates itself from the predominance of existing music. Thus, music theory becomes a critical force with the power to demarcate the limits of tonal harmony and to conjecture the future of music. By setting such standards, music theory takes an active part in musical progress.

Although Weitzmann's theory, as an example of the 'explicit' approach, is better equipped to be progressive in the sense developed above, on closer inspection it appears that, like Laurencin, he also failed to present a clear vision about the future of harmony. By developing his theoretical ideas to their ultimate consequence it turns out that anything and everything goes – or, in his words, 'any consonant chord can follow

---

[19] *Neue Zeitschrift für Musik* 50 (1859), p. 2.
[20] Giddens, *Modernity and Self-Identity*, p. 29. He concludes that paradoxically the search for certain knowledge casts radical doubt on its foundations. As we shall see shortly, this consequence also affects music theory.

any other consonant chord'. The 'organised future' that Weitzmann envisaged is one of disarray.

II

Thirteen years later, a young Hugo Riemann complained about the lack of forward-looking perspective in the theories of Weitzmann and Laurencin. His very first publication, the article 'Musikalische Logik' (1872), can be seen on one level as a rebuttal of such theoretical approaches:

> In light of the increasingly unfolding liberty of our modern harmony and the growing attitude that any chord could follow after any other chord [Weitzmann 1860, Laurencin 1861], I simultaneously pursue the purpose of demonstrating that a very definite barrier exists for such capriciousness, which is found in nothing but the logical meaning of the various scale degrees.[21]

To be sure, there are plenty of polemics against various earlier theorists in the article; no doubt Riemann was trying to create a discursive space for his own theories. Yet below the polemical surface there is a point that should be taken seriously, namely Riemann's anxieties regarding the future of music, and the careless way in which some theorists foster and legitimise a disorderly future with their theories. In other words, music theory has to bear a certain responsibility for music.

On the most basic level, the degree of reflexivity and foresight of the consequences, the need for responsibility, which Riemann presupposed for any music-theoretical approach, can be understood as an indication of music theory's participation in the mechanisms of modernity. Only when music theory assumes the burden of historical consciousness, it seems, does it have the possibility of becoming responsible. This begs the question of how Riemann's own theory was responsible in the sense that Weitzmann and Laurencin's were not.[22]

---

[21] Riemann (pseudonym Hugibert Ries), 'Musikalische Logik', in *Präludien und Studien* (reprint Hildesheim: Georg Olms, 1976), vol. 3, p. 2. 'Zugleich habe ich gegenüber der mehr und mehr sich entfaltenden Freiheit unserer modernen Harmonik und der aufkeimenden Ansicht, als könne überhaupt jeder Akkorde jedem Akkord folgen, den Zweck vor Augen, nachzuweissen [sic], dass eine ganz bestimmte Schranke für derartige Willkürlichkeiten existiert, die in nichts anderem zu suchen ist, als in der logischen Bedeutung der verschiedenen Tonstufen.' Reference to Weitzmann and Laurencin is made in a footnote. Strictly speaking, it was only Weitzmann – and not Laurencin – who made the claim that 'any chord can follow any other chord'. However, as I shall explore below, Riemann presumably considered it appropriate to include Laurencin too, because the same situation was also an implicit consequence of his approach.

[22] Leslie D. Blasius has broached ethical questions in Riemann, particularly concerning truth and conscience, in his article, 'Nietzsche, Riemann, Wagner: When Music Lies', in Clark and Rehding, eds., *Music Theory and Natural Order*, pp. 93–107.

The decisive criterion, Riemann had explained, was to 'show that a very definite barrier exists for such capriciousness'. In delineating these boundaries of what was harmonically possible, the notion of musical 'rightness' comes to the fore. In the immediate context of the criticism of Weitzmann and Laurencin, in the 1872 article 'Musikalische Logik', Riemann insisted that the immutable logic of harmony was restricted by the 'logical significance of the scale degrees'. He suggested, in close relation to Hauptmann's ideas, that all musical units could be traced back to the harmonic prototype $I - IV - V - I$.[23] (Later, in his dissertation, which in published form bore the same title, *Musikalische Logik*, Riemann added its dual, the minor prototype, $I - V - IV - I$.[24]) This basic prototype could be altered by substituting third-related scale degrees, expanding each element by means of subsidiary chords, as well as by repeating or omitting elements.[25]

Riemann evidently wrote this article before he had grasped the full implications of Arthur von Oettingen's idea of harmonic dualism, which, as has been amply documented, fundamentally changed his view of the nature of harmony.[26] However, where Oettingen was largely concerned with a physically sound explanation of the minor triad, Riemann misread him creatively, explaining Oettingen's theory as follows:

Among the higher partials of an interval or triads (i.e. among the partials of the individual tones of the triad and the combination tones of the partials) one is particularly prominent to the ear: it is the first common upper partial of the tones of the triad.[27]

In fact, Oettingen did not write anything at all about the *perception* of these common partials; nowhere did he state that the first common partial is perceived as salient. However, this misreading – bolstered by his belief that the undertone series was audible – allowed Riemann to refashion the basis of his theory of harmony. As Example 2.3 shows, in the early years of his career, at least from 1877 on, his theory of harmony relied on the notion of the dualistic *Klang*,[28] combining the upper triad with the lower one and its 'root' in the centre.

---

[23] Riemann, *Musikalische Logik*, pp. 2–3.   [24] Ibid., p. 58.

[25] Daniel Harrison discusses this article in greater detail in his *Harmonic Function in Chromatic Music* (Chicago and London: University of Chicago Press, 1994), pp. 266–73.

[26] Richard Münnich, 'Von [der] Entwicklung der Riemannschen Harmonielehre und ihrem Verhältnis zu Oettingen und Stumpf', in Carl Mennicke, ed., *Riemann-Festschrift* (Leipzig: Max Hesse, 1909), pp. 60–76.

[27] Riemann, 'Die Natur der Harmonik', in *Waldersees Sammlung musikalischer Vorträge* 4 (1882), p. 176. 'unter den höheren Obertönen eines Intervalls oder Akkordes (d.h. den Obertönen der einzelnen Akkordtöne und den Kombinationstönen der Obertöne) fällt derjenige ganz besonders laut ins Gehör, welcher der erste gemeinschaftliche Oberton der Akkordtöne ist'.

[28] See particularly Riemann, *Musikalische Syntaxis* (Leipzig: Breitkopf und Härtel, 1877; reprint Niederwalluf: Dr. Martin Sändig, 1971), p. 9.

Example 2.3a Riemann's dualistic *Klang*.

F   A♭   C   E   G

From this dualistic *Klang*, Riemann abstracted harmonic relations, in a manner reminiscent of Helmholtz's acoustical reasoning. Helmholtz had explained:

When we pass from C-e-G to G-b-D, we use a tone of the *Klang*, G, which is already contained in the first chord, and is consequently properly prepared, while at the same time such a step leads us to those degrees of the scale which are most distant from the tonic, and have only an indirect relationship with it. Hence this passage forms a distinct progression in the harmony, which is at once well assured and properly based.[29]

In a concept that became known as *Klang* representation (*Klangvertretung*), which was closely related to this line of thought, Riemann proposed that each element of the central *Klang* stood in for another *Klang* (with its own upper and lower triads around the central pitch) in its own right: 'It emerges that sonorities that are intelligible in succession are partly identical with respect to the partials of their overtone or undertone series.'[30]

As Example 2.3b shows, in this model of harmonic relations, therefore, the satisfying effect of the basic harmonic succession *I – IV – V – I* could be explained as a full presentation of the central *Klang*, the tonic, and its upper and lower fifths as present in the dual *Klang*. At the same time, the extremely chromatic harmonic succession of triads built on C – A♭ – E – C was admitted in *Musikalische Syntaxis* as effectively equivalent, as it simply exchanged the fifth relations of the central pitch C for its third relations. (In fact, as Example 2.3c shows, he used such a succession as an example of 'tonality' in his *Musik-Lexikon*.[31])

Riemann expanded this model into a 'grid of harmonic relations' (or *Netz der Tonverwandtschaften*), as shown in Example 2.4, which conceptualised harmonic relations in terms of spatial proximity, with axes of fifth relations and major-third relations. This grid, which he modified from Oettingen's original model, represented harmony on the same two

---

[29] Helmholtz, *On the Sensations of Tone*, trans. Alexander J. Ellis (London, 1885; reprint New York: Dover, 1954), p. 292 (translation modified). Not dissimilarly from Hauptmann's example in the previous chapter, Helmholtz expresses tuning differences by means of upper and lower case letters. These tuning differences do not bear on the argument here.

[30] Riemann, *Musikalische Syntaxis*, p. 9.

[31] See ibid., p. 39, and *Musik-Lexikon*, 5th edn (Leipzig: Max Hesse, 1900), p. 1143.

Example 2.3b Harmonic successions imagined on the basis of the dualistic *Klang*, in which third relations can replace fifth relations.

Example 2.3c From the entry of '*Tonalität*' in Riemann's *Musik-Lexikon*.

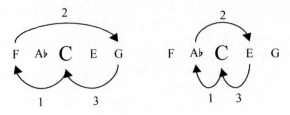

Example 2.4 Riemann's 'grid of harmonic relations', from *Große Kompositionslehre*, vol. 1.

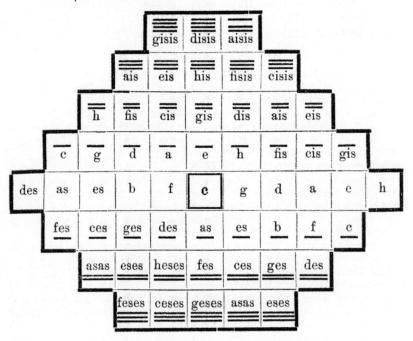

levels – chordal and relational – as his conception of the *Klang*. (Riemann reused this grid on numerous occasions in his harmony tutors, each time in a slightly different representation.[32] The differences between these grids, however, which are mainly related to tuning differences, need not concern us here, as the principle remains the same in all of them.)

In this grid of harmonic relations major and minor triads were represented as triangulations between adjacent squares, with the fundamental *Klang* at the right angle (bottom left for major triads, and top right for minor ones). At the same time, harmonic relations could be represented as manoeuvres across the harmonic space, as 'root-interval progressions' (*Harmonieschritte*) from fundamental to fundamental. Riemann invented a rather unwieldy terminology – which need not be discussed here in any depth[33] – describing the nature of these root-interval progressions from chord to chord. More complex relations were, as a rule, conceptualised as combinations of fifth and major-third relations.

Two features of the 'grid of harmonic relations' are particularly striking: first, the ease with which chromatically difficult relations – mostly mediated via the major-third relation – are accommodated. In fact, the entire conception of harmonic relations along the 'grid of harmonic relations' is distinguished by being completely independent of the diatonic scale. Second, the grid is striking for the open-endedness and the sheer number of harmonic moves it permits.[34] Fuelled by his belief in the objective existence of the undertone series, Riemann revelled in revealing how distant and seemingly impossible harmonic relations could still be

---

[32] These appear in *Musikalische Logik* (1874), 'Die Natur der Harmonik' (1882), *Systematische Modulationslehre* (Hamburg: J. F. Richter, 1887), *Große Kompositionslehre* vol. 1 (Leipzig: Breitkopf und Härtel, 1903), 'Ideen zu einer "Lehre von den Tonvorstellungen"', in *Jahrbuch der Musikbibliothek Peters* 21/22 (1914/15), *Allgemeine Musiklehre: Handbuch der Musik*, 8th edn (Berlin: Max Hesse, 1922). Many features of these are discussed in M. Kevin Mooney, 'The "Table of Relations" and Music Psychology in Hugo Riemann's Harmonic Theory', PhD dissertation (Columbia University, 1996).

[33] Riemann explains the basic idea behind *Harmonieschritte* in his *Musiklexikon* entry on '*Klang* succession', included in the glossary here. For detailed discussions see David Kopp, 'A Comprehensive Theory of Chromatic Mediant Relations in Mid-Nineteenth-Century Music', PhD dissertation (Brandeis University, 1995), and M. Kevin Mooney, 'The "Table of Relations" and Music Psychology'. A table of Riemann's *Harmonieschritte* is included in Klumpenhouwer's 'Dualist Tonal Space and Transformation in Nineteenth-Century Musical Thought', in Thomas Christensen, ed., *The Cambridge History of Western Music Theory* (Cambridge: Cambridge University Press, 2002), p. 471.

[34] In *Musikalische Syntaxis*, Riemann ignored tuning differences altogether. Oettingen and Helmholtz finely distinguished the intonation differences between third relations and fifth relations, that is to say, E as the third of C is not identical with E as the fifth of A. In equating these two slightly different pitches, Riemann opened up wide modulatory possibilities. He blithely wrote to the dedicatee of *Musikalische Syntaxis*, Arthur von Oettingen: 'I no longer require your distinction between third-tones and fifth-tones' (p. xiv). The importance of tuning differences will be considered further in Chapter 4.

explained. At the same time, however, this posed a problem with regard to the 'responsibility' of theory. With the 'grid of harmonic relations' Riemann offered a navigatory map of harmonic space, but he did nothing to show the limits of what is possible, as he had originally intended. Ultimately, Riemann's 'grid of harmonic relations' must succumb to the same kind of criticism that he had levelled at Weitzmann and Laurencin: in its infinite dimensions, allowing virtually any kind of harmonic relation, the 'grid' does not in fact explain anything.[35] Riemann's horror vision – 'any chord can follow any other chord' – is perfectly possible within the parameters of Riemann's 'grid of harmonic relations', as there is nothing to assert the centrality of one tonic *Klang* or pitch.

Riemann finally tackled this problem in *Vereinfachte Harmonielehre* of 1893, in which he introduced the taxonomy of harmonic function for the first time, and the third edition of his *Handbuch der Harmonielehre*, which followed a couple of years later. He appraised the advantages of the theory of harmonic function as follows:

The theory of tonal functions is nothing but the development of the ... notion of tonality. The sustained relation of all harmonies to one tonic has found its most concise expression in the denomination of all chords as a more or less modified appearance of the three primary pillars of the harmonic logical conception: the tonic itself and its two dominants.[36]

Example 2.5, taken from *Vereinfachte Harmonielehre*, shows how Riemann conceptualised this new tonal space, for both major and minor systems. In each, three fifth-related triads (labelled S^+, T^+, D^+ and ^oS, ^oT, ^oD respectively) are complemented by the dualistic opposite of the central triad, designated as ^oS in major, and D^+ in minor respectively.[37] Like the dualistic chordal shorthand, or *Klangschlüssel*, the taxonomy of function uses the signs $^+$ and ^{o} to indicate major and minor respectively. In practice, Riemann often omitted the $^+$ sign – if the function sign is left blank, a major function is always assumed.

---

[35] In *Musikalische Syntaxis* there are two control mechanisms in place: first, the notion of the dualistic sonority, and second, the postulate of harmonic units beginning and ending with the tonic. In the course of the book, however, Riemann frequently gets carried away, so that in effect neither of the two mechanisms poses any restrictions.

[36] Riemann, *Handbuch der Harmonielehre*, 6th edn (Leipzig: Breitkopf und Härtel, 1917), p. 214. 'Unsere Lehre von den tonalen Funktionen der Harmonie ist nichts anderes als der Ausbau des ... Begriffes der Tonalität. Die festgehaltene Beziehung aller Harmonien auf eine Tonika hat ihren denkbar prägnantsten Ausdruck gefunden in der Bezeichnung aller Accorde als mehr oder minder stark modifizierte Erscheinungsform der drei Hauptsäulen des harmonisch-logischen Aufbaues: der Tonika selbst und ihrer beiden Dominanten.'

[37] Riemann does not explain why the dualistic opposite should be added. It is safe to assume, however, that the D^+ needs to be added to the minor set so as to accommodate a harmony comprising the leading-tone. By dualistic analogy, the major set therefore requires its equivalent, the ^oS, which contains the 'minor leading-tone', or ♭6̂.

Example 2.5 Tonal space is reconceptualised using the notion of harmonic function, from *Vereinfachte Harmonielehre*.

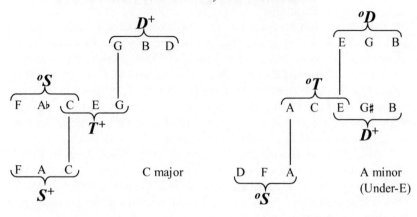

It would seem that these new function labels could be mapped onto the grid of harmonic relations without any problems.[38] However, the graphic representation conceals one feature that becomes clearer in the actual taxonomy: if the functional concept of tonality embraces the dualistic opposite of the central triad, why does its label not reflect a tonic relation? In other words, why does °c fulfil subdominant function when its dual c+ fulfils tonic function? (Or, in the minor system: why does e+ fulfil dominant function when its dual °e fulfils tonic function?) The dualistic conception of harmony would suggest different relations from those on which functional relations are based. However, this would suggest strongly that the theory of harmonic function is not based on a dualistic conception of harmony, but rather follows a conventional, 'monistic' model of harmony – which Riemann vehemently denied.[39]

There is one concept that helped Riemann out of this awkward situation, which he found in the work of the psychologist Carl Stumpf.[40] Stumpf reviewed the acoustical conceptions of consonance

---

[38] In fact, Renate Imig dedicates a whole book to this enterprise; see her *Systeme der Funktionsbezeichnung in den Harmonielehren seit Hugo Riemann* (Düsseldorf: Verlag der Gesellschaft zur Förderung der systematischen Musikwissenschaft, 1971).

[39] This criticism was made during Riemann's lifetime, and has been made continuously since. Riemann first responded to it in 'Das Problem des harmonischen Dualismus', *Neue Zeitschrift für Musik* 101 (1905), pp. 69–70, as quoted in the Introduction above, n. 22.

[40] Stumpf served as assistant professor there during Riemann's time at Göttingen University. It is not established whether there was any personal contact. Riemann's most incisive discussion of his views on harmony in the context of Stumpf's ideas can be found in *Die Elemente der musikalischen Aesthetik* (Berlin and Stuttgart: W. Spemann, 1900), pp. 91–9.

and dissonance and found them unsatisfactory. Since his experiments with musically trained and unmusical subjects, which showed different responses to musical dissonances, demonstrated that the laws of consonance and dissonance are not universal, he denied that the phenomena of consonance and dissonance reside in acoustical phenomena.[41] Instead, he posited the principle of tonal 'fusion' (*Klangverschmelzung*), which held that two tones sounded simultaneously are not perceived separately but as a single entity, depending on the interval they form. Stumpf's degrees of fusion comprised in descending order: octave, fifth, fourth, major/minor thirds, all other combinations. For Riemann, Stumpf's hypothesis of tone fusion was indeed the 'redeeming word', which he came to regard as the 'higher principle' that subsumed all previous acoustical speculation.[42]

To make Stumpf's concept work to dualistic ends, in fact, Riemann had to make some drastic changes to the concept, which resulted in a heated exchange between the two theorists.[43] This concerned mainly the nature of consonance: on the basis of his principle of fusion, Stumpf would consider the consonance of intervals the basic principle, of which the consonance of triads formed a special – and historically contingent – case. Riemann, by contrast, insisted that triads are the fundamental building blocks of all music, regardless of historical and cultural difference, and that each consonant interval is by necessity heard as representing a triad.

These polemics apart, Stumpf's concept of fusion became the 'redeeming word' for Riemann – once he had made it workable to his own dualistic ends – since it allowed him to introduce the new concept of tonality of Example 2.5, particularly in the premise that the sonorities F-A-C (f$^+$) and F-A♭-C ($^\circ$c) can fulfil equivalent functions. While this decision is nearly impossible to explain in the acoustical terms of harmonic

---

[41] See Carl Stumpf, *Tonpsychologie* (Leipzig: S. Hirzel, 1883), vol. 1, p. 14. 'Not even in dissonance, when regarded purely in terms of sensation, is there a hint to the consonance of the triad, nor is there a hint in the seventh chord [that would refer] to the triad. The so-called tendency to resolution is only present for those who are used to hearing consonant chords following after the earlier [dissonant] ones, and have memorised them ... Musically untrained subjects with a sharp sense of hearing do not [notice] anything of such a tendency to resolution even when they fully concentrate.'

[42] Riemann, *Handbuch der Akustik (Musikwissenschaft)*, 3rd edn (Berlin: Max Hesse, 1921), p. 93.

[43] On a number of occasions, Riemann criticised Stumpf for having effectively replicated Helmholtz's relative concept of dissonance. See *Handbuch der Akustik*, pp. 93–8, 'Zur Theorie von Konsonanz und Dissonanz', in *Präludien und Studien*, vol. 3, pp. 34–8, and 'Das Problem des harmonischen Dualismus', pp. 24–6. Stumpf in turn criticised Riemann's misappropriation of his ideas in 'Konsonanz und Konkordanz: Nebst Bemerkungen über Wohlklang und Wohlgefälligkeit musikalischer Zusammenhänge', *Zeitschrift für Psychologie und Physiologie der Sinnesorgane*, 1. Abt. Zeitschrift für Sinnesforschung 58 (1911), pp. 347–55.

Example 2.6 Common-tone relation of dualistic grid.

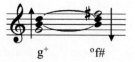

dualism, as a fused triadic entity, it no longer matters whether the root of the *Klang* is at the top or at the bottom.

It seems fair to say that Riemann's concept of harmonic function received its final and perhaps decisive impetus from Stumpf's work. At the same time, it is interesting to note Riemann's reluctance to bring Stumpf's concept of fusion to bear explicitly on his new concept of tonality. (In Chapter 3, I shall explore the reasons that held Riemann back.) In fact, the arguments that Riemann proposed in this situation were not very convincing.[44] He attempted to brush aside the differences between the dualistic and the functional aspects of his theory by asserting:

> It goes without saying that since the introduction of the taxonomy of function, the actual signpost through the maze of possible harmonic successions is no longer the nomenclature of root-interval progressions but rather that of functions.[45]

This again, is somewhat disingenuous, since Riemann never actually gave up the 'grid of harmonic relations'. Rather, as I shall pursue in more detail in the following chapters, it continues to exist *alongside* the theory of harmonic function, as a kind of supplement or corrective to it.

What is more, harmonic relations are imagined in radically different manners in both systems. Along the grid, harmony can be navigated freely. Root-interval progressions are based on compounds of third and fifth relations: the spatial lay-out of the grid shows that chord-to-chord harmonic relations are further imagined on the basis of common intervals, for instance as shown in Example 2.6. Here, the white noteheads mark the dualistic root.

---

[44] He asserts in *Vereinfachte Harmonielehre* (London: Augener, 1893), p. 54, that the sonorities F–A–C and F–Ab–C are virtually identical, 'since they have both tones of the interval of the fifth in common, and only differ in the third'. In stark contrast to this explanation, he suggests elsewhere that in C major °c should be heard as the lower fifth-relation 'of a tonic of the opposite harmonic gender'. He implied, in other words, that there is a kind of tacit 'tonic double' – in this case °g – to which the minor subdominant relates: 'For this reason we do not label the *Gegenklang* [the opposite half of the dualistic *Klang*] of the major tonic as °*T* but rather as °*S* . . . and the *Gegenklang* of the minor tonic not as *T*+ but rather as *D*+' (*Vereinfachte Harmonielehre*, p. 48). However, neither of the arguments explain the problem away, they merely relocate it.

[45] Riemann, *Handbuch der Harmonielehre*, p. 135. 'Es bedarf wohl nicht des Hinweises, dass der eigentliche Wegweiser durch den Labyrinth der möglichen Harmoniefolgen seit Aufstellung der Funktionsbezeichnung nicht mehr die Nomenklatur der Harmonieschritte sondern vielmehr diejenige der Funktionen ist.'

Example 2.7 Apparent consonances (*Parallele*, *Leittonwechsel* and *Variante*) in major and minor. These modifications can apply to all three main functions.

T^+ Tp ^oT ^oTp T^+ $\mathcal{L}$ ^oT $\mathcal{F}$ T^+ T^v ^oT $^oT^v$

The conception of harmonic space in terms of harmonic function, on the other hand, subsumes one axis under the other: harmonic function can only allow for harmonic relations other than the basic fifth relations by manipulating elements of the three 'harmonic pillars'. That is to say, each pitch of the three main triads can be exchanged for its neighbour note, by means of one of three modifications, as shown in Example 2.7. First, the parallel (added –*p*) exchanges the fifth of the triad for its sixth.[46] (Because the dualistic conception of chords applies here, the minor chord is reckoned from top to bottom: the dualistic minor root is what is conventionally regarded as its fifth.) Second, the *Leittonwechsel* or 'leading-tone change' applies to the root of the chord, which is exchanged for its leading-tone, as also seen above in Example 2.6. (Again, in accordance with dualistic principles, the minor 'leading-tone' is the flat scale-degree 6̂♭, resolving downwards into the 'minor root'.) To signify the leading-tone change, the function label receives a < sign in the major mode, and a > sign in the minor. Since these symbols already indicate the harmonic gender, Riemann dispensed with the usual markers $^+$ and $^\circ$ in this case. Finally, the variant (added –*v*), which was not introduced until 1914, changes the major third into the minor and vice versa.

The products of these modifications – parallels, leading-tone changes, and variants – Riemann called *Scheinkonsonanzen*, or apparent consonances, since they *sound* like consonant chords in their own right, but as modifications of the three main 'harmonic pillars', they *are* conceptually dissonant.[47] The differences between these conceptions of harmonic space are far-reaching: on the one hand, the succession of chords is imagined as potentially unlimited movements on the basis of the similarity between chords, and on the other, as modifications of three possible 'harmonic pillars'.

[46] Riemann's explanation of this apparent consonance changed over time. It was originally introduced as shorthand for the addition of the figures $^6_3$ to the function label. See Imig, *Systeme der Funktionsbezeichung*, pp. 70–6.

[47] Carl Dahlhaus has criticised this concept in a number of contexts. See 'Über den Begriff der tonalen Funktion', in Martin Vogel, ed., *Beiträge zur Musiktheorie des neunzehnten Jahrhunderts* (Regensburg: Gustav Bosse, 1966), pp. 93–102, and 'Terminologisches zum Begriff der harmonischen Funktion', *Die Musikforschung* 28 (1975), pp. 197–202.

Example 2.8 Opening of Franz Schubert's 'Im Frühling'. The boxed chord is here related to the preceding tonic function.

In other words, where the grid conceptualises the relation $g^+ - {}^\circ f\#$ as a root-interval movement of a semitone, on the basis of a common interval B–D, as it did in Example 2.6, the equivalent progression of functions proceeds in an entirely different fashion. The theory of function would hold that the latter harmony is a modification of a 'harmonic pillar'. Depending on the musical context, it would be considered either as a modification of the *same* function (in G major, $T^+ - \mathcal{T}$), or as the modification of a *different* function (in G major, $T^+ - Dp^+$).[48] As active listeners in Riemann's sense, we would have to make a decision between these two percepts.

These two possibilities can best be illustrated with two short excerpts. As Example 2.8 and 2.9 show, the context usually decides which interpretation is more appropriate. In the first excerpt from Schubert's 'Im Frühling' the B minor harmony (${}^\circ f\#$) proceeds from a G major tonic, it falls on the weak beat after the downbeat and is succeeded by the subdominant function. In this case, Riemann's theory would normally prefer the tonic leading-tone change: $\mathcal{T}$. In the passage from Dvořák's Quintet in G major, on the other hand, the equivalent harmony, which falls on the weak beat before the downbeat, is preceded by the subdominant, and followed by the tonic. In this position Riemann's theory would normally expect dominant function; it would therefore be appropriate to choose the Dp^+ label. In either case, the ${}^\circ f\#$ or B minor harmony needs to be related to one 'harmonic pillar', which it then represents sonically.

The precise nature of these 'harmonic pillars' is ambiguous – and as Carl Dahlhaus has observed, it is probably no accident that Riemann

---

[48] It might at first seem confusing that what sounds as a minor chord should be marked with a $^+$ sign. However, these indicators always refer to the main function – in this case, the *major* dominant – not to the sounding product.

Example 2.9 Excerpt from Antonin Dvořák's String Quintet in G major, first movement. While the boxed chord here could be considered as equivalent to that of Example 2.8, its context suggests that it fulfils a different harmonic function.

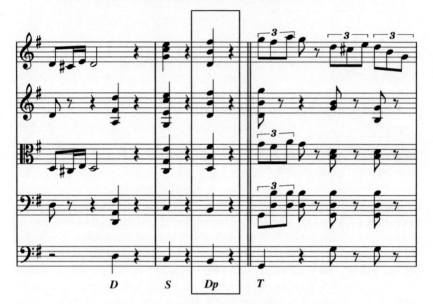

D   S   Dp   T

would choose such a vague metaphor at such a crucial point.[49] Riemann generally treated these 'harmonic pillars' as though they were chords, while it is clear that there are crucial differences between a chord and a harmonic function. Take, for instance, the above examples: the harmony in question – the third scale-degree in Roman-numeral nomenclature – is the same chord in both examples, yet it is assigned a different function in each context. The harmonic function is not itself a chord, but an *interpretation* of a chord, which tells us how the chord relates to its tonal-metrical context. (Conversely, we could also say that the chord is a *representative* of a function.) In the first instance, the chord is interpreted as fulfilling tonic function – it represents the tonic – and in the second as dominant function.[50] On the other hand, Riemann's postulate that each of these modifications should be traced back to one of these

[49] Carl Dahlhaus, *Studies on the Origin of Harmonic Tonality*, trans. Robert O. Gjerdingen (Princeton: Princeton University Press, 1990), p. 50.

[50] This interpretative notion of harmonic function has been pursued by David Lewin, 'Amfortas's Prayer to Titurel and the Role of D in *Parsifal*: The Tonal Spaces of the Drama and the Enharmonic Cb/B', *Nineteenth-Century Music* 7 (1984), pp. 336–49; Brian Hyer, 'Reimag(in)ing Riemann', *Journal of Music Theory* 39 (1996), pp. 101–36, and 'Tonal Intuitions in *Tristan und Isolde*', PhD dissertation (Yale University, 1989). Hyer has worked out further some specific ideas in 'The Concept of Function in Riemann', unpublished

Example 2.10 Major-third relations are simple to express in dualistic *Klang* shorthand but complex as harmonic functions.

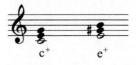

three 'harmonic pillars' is itself derived from a notion that identifies harmonies essentially with chords.[51] As we shall see, this equivocation between chords and their interpretation is a constant source of tension in Riemann's theory of harmonic function.

As a consequence of the diverging tonal spaces of the two components of Riemann's theory, there are some root-interval progressions that cannot be translated into the categories of harmonic function. For instance, as shown in Example 2.10, where the major-third relation between c^+ and e^+ was a basic step on the grid of harmonic relations – a 'directly intelligible interval' translated into a relation between chords – the theory of harmonic function does not allow for such a remote relation. The interpretative restrictions of harmonic functions mean that Riemann can only interpret the relation in rather clumsy fashion as a very indirect relation, namely as the dominant of the relative minor of the tonic, which itself is never sounded. In his function shorthand he usually expressed this relation in the following manner: *D[Tp]*.[52] This means that what was previously Riemann's prime example of 'tonality', the succession $c^+– ab^+– c^+– e^+– c^+$ shown in Example 2.3c above, can only be expressed in terms of harmonic function with the greatest difficulty. One recent commentator has noted with regard to such problems:

[Riemann's] unwillingness to grant chromatic relations equal rights with diatonic ones, reflected as well in the diatonic basis of the functional theory, is at odds with the assertions from his younger days about the equality of the strong third relations, and of an expanded notion of *Tonalität* reaching beyond the diatonic set.[53]

---

paper (AMS/SEM/SMT meeting Oakland, Calif., 1990); I am grateful to Professor Hyer for making a transcript of this paper available to me. See also my 'Trial Scenes at Nuremberg', *Music Analysis* 20 (2001), pp. 247–52.

[51] The *Musik-Lexikon*, 5th edn (Leipzig: Max Hesse, 1900), p. 259, shows an example where Riemann was unambiguous about the status of these 'harmonic pillars' when he stated in the entry on 'Dominante': 'the *chords* tonic, subdominant and dominant were identified as the actual pillars of tonal harmony' (my emphasis).

[52] The most elegant solution, $^+Dp^v$, he shunned until a very late stage in his career, as this would require two modifications at once: the parallel and the variant. See also Chapter 5 below, n. 13.

[53] Kopp, 'Chromatic Third Relations', p. 179.

Is Riemann's theory of function in fact regressive, or 'backpedaling', as the same commentator concludes? As we have seen, it is fair to say that his later theory does not allow certain successions that his former ideas accommodated. More pertinently, if such chromatic third relations are an important feature of the harmonic practice of the nineteenth century – which indeed they are[54] – we must ask what it means to exclude such possibilities from the theoretical framework.

A preliminary answer can already be given on the basis of Riemann's system of harmony as discussed so far. The two parts – the 'grid of harmonic relations', founded on Riemann's initial confidence in the objective existence of the undertone series, and theory of harmonic function, which interprets these chords in relation to the tonic – work in close conjunction. Their interrelationship is perhaps best understood in this manner: the grid is a demonstration of full harmonic potential (based on Riemann's aspiration to a scientifically true music theory), while the conception of harmonic function delimits how far one may move within a key. These two levels – loosely understood as 'what is possible' and 'what is permissible' – together constitute the notion of responsibility in Riemann's music theory.

At least it does so in principle: for we have already seen that the two levels do not fit together as snugly as Riemann pretends. Just as the edges turn out to be frayed, consequently, so does Riemann's notion of responsibility.

III

In this two-tiered scheme, we must now place the music-theoretical object. For this purpose we should return to the initial example of Riemann's analysis of Beethoven's 'Waldstein' sonata and consider what he makes of the second subject (which, incidentally, represents the $c^+ - e^+$ relationship to the first subject that caused Riemann's theory of harmonic function such problems). Example 2.11 shows his analysis of this passage. In bars 35–6, which open the example, all parts move down in a strictly sequential pattern with two interrupted cadences outlining a movement from E major to A major. In the detail of his analysis of this passage we can see the problems that arise between the two tiers of his conceptual model.

---

[54] Schubert in particular has been considered a paradigm of such third-relations. See for instance, Suzannah Clark, 'Terzverwandtschaften in der "Unvollendeten" von Schubert und der "Waldstein"-Sonate von Beethoven – Kennzeichen des neunzehnten Jahrhunderts und theoretisches Problem', *Schubert durch die Brille* 20 (1998), pp. 122–30. It is perhaps no coincidence that Riemann's model analysis in *Musikalische Syntaxis* is Schubert's Impromptu in G♭ (transposed to G). See also Chapter 3 below, n. 23.

Example 2.11 Riemann's analysis of Beethoven's 'Waldstein' Sonata, second subject area.

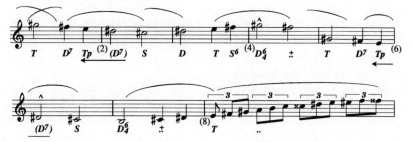

Example 2.12 The first two bars of the above passage expressed in dualistic *Klang* shorthand.

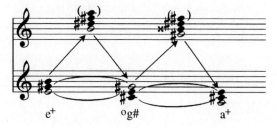

In his prose explanation, Riemann mentioned that the passage contains two interrupted cadences, and suggests that in isolation they could be labelled D^7 – Tp (in E major) and D^7 – $\maltese$ (in C# minor) respectively.[55] As Example 2.12 shows, the dualistic *Klang* shorthand, likewise, shows a pattern of regular, contiguous root-interval progressions for the chords that fulfil tonic functions in the same two bars. The observed parallelism is particularly striking in the graphic representation, with two common tones each between e^+ and $°g\#$, and $°g\#$ and a^+. As before, the white notehead indicates the dualistic root.

The analysis of the same passage in terms of harmonic function, however, does not allow us to transfer these relations: the problem is the second interrupted cadence, which Riemann labels *S*, rather than treating it as a further modification of the tonic E major (as was the case with the C# minor chord as *Tp*). By doing that, he breaks up the parallelism in the phrase. He bolsters his decision by suggesting that the preceding chord in its dominant function must not be related to this A major harmony, but rather – as the arrow pointing left in Example 2.11 indicates – backwards to the *Tp*.

---

[55] Riemann, *Ludwig van Beethovens sämtliche Klavier-Solosonaten*, 2nd edn (Berlin: Max Hesse, 1920), vol. 3, p. 6.

In other words, while Riemann is aware of the harmonic parallelism in principle, he does not make room for it in the final analysis. Instead, he reinterprets the context to avoid the alternative interpretation. Moreover, Riemann's decision to label the A major harmony *S* is precisely an instance of the confusion mentioned above, between the actual meaning of harmonic function as a chord, or as an interpretation of a chord: in calling the A major harmony *S*, regardless of the context in which it appears, Riemann holds on to the chordal aspect of this 'harmonic pillar' here by considering the full congruence of the A major triad with the subdominant 'harmonic pillar' of E major. However, as Brian Hyer reminds us, harmonic function is not a chord but something one *does* to a chord.[56] The fact that a chord *sounds* like an A major triad in E major does not necessarily mean that it must *function* as a subdominant.

Even without being able to put a finger on it at this stage, we can see that there is a problem in Riemann's vacillation between the chordal properties and the relational properties of the notion of harmonic function: he evidently cannot accommodate both these relations – $D - Tp$ (in E major) and $D - \mathit{T}$ (in C# minor) – in terms of his harmonic function within one tonal unit at the same time. There is no room for this relation in the tonal space opened up by his theory of harmonic functions.

This is of crucial significance, for if we follow Riemann's contention, as quoted earlier, that the 'taxonomy of function [is] the actual sign-post through the maze of possible harmonic successions', this means no less than that the parallels are irrelevant. Or, to put it more strongly: in the world of harmonic function, there exists no interrupted cadence from g#+ to a+; it would be located outside the tonal boundaries set by Riemann's theory. In this way, Riemann fulfilled his promise of 'demonstrating that a very definite barrier exists for such capriciousness', as he had decreed at the outset of his career. He had created a responsible theory. At the same time, this 'definite barrier' is also a demonstration of the conceptual power such an 'explicit' theoretical approach may exert over a musical composition.

Riemann's analyses of Beethoven's sonatas stand in isolation in his theoretical work as his most sustained and detailed analytical effort. Carl Dahlhaus has suggested that the analyses themselves function as a kind of exemplary proof of the validity of Riemann's theory of harmony.[57] In

---

[56] Hyer, 'The concept of harmonic function in Riemann', p. 6. Similarly, David Lewin explains that the equation of IV and subdominant is only a 'matter of convention'. See 'Amfortas's Prayer to Titurel and the Role of D in *Parsifal*', p. 344.

[57] See Dahlhaus, *Musiktheorie im 18. und 19. Jahrhundert; Erster Teil: Grundzüge einer Systematik*, p. 30. A recent commentary can be found in Wilhelm Seidel, 'Riemann and Beethoven', in Tatjana Böhme-Mehner and Klaus Mehner, eds., *Hugo Riemann (1849–1919): Musikwissenschaftler mit Universalanspruch* (Cologne, Weimar, Vienna: Böhlau, 2001), pp. 139–51.

other words, the works (supported by the canonical status of their composer) function as a legitimation device of the theory. This would explain why Riemann was so anxious to stress the ordinariness of the opening of the 'Waldstein' sonata, as observed initially: what matters for purposes of legitimation is its normative regularity, not its particularity. However, it must be remembered that the normativity of the passage is not so much a feature of the music, as of the theory. In other words, it is Riemann's theory that *made* the passage ordinary, just as the second subject was truncated by the theoretical parameters. While partaking of the canonical status of the music it works on, Riemann's music theory effectively shapes and recreates the music within its boundaries.

With this model in mind – which effectively reverses the commonplace understanding of music theory and musical works – it is possible to rethink the widespread reproach as to how little interest Riemann showed in issues in contemporary composition. Numerous commentators understand this incongruence between the features of Riemann's theory and those of harmonic practice as a mark of his failure. It has been asserted, for instance, that the daring chromatic harmonies of works such as Wagner's *Tristan und Isolde*, written half a century previously, already relativised the universal aspirations of Riemann's theory before he had even articulated it.[58] However, with a view to the self-assumed responsibilities of music theory, there is an alternative interpretation. The observed failure of Riemann's theory with regard to *Tristan* can also be construed as a failure of the music with regard to the theory: in *not* engaging with the music successfully, Riemann's theory is implicitly commenting on it, and seems to suggest that there is something wrong with the music. And here we must remember Riemann's obsession with a quasi-scientific epistemology discussed in the previous chapter – whose full significance comes to the fore with respect to the ethical and historical work that he envisaged his theory doing.

In other words, his theory filtered that which is possible through that which – according to the parameters of his theory – is permissible. From this angle, there is something highly charged when we consider that at a time when it became increasingly clear that plenty more categories would be needed to come to terms with the compositional reality of harmonic structures, Riemann focused his attention on two harmonic modes, major and minor.

It would be wrong-headed simply to dismiss this attempt as musically insensitive or reactionary. Rather, it is concerned with the music of the

---

[58] Helga de la Motte-Haber and Carl Dahlhaus, *Systematische Musikwissenschaft* (Wiesbaden: Akademische Verlagsgesellschaft Athenaion, 1982), p. 5.

later nineteenth century in a much more complex, utopian fashion: his music theory works against musical works as much as it works on them. By means of his music theory, as we shall see in the following chapters, he hoped to instruct composers and listeners what music ought to be. This concern of Riemann's music theory – leaving its object, 'music', conspicuously unqualified – is not merely concerned with autonomous harmonic structures. Rather, its concerns are far more wide-ranging and, in the final analysis, turn out to take an active part in music history and cultural politics.

These wider dimensions of the responsibility of music theory may not always be immediately obvious. We can catch an initial glimpse of it, however, in *Musikalische Syntaxis*, written five years after his initial attack on Weitzmann and Laurencin, in which Riemann made a similar point when he pointedly dismissed the theorists Melchior Sachs, Albert Hahn and Heinrich Vincent with the bewildering epithet 'Social Democrats'.[59] All three theorists, the core members of a 'chromatic movement' in harmonic theory, were interested in using the chromatic scale as the foundation of a harmonic system and in abolishing chromatic differentiations such as G#/A♭. This move would open the door to total chromaticism: Vincent's theory adumbrated a pitch-class set approach to harmony, in that he labelled all semitones from 0 to 11.[60] In the light of the programme of those three theorists of harmony, the overtly political name Riemann invented for them is poignant: August Bebel's Social Democratic Party was to be severely legislated under Bismarck's administration in the following year. Indeed, it has been argued that Bismarck's attacks against the Social Democrats were more acrimonious than those against any of Germany's external adversaries.[61] The common conservative reproaches against the political Social Democrats can indeed be easily transferred to the music-theoretical realm: they promoted a society without hierarchy, and their internationalism was held against them, as was, in a closely related criticism, their rootlessness and denial of tradition.

The music critic Rudolf Louis once pointed out, apropos a turn-of-the-century debate about musical progress, that whenever parallels are drawn between musical and political situations, this is a sure sign that

---

[59] Riemann, *Musikalische Syntaxis*, p. 34. (Riemann wrote, probably erroneously, 'I. Sachs'.) Whilst totally forgotten nowadays, the three theorists were prominent in the 1870s, particularly after the foundation of Hahn's journal *Die Tonkunst* in 1876, which promoted the chromatic scale. The polemical mention of the three is thus primarily a topical concern of Riemann. He exorcised them in his article 'Das chromatische Tonsystem', in *Präludien und Studien* (reprint, Hildesheim: Georg Olms, 1967), vol. 1, pp. 183–219.

[60] See Wason, 'Progressive Harmonic Theory', pp. 61–5.

[61] Gordon A. Craig, *German History 1866–1945* (Oxford: Oxford University Press, 1981), p. 93.

art is considered within a covert historical trajectory.[62] And such a politicised name for a musical tendency was by no means a singular phenomenon. To cite just one example from Riemann's immediate context, we find the same derogatory label with all these implications in a polemic by Felix Draeseke, to which Riemann would contribute a few years later:

Even worse is the impression of increasing crudeness, coupled with a disdain for all previous traditions, that a cult of the ugly necessarily evokes in the entire musical world, on artists and amateurs alike. It is impossible that this defamiliarisation with beauty, simplicity and euphoniousness could bear fruit – it can only exacerbate the already noticeable decay of art. Indeed, if no one stood up to fend off [this tendency], it could lead us to utter ruin: if the Social Democrats came to power and wanted to turn art upside down, just as they do with any existing order, they would not find a lot to get rid of.[63]

The chromatic freedom that Vincent, Hahn and Sachs advocated negated the diatonic hierarchy of tonal music; its semitonal order not only denied the tonal tradition of Western music, but, as we shall see, apparently even contradicted the basic facts of nature. Altogether, the name 'Social Democrats' resonates with reproaches of disorder and chaos; social and tonal order converge in this rather outlandish label. To promote such a music-theoretical approach lacking any kind of limitation would be nothing short of irresponsible – as Riemann's criticism leaves us in no doubt, harmonic chaos would ensue. While there is nothing in their theoretical approaches that would make 'chromatic' theorists of Vincent, Hahn and Sachs's ilk obvious bedfellows of the likes of Weitzmann and Laurencin, this lack of music-theoretical responsibility connects the two groups.

---

[62] Rudolf Louis, *Die deutsche Musik der Gegenwart* (Munich and Leipzig: Georg Müller, 1909), p. 19.

[63] Felix Draeseke, *Die Konfusion in der Musik*; reprinted in Susanne Shigihara, *'Die Konfusion in der Musik': Felix Draesekes Kampfschrift (1906) und die Folgen* (Bonn: Gudrun Schröder, 1990), p. 61. 'Was uns übrigens noch schlimmer dünkt, ist der verrohende Eindruck, den ein Kultus des Hässlichen, verbunden mit der Verachtung aller bisher gültigen Traditionen, auf die gesamte musikalische Welt, Laien wie Künstler, hervorrufen muß. Denn diese Entwöhnung vom Schönen, Einfachen und Wohlklingenden kann unmöglich gute Früchte tragen und den bereits merklichen Verfall der Kunst nur noch weiter steigern. Ja, sie könnte, wenn niemand sich wehrte und ihr kein Einhalt getan würde, sogar zum völligen Ruin führen, so daß die Sozialdemokraten, im Fall sie zur Herrschaft kämen und, wie mit allem Bestehenden, auch mit der Kunst aufräumen wollten, bei uns nicht viel zu beseitigen finden würden.' On the development of a related trope after 1917 into political extremism, see particularly Eckhard John, *Musikbolschewismus: Die Politisierung der Musik in Deutschland 1918–38* (Stuttgart and Weimar: Metzler, 1994). Riemann's contribution to this debate resulted in the row with Reger, see Introduction above, n. 25.

IV

The complex power relations between the musical repertoire and the music theory can perhaps be best understood with the help of two terms that Riemann used to classify music theory: he habitually differentiated between 'speculative' and 'practical' aspects.[64] Speculative theory was concerned with the metaphysics of musical phenomena, with the attempt to find the basis of what is harmonically admissible and what is not, whereas practical music theory sought to formulate rules and to present them as a theoretical system which would be used primarily for purposes of teaching. These two parts of music theory, which, Riemann admitted, cannot in effect be completely separated, closely reflected two of the main concerns of the German nineteenth-century music-theoretical tradition: the preoccupation with pedagogy on the one hand, and the urge to find quasi-scientific rules as a basis of a universal aesthetics on the other. On the most basic level, the interaction between speculative and practical music theory can be imagined thus: speculative music theory searches for the epistemological foundations of music, which practical music theory then perpetuates in teaching. Riemann's sedulous concern with the speculative side of music theory suggests how seriously he took the responsibility of his theoretical work. (It is no coincidence that the works Riemann analysed extensively – besides Beethoven's piano sonatas, Bach's *Well-Tempered Clavier* and *The Art of Fugue* – were perceived in the nineteenth century as eminently pedagogical works.)

In this sense, Riemann's dualistic theory of harmony is lodged between apparently immutable laws on which the rules of the music theory are built, and a canonical repertoire of musical works that it seeks to (re)interpret on the basis of those rules. From this angle, then, apparently straightforward comments, such as the following, must be read very carefully:

It would be a strange enterprise to attempt to teach how to make music other than the type written hitherto. A reasonable theory of art can only strive to find the most convenient and instructive form of communication of that which is common technical knowledge of the artist, to gain an understanding of how the masterworks are made, to facilitate the assimilation and the acceptance of the achievements of others in one's own imagination, altogether to practise [the creative] imagination and to protect it from one-sidedness.[65]

---

[64] See, for instance, the entry 'Theorie' in Riemann, *Musik-Lexikon*, 5th edn (Leipzig: Max Hesse, 1900), p. 1131. Also see Peter Rummenhöller, *Musiktheoretisches Denken im 19. Jahrhundert* (Regensburg: Gustav Bosse, 1967), pp. 27–38.

[65] Riemann, *Systematische Modulationslehre*, p. viii. 'Es wäre ein seltsames Beginnen, etwa lehren zu wollen, wie man andere Musik machen könne als die bisher geschriebene. Eine vernünftige Kunstlehre kann nur anstreben, die bequemste und nutzbringendste

When taken at face value, this assertion would appear to contradict flatly the above ideas concerning the power and responsibility of music theory: Riemann simply seems to submit his theoretical postulates to the course of music history. The interpretation of Riemann's theories in the following chapters, however, will show that his theory of harmony was actually not as modest as his statement would lead us to believe. And from the ground already covered, we can gauge that Riemann was being disingenuous in this statement: his insistence on harmonic dualism sufficiently demonstrates that he by no means urged his students to adhere to conventional musical patterns. Rather, the first sentence – 'it would be a strange enterprise to teach how to make music other than the type written hitherto' – rings rather differently when it is considered against the background of the increasingly chromatic music with which Riemann battled. While the statement may superficially appear to be in contradiction to Riemann's music-theoretical ambition, it is in fact an integral part of it: it implies that his theories should not be understood as a radical departure to an essentially new music, but rather as a revision of the foundations of the Western musical tradition.

In this sense, one must understand the above statement – as Riemann's theory on the whole – in terms of its cultural, historical and political dimension. From a practical viewpoint, Riemann's ambition to devise a universal theory of harmony on the basis of his harmonic dualism may now be regarded as a failure. From the viewpoint of the responsibility of music theory, however, what remains is a utopian vision of an everlasting realm of tonal order.

Form der Mittheilung dessen zu finden, was technisches Gemeingut der Künstler ist, das Verständnis der Faktur der Meisterwerke zu erschliessen, den Prozess der Assimilation, der Aufnahme des von andern geleisteten in das eigene Vorstellungsvermögen zu erleichtern, überhaupt die Phantasie zu üben und vor Einseitigkeit zu bewahren.'

3

Riemann's musical logic and the 'As if'

With his taxonomy of harmonic function Riemann hoped to introduce systematic order to the boundless dualistic harmonic grid. Yet he still felt the need to employ an additional category: cadential succession. In fact, Riemann's use of the term 'cadence' differed significantly from contemporary Anglo-American usage and may need some words of clarification: a cadence for Riemann was not a momentary event but rather a succession of chords that establishes a tonic. He explained the relation between the two concepts as follows:

The theory of cadential construction expands increasingly, from the conclusions of the parts to the order of succession of harmonies within these [parts]. Finally, a complete theory of the immanent logic of harmonic succession emerges, a theory of the natural, law-abiding order of harmonic motion.[1]

As with many aspects of Riemann's harmonic system, there is some controversy about the validity and significance of Riemann's notion of cadential succession: most critics either ignore it,[2] or argue that it is self-contradictory.[3] Moreover, the criticism that Riemann himself did not comply with the restrictions he set himself has also been levelled.[4]

---

[1] Hugo Riemann, *Geschichte der Musiktheorie*, 2nd edn (Berlin: Max Hesse, 1921; reprint Hildesheim: Georg Olms, 1990), p. 473. 'Die Lehre von der Kadenzbildung greift immer mehr von den Abschlüssen der Teile auch auf die Folgeordnung der Harmonien innerhalb derselben über und schließlich entwickelt sich eine vollständige Lehre von der immanenten Logik der Harmoniefolgen, eine Lehre von der natürlichen Gesetzmäßigkeit der Harmoniebewegung.' See also Siegfried Schmalzriedt, 'Kadenz', in Hans Heinrich Eggebrecht and Albrecht Riethmüller, eds., *Handwörterbuch der musikalischen Terminologie* (Stuttgart: Franz Steiner, n.d.), p. 17.

[2] David Lewin, *Generalized Musical Intervals and Transformations* (New Haven: Yale University Press, 1987), pp. 175–92, and Brian Hyer, 'Reimag(in)ing Riemann', *Journal of Music Theory* 39 (1995), pp. 101–36.

[3] Carl Dahlhaus, 'Über den Begriff der tonalen Funktion', in Martin Vogel, ed., *Beiträge zur Musiktheorie des neunzehnten Jahrhunderts* (Regensburg: Gustav Bosse, 1966), pp. 96–7.

[4] Daniel Harrison, *Harmonic Function in Chromatic Music* (Chicago: University of Chicago Press, 1994), p. 278.

All these criticisms have a certain validity, especially when applying Riemann's theory to musical works for analytical purposes. Despite the tension between practice and theory, as we shall see, in Riemann's thought cadential order did serve a supremely important purpose. No less than the rigorous, scientific appeal of Riemann's musical thought rested on the notion of cadential order: it can tell us how music ought to work.

I

Riemann had first developed a notion of cadential order in his doctoral dissertation *Über das musikalische Hören* (*On Musical Hearing*, 1873), a preview of which was also published in excerpts in 1872 as an article entitled 'Musikalische Logik'; the published form of his dissertation bore the same title.[5] Significantly, harmonic dualism played no part in the concept of musical logic as it was elucidated in the article, although Riemann was already familiar with Oettingen's work.

In the article, Riemann explained that musical logic resides in the cadential succession $I - IV - I - V - I$. His 'logic' here was presented in dialectical terms *à la* Hauptmann, but Riemann promised to go beyond him. Hauptmann had explained that a central chord is recognised in its role as a tonic by virtue of its lower and upper dominants and expressed his dialectical idea of tonality by means of a 'triad of triads', as is shown in Example 3.1, where tonality is established in three stages.

What Hauptmann described in the 'triad of triads' is essentially the logical process from an unmediated triad to its dialectically asserted position as the centre of a tonality. After stating the triad (at I), another fifth-related triad is sounded to challenge the first in its central significance. Stage (I) – (II) depicts the two possibilities. Since the position between two fifth-related triads is always ambiguous, it is impossible to decide whether the relation should be heard as a tonic–dominant or subdominant–tonic. The central triad has thus come into opposition with itself, which is expressed by the antithetical (II). It is only when the other fifth-related chord is introduced that tonal order is regained, and the first chord can be reinstated as a central triad – now as confirmed tonic. The synthetic task of the tonic, as (III), consists in simultaneously 'being' dominant to its subdominant and 'having' a dominant itself.[6]

---

[5] For a recent reappraisal of the notion of 'musical logic' see Adolf Nowak, 'Wandlungen des Begriffs "musikalische Logik" bei Hugo Riemann', in Tatjana Böhme-Mehner and Klaus Mehner, eds., *Hugo Riemann (1849–1919): Musikwissenschaftler mit Universalanspruch* (Cologne, Weimar, Vienna: Böhlau, 2001), pp. 37–48.

[6] Moritz Hauptmann, *The Nature of Harmony and Metre*, trans. William E. Heathcote (London: S. Sonnenschein, 1893; reprint New York: Da Capo Press, 1991), p. 9.

Example 3.1 Moritz Hauptmann's 'triad of triads', from *Die Natur der Harmonik und Metrik*. The 'triad of triads' indicates the dialectical passage from one simple chord, at stage (I), to fully fledged tonality, at stage (III).

(I)

I - III - II
C   e   G

(I)   -   **(II)**

I - III - II   I - III - II
F a C e G   C e G b D
I - III - II   I - III - II

(I) - **(III)** - **(II)**

I - III - II   I - III - II
F a C e G b D
I - III - II

Riemann was critical of this model. For Hauptmann, he explained, it sufficed that the tonic triad is surrounded by both dominants, that in this way the tonality was 'shown from all sides', but Hauptmann did not distinguish any further between the two dominants. (The two possibilities at stage (II) of the triad of triads illustrate the equivalence of the upper and lower dominants.) Riemann, then, sought to improve on this model by adding a temporal perspective.

Having ascribed a 'cold and meagre' effect to the plagal cadence *I – IV – I*, and a 'full and satisfying' one to the perfect cadence *I – V – I*, Riemann combined the two, to form *I – IV – I – V – I* with the satisfying close last. He explained this dialectically, but with a different approach from Hauptmann: 'Thesis is the first tonic, antithesis the subdominant with the six-four chord of the tonic, synthesis the dominant with the closing tonic chord in root position.'[7] To us, this conception is striking since the middle tonic chord *I* is more often regarded – even by Riemann himself in subsequent writings[8] – as a double suspension of the following *V*. (Both interpretations are outlined in Example 3.2.) Yet Riemann described a clear disjunction in the dialectical moments between the suspension and its resolution. This may partly be because he was altogether

---

[7] Hugo Riemann (pseudonym: Hugibert Ries), 'Musikalische Logik', in *Präludien und Studien* (reprint Hildesheim: Georg Olms, 1967), vol. 3, p. 3. 'These ist die erste Tonika, Antithese die Unterdominante mit dem Quartsextakkord der Tonika, Synthese die Oberdominante mit dem schließenden Grundakkord der Tonika.'
[8] See *Systematische Modulationslehre* (Hamburg: J. F. Richter, 1887), p. 54.

Example 3.2 Riemann's dialectical cadential order, as discussed in 'Musikalische Logik'.

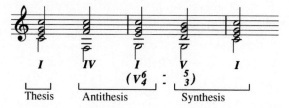

suspicious of voice-leading,[9] but the main reason for this unorthodox view resides in the argument itself: the six-four is presented as a direct result of the 'cold and meagre' plagal cadence, which causes the tonic to come into 'disagreement with itself'. As a triad in second inversion, this 'tonic' is incapable of attaining full closure.

In this conception, the upper and lower dominants are operators that exert their power over the tonic: the tonic itself is viewed as the result of the dialectics to which it is subjected. Riemann drew on Fichte's dialectical model of the Self as '*I – not I – limiting I-not-I*' ('*Ich – nicht-Ich – limitierend Ich-nicht-Ich*')[10] to explain this mechanism as follows: a chord has to be both given and denied its central position in the tonality in order then to arrive at the synthetic position of a fully fledged tonic. The outer two statements of *I*, usually in root position, would appear identical, yet the meaning of the latter *I* would be mediated and understood as the central chord of the tonality, while the initial *I* is a mere statement, the assumption of a tonic. The denial of a central position to *I* is achieved between *IV* and *I*, since the root of *I* is re-sounded in *IV*, but in a different position; it must be reinterpreted as the fifth of *IV*. Following the acoustical line of argument advanced by Helmholtz – that the main partials in the sound wave (or in the compound *Klang*) could be translated into harmonic relations – one could argue that *V* is acoustically implied in the overtone *Klang* of *I*, and in this way anticipates the sounding of *I*. As for *IV*, however, the problem is twofold: not only is there no acoustical

[9] In his thesis, *Über das musikalische Hören*, Dr phil. dissertation (Göttingen University, 1873), publ. as *Musikalische Logik* (Leipzig: C. F. Kahnt, 1874), pp. 53–4, Riemann suggested that dissonance might arise if individual voices go through different stages of the dialectics at the same time. Such a dissonant clash would occur if, say, the bass were 'in antithesi' while the treble were 'in synthesi'. Riemann thus effectively declared counterpoint as the source of dissonance. However, he did not fully develop this thought either in this work or in any subsequent publication.

[10] Riemann, *Musikalische Logik*, p. 52. The Fichtean model (taken from his *Wissenschaftslehre*) was absent in the early article 'Musikalische Logik', where instead reference was made to Hauptmann. Elmar Seidel has juxtaposed the two versions in his 'Die Harmonielehre Hugo Riemanns', in Martin Vogel, ed., *Studien zur Musiktheorie des neunzehnten Jahrhunderts* (Regensburg: Gustav Bosse, 1966), p. 48.

anticipation of the root of the chord in *I*, but the Helmholtzian *Klang* of *IV* in turn implies *I*. In this case, however, it is tempting to interpret the chord succession not as *I – IV* but rather as (*V – I*) of *IV*. In other words, it is specifically the subdominant, not the dominant as Hauptmann had equivocated in his triad of triads, that challenges the central position of the tonic. It is impossible to judge outside a precise context which interpretation is correct. The occurrence of *IV* thus carries an inherently conflicting element. The *I* in six-four position, the *'nicht-Ich'*, Riemann viewed as the external manifestation of this conflict: *I* becomes in this position, so to speak, its own dominant.

However, in an appeal to compositional practice, Riemann then went on to eliminate the central *I* from his model cadence, arguing that 'in freer composition *I – IV – V – I* is by far the most used form'. The central *I*, he explained, did not 'actually present anything new' and could therefore be removed without any further ado.[11] On the basis of this new four-chord model, he located the dialectical moments in the chords themselves: 'thetic is the tonic, antithetic the subdominant, synthetic the dominant'. In the light of the above explanation, this must be a false conclusion: the dialectical moments are not located in the chords themselves, but rather in the relations between chords, between the dominants and the tonic. *IV* itself is meaningless, it is only in its relation to *I* that it functions as the antithesis. This is nothing but another manifestation of one of the problems we were left with at the end of Chapter 2 above. In fact, Brian Hyer has suggested the felicitous phrase 'linguistic Midas touch' to describe this phenomenon of referring to a dominant as a chord instead of a relation, in the sense of 'something that one does to a chord'.[12]

That said, it seems that Riemann left himself a back door open: his decision to locate the dialectical moments in the chords themselves is perhaps not necessarily a 'Midas touch', a false likening of relation with chord. For it would seem that in Riemann's conception relations are not actually irreconcilably opposed to chords:

If I imagine the C major triad in its meaning in the key of C major, it is the tonic itself, centre, closing chord. The image of it contains nothing that would contradict its consonance. It appears stable, pure, simple. If I imagine, on the other hand, the G major chord in the sense of the key of C major, then I imagine it as the *Klang* of the upper fifth of the C major triad, i.e. the C major triad itself is part of the imagination as that *Klang* by which the significance of the G major

---

[11] Riemann, 'Musikalische Logik', pp. 3–4.

[12] Brian Hyer, 'The Concept of Harmonic Function in Riemann', unpublished paper (AMS/SMT/SET Oakland, 1990), p. 6. We can see here that the petrification of a relation into a chord is not only due to discursive laxness but was part of Riemann's rhetoric from the start.

triad is determined as something deviating from it – the centre of its imagination lies, so to speak, outside of it. That is to say, a moment of instability emerges, a desire to progress to the C major triad, dissonance.[13]

In the realm of mental representations of tones (*Tonvorstellungen*), a concept that Riemann did not fully develop until the final years of his life, the sounding of chords is always a mental act of comparing. A chord may in itself be nothing but a chord, but in the framework of tonality, Riemann explained, every chord is invariably compared with the harmonic centre, and demands progression according to a certain pattern, which he called musical logic. It is not necessary to sound the tonic itself to make this act of comparing possible. Due to the mental comparison, the only true consonance – the consonance of the full cadence, as it were – is the tonic triad. Viewed in this light, the sounding of the central *I* is indeed not necessary, because it is implicit. A chord in Riemann's theory of tonality, then, is also a relation.

At least in principle this is so. To be sure, Riemann did not act accordingly when he developed the concept of the model cadence – and ultimately of musical logic – in his books. A first attempt to bring the cadential model to bear on his mature musical thought came to the fore in *Systematische Modulationslehre* (1887), the immediate precursor of his function treatises. In this work, the two principal factors of form, 'harmonic cadence and rhythmic symmetry',[14] were treated together. This was no small achievement, as previously Riemann had largely developed the two separately, and had only alluded to their combination in musical practice. In fact, perhaps the most notable feature of *Systematische Modulationslehre* is its wealth of real musical examples, rather than the schematic models that Riemann habitually employed in his books on harmony.[15] This practice was common among his theory books on metre, but very rare among his harmony textbooks. In the context of this book, and his ambitious attempt to join metric and harmonic ideas, it seems he resorted to this strategy because he had no sound theoretical foundation for the harmonic–metric unit in the abstract. Riemann's

---

[13] Hugo Riemann, 'Die Natur der Harmonik', *Waldersees Sammlung musikalischer Vorträge* 4 (1882), p. 188. 'Denke ich mir den c-Durakkord im Sinne der c-Dur-Tonart, so ist er selbst Tonika, Centrum, schlußfähiger Akkord, seine Vorstellung enthält also nichts seiner Konsonanz Widersprechendes, erscheint ruhig, rein, einfach; denke ich mir dagegen den g-Durakkord im Sinne der c-Durtonart, so denke ich ihn mir als Klang der Oberquinte des c-Durakkordes, d.h. der c-Durakkord selbst geht mit in die Vorstellung ein als derjenige Klang, an welchem sich die Bedeutung des g-Durakkordes bestimmt als etwas von ihm Abweichendes – das Centrum der Vorstellung liegt also sozusagen außer ihr, d.h. es kommt ein Moment der Unruhe in dieselbe, das Verlangen der Fortschreitung zum c-Durakkord, die Dissonanz.'

[14] Riemann, *Systematische Modulationslehre*, p. 2.

[15] Daniel Harrison, *Harmonic Function in Chromatic Music*, p. 278, draws special attention to this book and notes how it seemed to lead into a cul-de-sac.

Example 3.3 Riemann's 'double-sided' cadence, embracing both upper and lower dominants, indicating the relative metric weight of each main function.

theory of metre, in particular, lacked the quasi-scientific rigour that, as we saw before, his theories of harmony seemed to possess. The ultimate authority that he appealed to in his ideas on metre was common sense.

The basic assumption of Riemann's theory of metre was the constant iambic alternation of light and heavy beats. While the axiomatic anacrusis (*Auftaktigkeit*) has gained a certain notoriety as the cornerstone of Riemann's theory of metre,[16] it is perhaps more enlightening to speak of a postulate of a downbeat ending instead. The initial upbeat is then a consequence of the conjunction of this final downbeat with the underlying doctrine of symmetry: if the last beat is heavy, then the corresponding antecedent must be light. As Example 3.3 shows, this metrical model is matched with the basic cadential model of $I - IV - V - I$ to form a quadratic stress pattern with bar lines after the light beats, which becomes normative.[17] In this coexistence of the two factors, harmony and metre, Riemann remained ambiguous as to whether harmonic function is dependent on metrical stress or vice versa.[18]

Despite these uncertainties, Riemann analysed some rather sophisticated examples, for instance the long opening phrase of Chopin's Nocturne in E♭ major (Example 3.4).[19] Even though this phrase is rich in harmonies, and several of them seem to escape from the domain of E♭ major, Riemann managed to interpret the entire eight-bar phrase as one cadence. Perhaps the most suspicious-looking formations in this excerpt

---

[16] See for instance the entry 'Auftakt' (upbeat), translated in the glossary. For a modern response to *Auftaktigkeit* see Edward T. Cone, 'The Picture and the Frame: The Nature of Musical Form', in *Musical Form and Musical Performance* (New York: Norton, 1968), pp. 18 and 25.

[17] See Riemann, *Systematische Modulationslehre*, p. 16.

[18] The metrical implications of the concept of function were first explored by Hans Joachim Moser in 'Die harmonischen Funktionen in der tonalen Kadenz', *Zeitschrift für Musikwissenschaft* 1 (1919), pp. 515–23. Carl Dahlhaus has written extensively about this aspect, for instance in Erwin Apfel and Carl Dahlhaus, *Studien zur Theorie und Geschichte der musikalischen Rhythmik und Metrik* (Munich: Dr. Emil Katzbichler, 1974), vol. 1, pp. 184–203. A more recent contribution in English can be found in William Caplin, 'Tonal Function and Metrical Accent: A Historical Perspective', *Music Theory Spectrum* 5 (1983), pp. 1–14.

[19] Riemann, *Systematische Modulationslehre*, pp. 43–5.

Example 3.4 Riemann's analysis of Chopin's Nocturne in Eb major, from *Systematische Modulationslehre*.

are the g^7 and the $f^{9>}$, where the crossed-out letter signifies that the root is not sounded, and the Arabic-numerals signify pitch additions (with the ninth flattened, as the > indicates). Another way of describing the second chord in question would therefore have been $a^{7>}{}_{5>}$, but the fact that Riemann did not choose this label, and rather decided in favour of a chord label that builds on a non-sounding root, indicates that a strong interpretative element was at play here. That is to say, Riemann recognised these two chords, g^7 and $f^{9>}$, as intermediary dominants, which, rather than introducing a modulation, merely underline the gravity of the main chords. In fact, every harmony of this phrase is preceded by an applied dominant. What is more, Riemann did not hesitate in the explanation accompanying the example to call the F minor triad ($^\circ$c) the subdominant, rather than ab^+, which would be *IV* of Eb. He was obviously already thinking in terms of harmonic functions, a concept that he did not present formally until his next book, *Vereinfachte Harmonielehre*.[20] We can therefore – violating chronology here for reasons of intelligibility – easily translate the interpretation into functions.

The eight-bar period (which in Chopin's original only comprises four bars in 12/8) can then be interpreted as opening with a short *T – D – T* phrase (eb^+–bb^+–eb^+), which opens up the harmonic space to *Sp* ($^\circ$c) via an applied dominant, c^7 (which Riemann will always mark as *D* in parentheses). The appoggiature in bars 2 and 4 are metrically emphasised with an accent over the downbeat. While the second half of this eight-bar unit begins with a restatement of tonic (which Riemann forgot to label in this example) and dominant at bar 5, Riemann's rebarred version actually de-emphasises the metric weight of this dominant, as in

---

[20] He first introduced a modified version of function terminology in the article, 'Die Neugestaltung der Harmonielehre', *Musikalisches Wochenblatt* 22 (1891), pp. 513–14, 529–31, 541–3. See Renate Imig, *Systeme der Funktionsbezeichnung in der Harmonielehre seit Hugo Riemann* (Düsseldorf: Gesellschaft zur Förderung der systematischen Musikwissenschaft, 1971), pp. 67–9.

Example 3.5 Interrupted cadences that are difficult to reconcile with
the limitations of harmonic function, from *Handbuch der
Harmonielehre*.

his metric scheme bar 6 is considered weightier. The harmonies, whose
rhythm speeds up towards the end, traverse *Tp* (°g at bar 6) and *D*
(b♭⁷at bar 7), both preceded by applied dominants. In this way Riemann
manages to represent this structure – which other theorists might well
regard as a *Satz* – as a full eight-bar period, touching on both subdominant and then dominant regions.

Because of the consideration given to cadences in the book, he could
also explain interrupted cadences in proto-functional terms, defining
them as 'a real close, but…disturbed by a simultaneously sounding
alien tone'.[21] Yet the closing chord is not a different function altogether:
its tonic meaning is not affected. In other words, the interrupted cadence
is conceptualised on the basis of the cadential model, as a deviation from
it, which, however, does not change its significance.

The cadence, then, formed the context in which Riemann's theories
of function and metre conjoined as mutually determining forces. Deviations from the model, however, were not unrestricted. In the – admittedly rare – example of an interrupted cadence *V – IV*, Riemann
would suggest an interpretation using the functions *D – S* (Example 3.5
also shows the minor dual). In fact, this interpretation corresponds
to Riemann's analysis of the 'Waldstein' Sonata, discussed above in
Example 2.11. Drawing on his explanation of the interrupted cadence,
we should expect the last chord to fulfil a tonic *function* in the phrase,
even though it is not the tonic *triad*. In accordance with the above
definition, we could derive this interrupted cadence in Example 3.5
as a tonic chord with two altered tones. The function label *S*, which
Riemann prefers, draws attention to the fine print of his definition of an
interrupted cadence: it seems to insist that only *one* tone may deviate
from the expected tonic chord. If this is so, then *S* remains the only
option, but the usage of *S* then attains clear chordal connotations. As
in the 'Waldstein' example in Chapter 2, however, a certain automatism
is discernible with which *S* is equated with *IV*, which would seem to
ignore the requirements of the metrical context.

Not until 1914, when he pursued his concept of *Tonvorstellungen* further, did Riemann take the first steps towards reconciling this tension

---

[21] Riemann, *Systematische Modulationslehre*, p. 14.

in his theory.[22] In the fifth edition of his *Handbuch der Harmonielehre*, he offered the 'more complicated' option of interpreting the interrupted cadence $V - IV$ as $D^7 - \overline{\overline{S}}p$.[23]

The label $\overline{\overline{S}}p$ represents an unusual apparent consonance; it is 'twice removed' from the tonic triad, by a major and a minor third. In arithmetical terms the combination of a major and a minor third may contain the same number of semitones as a perfect fifth, but it would be wrong, in Riemann's harmonic space, to conclude that the two actually *are* the same: S might tell us in the most straightforward way what the harmony *is*, whereas $\overline{\overline{S}}p$ tells us how we should *understand* it, and how we get there.

At the same time this 'more complicated' solution – which is at once far more adequate for Riemann's conceptual framework – meant that the cadential model, not the chord, is the basis of this decision: the actual chord progression would suggest $D - S$, just as Riemann wrote initially (in contradiction to his own express ideas about the order of succession in musical logic); meanwhile, the requirement that a full cadential statement must end with a tonic function would make a subdominant function an impossible choice. Only when the actual chord progression is mentally compared with the way an ideal cadence ought to go can harmonic function be fully determined; the appearance of the chord is often less relevant than its metrical position within the cadence.

Riemann's later writings show that he asserted the cadential model over the identity of chords. This often leads him to apparently radical interpretations, which, however, are really no more than attempts at consistency. It is doubtful, for example, that the earlier Riemann would have decided upon such an extravagant interpretation as the one he put forward in his late Beethoven analyses concerning a phrase in Op. 54, reproduced in Example 3.6: the final chord of the phrase is labelled T although it is clearly an augmented sixth chord which has not a single note in common with the tonic chord ($°a$ or D minor). An explanation that simply proceeds harmonically would not arrive at this label; the tonic function is here assigned to this unlikely chord on the basis of its metrical position, because it follows the dominant on a phrasal downbeat

---

[22] Strictly speaking, not even then: there is still a rather odd example in the late 'Ideen zu einer "Lehre von den Tonvorstellungen"', in *Jahrbuch der Musikbibliothek Peters* 21/22 (1914/15), pp. 7–8, where Riemann evidently labels functions as chords. Even though he warns that this example is meaningless, the fact that he did write and discuss it raises a number of issues.

[23] Hugo Riemann, *Handbuch der Harmonielehre*, 6th edn (Leipzig: Breitkopf und Härtel, 1917), p. xv. A corresponding example can be found in Schubert's G♭ major Impromptu at bar 139. As mentioned before, in Chapter 2, n. 54, Riemann's very first music analysis, which is included in *Musikalische Syntaxis*, tackled this piece. In this context, however, Riemann's analytical observations are only interesting in so far as he does not perceive this 'interrupted cadence' as a problem.

Example 3.6 From Riemann's analysis of Beethoven's Sonata in
F major, Op. 54, in *L. van Beethovens sämtliche Klavier-Solosonaten*,
vol. 3. The surprising augmented-sixth chord that concludes the
period is interpreted as fulfilling tonic function.

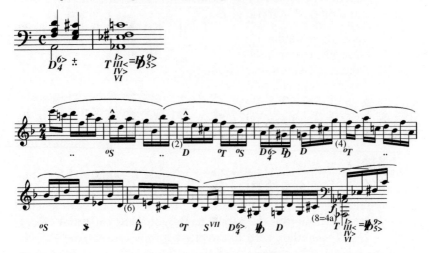

('bar' 8 of the period). In this position, at the close of the eight-bar period, the tonic is necessarily expected. The chord which actually sounds
must therefore fulfil this tonic function, regardless of its appearance.
Here Riemann shows that the notion of function (certainly in this late
conception) was not strictly dependent on the sounded chord but rather
on an expectation–fulfilment pattern. The phrase comes to an irrevoca-
ble end with the emphatic $\frac{6}{4}$ – $\frac{5}{3}$ pattern of the dominant on the relatively
weaker beat, which resolutely demands the tonic. The fact that the tonic
chord itself does not appear cannot change anything about this; the
sounded augmented-sixth chord represents the tonic function. In other
words, function here is predicated upon cadential order. 'Musical logic'
here, as mostly in the late works of Riemann, becomes an ideal type, an
a priori model resting on phrase rhythm, which determines the interpretation of functions.

After this global exposition of Riemann's changing views of the cadential order in his theory, one thing will have become obvious: there is
a problem that seems to beset the theoretical works between 1887 (the
year which saw the publication of *Systematische Modulationslehre*) and
1914 (when he revised many of his assumptions in light of his concept
of 'tone imaginations'). All the elements – harmony, metre, cadence –
were in place by 1887; even the theoretical intention was stated explicitly. And yet, the three did not seem to work together as well as they
could; the rift between what Riemann wanted, namely to coordinate the
eight-bar period with the cadential harmonic 'logic', and what he could

(or dared to) do, could not be closed. The problem can, at least provisionally, be located in his associating too closely the notion of function with the chord, which we already encountered in Chapter 2 above. A further indication of this can be found in the general cadential model that Riemann offered in those years:

    I. Tonic (first statement)
    II. Subdominant (conflict)
    III. Dominant (solution of conflict)
    IV. Tonic (reconfirmation, close).[24]

The early dialectics of 'musical logic' have become atrophied and insignificant; rather than three relational moments, the 'natural circular succession' (*naturgemäßer Rundlauf*)[25] of harmony now contains four stations.

Indeed, the rift between what Riemann said ('function as relation in the cadence') and what he did ('function as chord') had considerable consequences. Witness, for instance, a criticism that has been levelled at Riemann on numerous occasions, namely that the cadential models $T - S - D - T$, together with its inverted minor counterpart $T - D - S - T$ do not actually comply with the idea of dualism. Dahlhaus, for instance, formulates the problem as follows: if the subdominant is the 'antithesis' – or 'conflict', we might add, in accordance with the second stage of Riemann's current terminology, which refrained from using the early dialectic vocabulary – and the dominant the 'synthesis' (or 'solution'), then the inverse order of the minor model becomes nonsensical: the solution would precede the conflict. Cadential order and dualism are irreconcilably opposed.[26] In other words, by choosing to call 'subdominant' a fixed tonal area, one that is associated with *IV*, irrespective of whether the mode is major or minor, Riemann seemed to sacrifice the basic idea of dualism. An appropriate notion of 'subdominant', by contrast, would have to be context-sensitive: it would have to embrace *IV* in the major mode, and *V* in the minor mode, in order to express a form of 'conflict' in compliance with the idea of dualism.

We can let Riemann speak in his own defence. For he answered a related criticism in 1905:

[The critic] forgets that these terms are not chosen by me, but have been in general use since Rameau, and that I have kept them with the same right and for the same reasons as the terms major, minor, relative, root and a lot of others.

---

[24] Riemann, *Systematische Modulationslehre*, p. 16. Although this model is introduced as generally valid in major and minor, a special section is later devoted to the minor cadence.

[25] Hugo Riemann, *Große Kompositionslehre* (Stuttgart: W. Spemann, 1902), vol. 1, p. 34.

[26] Dahlhaus, 'Über den Begriff der tonalen Funktion', pp. 96–7 and 100–1.

[The critic further forgets] that at the very beginning and also in my very latest works, I have introduced the precise terms *schlichter Quintklang, Gegenquintklang, Seitenwechselklang* and the entire terminology of *Harmonieschritte*, of interval progressions between principal tones (*Gegenquintschritt* etc.), in order to clarify the completely different meaning of the dominants in major and minor.[27]

But this argument is insufficient for a number of reasons. For one, it undoes itself: Riemann admitted that he introduced new categories and drew on existing ones. However, he remained suspiciously silent about those categories that had already existed but which he had reinterpreted. Among these are terms such as 'major, minor, relative, root, and a lot of others', which all received a radically new meaning from Riemann. What is more, Oettingen had in fact introduced new symbols (*Phonica, Regnante, Oberregnante*) to characterise functions of the minor mode, which Riemann could well have adopted.[28] In the light of these observations, however, one must ask why he should not have reinterpreted the pre-existing terms dominant and subdominant as well, to suit the needs of his dualism.

A satisfactory answer to Riemann's problem can only be found if we turn to the alternative interpretation, and regard function in its meaning as a chord. For only under that premise can the contradiction be resolved. If subdominant *is IV*, and dominant *is V* in both major and minor, then the meaning of the function label is not subject to the dialectical (or conflict–solution) chronology, as Dahlhaus suggests, but can be inverted without problems. The 'logic', or 'natural circular succession of harmony', on the contrary, resides in the conception of the chord itself: the subdominant is defined in its meaning as *IV*, not as 'conflict'.

To explain this, we must return to *Systematische Modulationslehre*. There Riemann argued on the basis of the harmonic series (in obvious response to Helmholtz), that the major dominant is in a relation of 'natural descendancy' to the tonic, 'as it is only composed of overtones of the tonic'. The subdominant, by contrast, comprises the tonic chord in its overtones; the

[27] Hugo Riemann, 'Das Problem des harmonischen Dualismus', *Neue Zeitschrift für Musik* 101 (1905), pp. 69–70. 'Er vergisst, dass diese Namen gar nicht von mir gewählte, sondern seit Rameau allgemein gebräuchliche sind, und ich sie mit demselben Rechte und aus denselben Gründen beibehalten habe wie die Bezeichnungen Dur, Moll, Parallele, Grundton und eine Menge anderer, und dass ich deshalb von allem Anfange an und auch in den allerneuesten Arbeiten zur Klarstellung des gänzlich verschiedenen Sinnes der Dominanten in Dur und in Moll die scharf präzisierten Bestimmungen schlichter Quintklang, Gegenquintklang, Seitenwechselklang und die gesamte Terminologie der Schritte (Gegenquintschritt etc.) eingeführt habe.'

[28] Arthur v. Oettingen, *Harmoniesystem in dualer Entwickelung* (Dorpat: W. Glässer, 1866), p. 67.

tonic may easily be mistaken for the dominant, a partial *Klang*, of the subdominant. (The minor variant of the subdominant chord – or '*Seitenwechsel*' [side-change], as his terminology of *Harmonieschritte* calls it – cannot have the same effect, as it does not relate to the tonic chord in the same way as the major subdominant does.[29]) The descending fifth between tonic and subdominant, which mirrors the dominant close and causes a 'conflict' in the tonal order, must precede the stabilising move from dominant to tonic, which provides for the closure of the cadence.

The minor mode, on the contrary, can form one of two possible cadences: one emulates the order of the major cadence and is, as Riemann argued, a result of the underdeveloped autonomy of the minor system. The other is the 'pure' minor cadence, following the special properties of the minor mode, which, based as it was for Riemann on the undertone series, works in diametric opposition to the major model, to form the cadence tonic – dominant – subdominant – tonic.[30] The minor cadence is thus based, analogously, on two plagal cadences. The minor dominant represents in this conception the 'conflict', since, in analogy to the overtones of the major mode, the tonic is implied in the undertones of the minor dominant.

Following this explanation, the cadential order is only understandable in terms of the acoustical properties of the tonic chord. It appears that what kept Riemann from carrying through his theory to the end (where he would regard cadential order as an ideal type, as indicated above) was related to this problem: he had not yet found a satisfactory basis on which to reconcile the relational nature of the functions with the principles of chordal dualism. As we have seen, his 'pure minor' model cadence hinged on the undertone series. This did not change after 1893, when he introduced his function taxonomy: although he avoided mentioning the physical properties of the individual chords in favour of the functions, and used instead imagery of 'pressing downwards' and 'screwing upwards'[31] of the harmony, it is obvious that this explanation was a prevarication – Riemann made no attempt to explain these pointedly physical metaphors, or what brings about these effects. The cadential model simply does not have the same stringent necessity without the chords themselves. (It must be remembered that Riemann always used functional symbols alongside – not instead of – the *Klang* shorthand developed in the earlier theories.) In the end, he clarified what he actually meant – namely, the properties of the chords – with a graphic example, shown in Example 3.7.

The Roman numeral v in the example denotes the 'lower fifth' of C major, according to the minor principle, and the Arabic 5 denoting the

---

[29] Riemann, *Systematische Modulationslehre*, p. 15.   [30] Ibid., pp. 29–32.
[31] Riemann, *Vereinfachte Harmonielehre* (London: Augener, 1893), p. 30.

Example 3.7 Riemann's attempt to explain cadential logic in the context of his new concept of harmonic functions, from *Vereinfachte Harmonielehre*. The arrows and the Arabic/Roman numerals indicate the principles of harmonic dualism at work.

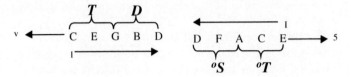

'upper fifth' of °e, according to the major principle. However, the example is misleading in so far as these two numerals in the extreme positions suggest the *Gegenklänge* (opposite sonorities)[32] of the respective tonics (°*S*, as °c in major, and *D*$^+$, as e$^+$ in minor, respectively). Riemann presumably added them in order to support the imagery of tension and forces exerted on the tonic illustrated by the arrows in the example, but this is not in fact what he was discussing in the accompanying text. On the contrary, he explicitly warned the reader not simply to equate these:

To replace the *Gegenquintklang* [in major *S*$^+$, in minor °*D*] simply with the *Gegenklang* [in major °*S*, in minor *D*$^+$] in the two complete cadences *T* – *S* – *D* – *T* and °*T* –°*D* –°*S* –°*T* would not be the right thing to do; one would only dispose of a highly relevant element of the cadence (the tension of the *Gegenquintklang* is not replaced by the *Gegenklang*).[33]

We saw in Example 2.5 that Riemann conceived of the major tonality as the arrangement of G major and F major *or* minor around the C major triad (and for A minor, the arrangement of D minor and E major *or* minor around the A minor triad). We noted there that, thanks to Stumpf's concept of 'tonal fusion', in this conception it did not matter whether the starting point was at the top or at the bottom. However, the above quotation stands in stark opposition to all this. In particular, the final remark in parentheses speaks volumes: although the *Gegenquintklang* received the same function sign as the *Gegenklang*, Riemann still noted a difference. This difference can only be predicated upon the demands of harmonic dualism; it is a consequence of the essentially chordal nature of

---

[32] Riemann's terms *Gegenklang* and *Seitenwechsel* (which was used above in n. 29) both draw on the idea of the dualistic *Klang* consisting of two opposing halves and are used interchangeably in this context.

[33] Riemann, *Vereinfachte Harmonielehre*, p. 49. 'In den beiden vollständigen Kadenzen *T* – *S* – *T* und °*T* –°*D* –°*S* –°*T* etwa den Gegenklang einfach an Stelle des Gegenquintklanges einstellen zu wollen, hiesse nicht das rechte treffen; man würde damit nur ein hochbedeutsames Element der Kadenz beseitigen (die Spannung des Gegenquintklanges wird durch den Gegenklang nicht ersetzt).'

the elements in the full cadence. Riemann's qualifications of the cadence are mirrored in the restrictions made earlier in *Systematische Modulationslehre*, apropos the interrupted cadence. Apart from the new taxonomy of function, there is no real change in the conception of the cadence as presented in *Systematische Modulationslehre* and *Vereinfachte Harmonielehre*.

We have thus a triple task at hand: we must first explore the epistemological status of the undertone series, which makes possible the pure minor model. Second, we must propose a reason for Riemann's urge to suppress chordal dualism – even though it was clearly in use – and third, we must find out why he refused to introduce separate function symbols for major and minor. To begin with, it is helpful to examine the aspirations of nineteenth-century science, among which, Riemann professed, music theory actually belonged.

II

Hermann von Helmholtz, in many ways the epitome of the nineteenth-century scientist, summarised his understanding of 'real science' succinctly as 'nothing but methodically and deliberately completed and purified experience'.[34] This position was in line with the nineteenth-century vogue for positivism and inductive science.[35] Hand in hand with this apotheosis of empiricism, which was confirmed by the high prestige that science – particularly German science[36] – enjoyed, went severe distrust in the speculative philosophical systems of German Idealism, and Hegelian metaphysics especially. In this climate of scepticism, existence and meaning drifted apart. German philosophy of the later nineteenth century had to face the demise of one of the cornerstones of absolute Idealism: the separation of the trinity of the good, the true and the beautiful from the notion of existence. The former were reduced to a mere value, while existence in turn was reduced to a mere state of facticity.[37]

This was not merely an abstract philosophical problem. An idea of how important academic philosophy was in German science – and how

---

[34] Hermann von Helmholtz, *Vorträge und Reden*, cited in Herbert Schnädelbach, *Philosophy in Germany 1831–1933*, trans. Eric Matthews (Cambridge: Cambridge University Press, 1984), p. 85.

[35] This was, however, never quite as pronounced as in other European countries. See W[alter] M. Simon, *European Positivism in the Nineteenth Century* (Port Washington, NY, and London: Kennikat Press, 1972), pp. 238–63.

[36] See for instance, David Knight, *The Age of Science* (Oxford: Blackwell, 1986), pp. 140 and 167, or Helge Kragh, *An Introduction to the Historiography of Science* (Cambridge: Cambridge University Press, 1987), p. 14.

[37] Schnädelbach, *Philosophy in Germany*, pp. 162–6.

intertwined the two were – can be gained from the university structure, which (until the early twentieth century) regarded natural science as a subordinate branch of the philosophical faculty.[38] The advance of science in the nineteenth century may have dealt a heavy blow to the supremacy of philosophy, but it did not deliver the *coup de grâce*, as is sometimes assumed. Rather, as far as Hermann Rudolf Lotze, Riemann's teacher at Göttingen, was concerned, it led in turn to the dismantling of the 'noisy glorification of experience'[39] that Helmholtz had essentialised in science. For it became more and more evident that hard science did not simply rely on 'purified experience' but was itself highly speculative – and this, as philosophers triumphantly pointed out, required their professional help. In this situation, German academic philosophy sought alternative paths; it turned increasingly to methodological issues, which, particularly in the neo-Kantian schools of Marburg and Baden, sought to attain mediation between scientific positivism and idealism. While it became the domain of science to determine what actually *is*, philosophy still kept its privilege to explain what this existence meant.

Witness for instance the nineteenth-century debate about atomism, which by the very nature of the subject matter escaped experience. After the success of Dalton's theory at the beginning of the century, which posited that chemical elements could only react in integer proportions, making redundant the complicated percentages of elements that had been common prior to it, atomism became one of the central issues of nineteenth-century science. The rediscovery of the atom marked the beginning of modern chemistry. In physical terms, however, the atom was an inexplicable object – even to describe the atom as an object made a major assumption that was better located, one imagines, in the speculative realm.

At the heart of atomic theory after Dalton was a conception of the atom as a definite material entity, a kind of 'billiard ball'. But whilst the model went a long way to explain the behaviour of chemical reactions, it begged as many questions as it answered: how, for example, could the void space between two atoms – an impossible scenario according to nineteenth-century sceptics – be explained? Clearly, the atom was a useful concept, but could one claim that it was real? Pragmatic scientists, such as the

---

[38] In fact, the institutional factors are much further reaching than this: witness, for instance, the rule that *Realgymnasium* graduates had to be given special permission to enter university (and the reluctance with which this permission was granted), because they lacked a thorough humanistic education. See Hans-Peter Ullmann, *Das deutsche Kaiserreich* (Darmstadt: Wissenschaftliche Buchgesellschaft, 1997), pp. 185–6.

[39] Hermann Rudolf Lotze, *System der Philosophie; Zweiter Theil: Metaphysik*, 2nd edn (Leipzig: S. Hirzel, 1884), p. 6. Lotze's work is discussed in the context of neo-Kantianism by Thomas E. Willey, *Back to Kant: The Revival of Kantianism in German Social and Historical Thought* (Detroit: Wayne State University Press, 1978), pp. 40–57.

French chemist Charles Gerhardt, chose to ignore the question of the verisimilitude of the atom and to make the most out of the explanatory power that the concept provided. But in the long run, this was not an acceptable way out: a tree bearing fruit like atomism, complained the physiologist-philosopher Theodor Fechner, must also have roots.[40] If science was to make a claim to facticity and truth, it would need a definite concept of reality. In the course of the century, an alternative view of the atom became prevalent: it was increasingly seen as unreal, as a material concept that had been necessary as long as force was believed to be mediated by matter. Nevertheless, the concept of the atom was not abandoned even then. In fact, the issue about the nature of the atom was so contentious that in the end chemists resorted to an unusual measure: at the international chemistry conference at Karlsruhe in 1860, chemists tried to reach an agreement by casting a vote.[41]

Riemann's teacher Lotze was one of the foremost philosophers at that time, who grappled with science and sought to coordinate philosophical speculation with it. Lotze's philosophy, a tightrope walk between realism and idealism, is now largely forgotten, but in the second half of the nineteenth century he was a prominent philosopher, and a central figure in German (as well as Anglo-American) philosophical discourse.[42] Lotze, for one, dismissed any notion of reality for its 'utter uselessness' (*völlige Unbrauchbarkeit*): the common understanding of 'reality' as an empirical existence of things was for him subsumed under the much broader reality of ideas, as a network of logical relations.[43]

He reminded his readership that recognition of any form of being was impossible, as it was invariably reliant on sensual perception. Even the most detailed sensations can only provide information about the 'How?', the qualities of a thing. But 'How?' is the wrong question altogether: it would be a fallacy to assume that recognition of the thing itself – the 'What?' – can be arrived at via our senses; the sum of the qualities of an object gives no information about the ontological status of the thing itself.[44] Thus Lotze even questioned the meaning of a 'thing':

---

[40] Gustav Theodor Fechner, *Atomenlehre*, p. 4, cited in Hans Vaihinger, *Philosophie des Als-Ob* (Berlin: Reuther und Reichard, 1911), p. 436.

[41] See Knight, *Age of Science*, p. 157.

[42] George Santayana, *Lotze's System of Philosophy*, ed. Paul G. Kuntz (Bloomington, London: Indiana University Press, 1971), pp. 48–87. For a further discussion of Lotze's influence on Riemann's conception of music theory, see Gerhardt Wienke, *Voraussetzungen der Musikalischen Logik bei Hugo Riemann*, Dr phil. dissertation (Freiburg/Br., 1952), and more fleetingly, Heinrich Besseler, 'Das musikalische Hören der Neuzeit', in *Bericht über die Verhandlungen der Akademie der (königlich) Sächsischen Wissenschaften zu Leipzig, philologisch-historische Klasse* 104 (1959), pp. 6–7.

[43] Lotze, *Metaphysik*, p. 67.   [44] Ibid., pp. 46–7.

If we are speaking of the essence of things, we mean by this term either that which distinguishes one thing from another so that each is that which it is, or that which causes them to be things as opposed to that which is not a thing.[45]

The second possibility proved decisive: as mere sensation cannot give us any information about the ontology of a thing, we cannot tell whether this thing exists in actuality, or is only a thinkable, possible category. Lotze therefore came to regard things in this latter sense as valid in the form of logically coherent concepts. The only reality, Lotze claimed, is one of validity; it is constituted by eternal laws that govern the relations between all things. He defined:

Things *are* not on account of some substance which is inside them, but rather when they can create the semblance of substance inside them.[46]

This was Lotze's clinch: he problematised the hard-and-fast distinction between things that *are* and things that are valid (in other words, *ought* to be).[47] The immediate phenomenal world exists, in that sense, for something that ought to be.[48] It goes without saying that this 'idealism of values', which fell barely short of a tacit reidentification of being and values, provoked major criticisms of Lotze in later generations and opened the door to irrationalism.

If Lotze was wrestling with the problem of science in his age,[49] then the Kantian philosopher Hans Vaihinger tried to reconcile the demands of science with the rigours of a philosophical system. He effectively moved Lotze's scepticism of reality onto a more pragmatic basis in his important *Philosophy of the As-if* (1876–7, published 1911): Vaihinger, too, claimed that thought and reality are fundamentally different. All knowledge can only be symbolic; the nature of the world, its ultimate reality, is unknowable. Scientific theories are but instruments used in order to come to terms with a reality that cannot be grasped itself. Needless to say, the atomism debate is a prime example in Vaihinger's work.[50] Although thought processes follow a different path from objective reality,

---

[45] Ibid., p. 45. 'wenn wir von dem Wesen der Dinge sprechen, so meinen wir mit diesem Ausdruck bald das, wodurch die Dinge sich unterscheiden und jedes das ist, was es ist, bald dasjenige, wodurch sie alle Dinge sind im Gegensatz zu dem, was nicht Ding ist'.

[46] Ibid., p. 84. 'Nicht durch eine Substanz, die in ihnen wäre, seien die Dinge, sondern sie seien dann, wenn sie einen Schein der Substanz in sich zu erzeugen vermögen.' See also A. Lichtenstein, 'Lotze und Wundt: Eine vergleichende philosophische Studie', *Berner Studien zur Philosophie und ihrer Geschichte* 24 (1900), p. 25.

[47] Lotze, *Grundzüge der Logik und Encyclopädie der Philosophie* (Leipzig: S. Hirzel, 1883), p. 115.

[48] See Thomas E. Willey, *Back to Kant*, p. 49.

[49] See Santayana, *Lotze's System of Philosophy*, pp. 109–29.

[50] Vaihinger, *Philosophie des Als-Ob*, pp. 101–5 and 429–51.

Vaihinger posited, they will eventually coincide.[51] This is possible by virtue of 'fictions'. A fiction, Vaihinger explained, is a temporary deviation from reality, variously described as a scientific fabrication to practical ends, and as a conscious, purposive, but false assumption. A scientific fiction is distinguished from a scientific hypothesis in that the latter seeks verification, the former is necessarily false. As such, the fiction is provisionally equated with reality and thus forms a working basis for science *as if* the fiction were real (it becomes 'true', according to Vaihinger, as long as it is purposive).[52] The concept of fiction is characterised by four conditions:

1. A fiction is an arbitrary deviation from reality.
2. Its nature is expediency, the truth content of a fiction lies in its utility.
3. An awareness of the unreal character of the fiction is necessary.
4. It is a 'logical crutch', which is dismissed eventually, on either historical or logical grounds.[53]

These categories can be applied to Riemann's concept of the undertone series.[54] Naturally, the undertone series fulfils the first condition; it is an arbitrary deviation from reality, as Riemann's critics were eager to point out. In this respect, however, it is essential to note the change of Riemann's argument which took place in 1891. Again, the temporal proximity to Stumpf's concept of tonal fusion is not accidental, but rather suggests to what extent Riemann's new argument relied upon it: in a much-discussed paragraph Riemann explained that the undertone series is rendered inaudible by the phenomenon of interference (Example 3.8).[55] Riemann asserted that it is possible to analyse the wave of the sounded tone into its undertone components, which would be n times as long as the sound wave. Since each lower partial would be present in the soundwave as n complements (in different phases), he claimed that these equivalent components would automatically cancel each other out. The undertone series, unlike the corresponding overtone series, cannot, according to this argument, but be inaudible.

---

[51] Ibid., pp. 10–12.   [52] Ibid., p. 193.

[53] Ibid., pp. 171–5, in different order. Incidentally, Lotze briefly introduced 'fictions' in his *System der Philosophie; Erster Theil: Logik*, 2nd edn (Leipzig: S. Hirzel, 1880), p. 412.

[54] To be more precise, the undertone series would feature as a semi-fiction (a concept that does not have a correlate in reality, but which is in itself – in a relative reality – logical) with a tendency towards the category of total fiction. Although Vaihinger introduced these two types, there is a gradual shift between them. As we shall see later, the undertone series may also exhibit certain features of what Vaihinger called the 'lie'.

[55] Hugo Riemann, *Handbuch der Akustik (Musikwissenschaft)*, 3rd edn (Berlin: Max Hesse, 1921), p. 80. It was not until after this physical demonstration that Riemann was prepared to give up the undertones but only if – following Stumpf – the overtone argument is discarded, too.

Example 3.8 Riemann's demonstration of the inaudibility of undertones by means of interference between waves out of phase, from *Handbuch der Akustik*.

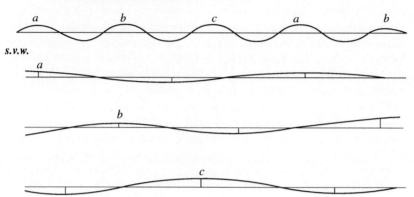

Various commentators are quick to conclude that this explanation should constitute a renunciation of the undertones.[56] It seems rather that, on the contrary, by claiming that the undertones are inaudible Riemann did in fact confirm their existence. The fact that we cannot perceive an object, following Lotze's argument, does not mean that it cannot exist. In this sense, then, Riemann demonstrated the Lotzean validity of the undertone series: even though we cannot hear it – for acoustical reasons – the undertone series ought to exist. By positing the inaudibility of the undertone series Riemann recanted his earlier nocturnal experiments with his grand piano, as seen in Chapter 1 above, but no more than that. This was truly a small price to pay for what Riemann gained from this argument. By moving the undertone series away from the perceptual realm into a state of inaudibility, he achieved, paradoxically enough, a solid theoretical foundation on the basis of Lotze's epistemology. In this way the undertone series could – that is: ought to – be a fact of nature. This was the precondition of his aesthetics, and the indispensable cornerstone of his theory of function.

---

[56] Seidel baldly asserts in 'Die Harmonielehre Hugo Riemanns', p. 44, that Riemann 'yielded to the illusion of the objective existence... only for a short time'. In fact, sixteen years had passed between 'Die objective Existenz der Untertonreihe' (1875) and *Handbuch der Akustik* (1891), and there is no indication that Riemann had expressed any doubts in the interim. It seems that Seidel plays the undertone series down in order then to conclude that harmonic dualism was unnecessary altogether. Mickelsen also asserts that Riemann gave up his belief in undertones, assessing the explanation that the undertones are inaudible as 'futile but entertaining'. See William Mickelsen, *Hugo Riemann's Theory of Harmony and History of Music Theory Book III* (Lincoln: University of Nebraska Press, 1977), p. 53. He takes Riemann at face value when the theorist explained in 1905 that he was 'deceived by the pseudo-logic of an undertone series' (p. 55).

In the wake of this new argument Riemann redefined the undertones in his *Musik-Lexikon* as 'that series of tones which... *must be drawn on* for the explanation of the consonance of the minor triad'.[57] This definition exhibits how the undertone series is clearly seen as an ethical postulate: undertones ought to exist if we want to explain the minor consonance in terms equivalent to the major consonance. Their existence is motivated by their explanatory power. This condition is precisely what Vaihinger circumscribed in his second criterion, the postulate of expediency: a fiction is characterised by its utilitarian nature.

However, Riemann's conception of the undertones as an expediency does not merely concern the nature of the undertones themselves but has far-reaching ramifications. It must be borne in mind that Riemann's effort was further to assign the undertone series a place in nature. When treating the undertones as an expediency, as a 'fiction' in Vaihinger's sense, Riemann effectively extended the category of 'fiction' to the entire conception of nature in his music theory. We should therefore cast a sideways glance at the way nature is employed by Riemann in general, before returning to Vaihinger's categories.

III

More often than not, the idea of nature in music theory is conceptualised broadly as that 'which is not human and distinguished from the world of humanity'.[58] The employment of a concept of nature in music theory must therefore be seen as an attempt to remove the principles of music theory from the sphere of transitory human endeavour. By grounding music theory outside itself, outside the cultural context that produced it, the theorist can apparently gain access to a locus of truth, and present the theoretical principles as universal.

Nature did indeed occupy a central place in Riemann's conception of music theory. At the beginning of the last chapter of Riemann's theoretical magnum opus, the *Geschichte der Musiktheorie*, conspicuously entitled like the early work 'Musikalische Logik', he outlined his position as a theorist:

If one asks what the task of a theory of art consists of, the answer can only be that it should explore the natural laws which consciously or unconsciously govern artistic creation, and present them in a system of logically coherent rules.[59]

---

[57] Riemann, 'Untertöne', in *Musik-Lexikon*, 5th edn (Leipzig: Max Hesse, 1900), p. 1174. My emphasis.

[58] This definition is taken from Kate Soper, *What is Nature?* (Oxford: Blackwell, 1995), p. 15. Further see Raymond Williams, 'Ideas of Nature', in *Problems in Culture and Materialism*, 2nd edn (London and New York: Verso, 1997), pp. 67–85.

[59] Hugo Riemann, *Geschichte der Musiktheorie*, p. 470. 'Fragt man sich, worin eigentlich die Aufgabe der Theorie einer Kunst bestehe, so kann die Antwort nur lauten, daß dieselbe

His definition draws a clear link between nature and logic – the logic inherent in the theoretical rules is to reflect the nature in which art is rooted. While for Riemann the artist was 'graced by God' and by necessity evaded musicological enquiry, art itself could be captured by the rules of music theory.[60] The direction of Riemann's aesthetic position, particularly in his equation of nature with the object of scientific investigation, could perhaps be described as industrially orientated: it is the task of the music theorist (who need not be different from the artist) to discover and explore these pre-given rules of nature, so as to make them generally accessible and make possible further production of rule-based music.

In his essay 'Die Natur der Harmonik' (1882) Riemann outlined the study of *'musikalische Naturforschung'*, the investigation of the natural basis of music. In this, the category of nature in Riemann's theory turned out to be defined along institutional lines in the first instance: it connotes the object of scientific (musical) research – it can draw on physics, physiology and psychology. The last discipline, psychology, seems unusual in this list, and it is not by chance that Riemann increasingly drew on psychology in his later works.[61] In the late nineteenth century psychology was an ill-defined discipline. It occupied a comfortable middle position between the natural and the human sciences, which were in the process of forming discrete faculties with distinct methodologies; psychology was repeatedly claimed by both.[62] Riemann, for one, referred to psychology as a 'hard' science:

If experience tells us that we are capable of conceiving of a tone as a representative of a minor chord as well as a representative of a major chord (without either *Klang* actually being sounded), then this is a scientific fact on which we can build as well as on acoustical phenomena. Once we have arrived at this conclusion, we need hardly be concerned with a physical explanation.[63]

die natürliche Gesetzmäßigkeit, welche das Kunstschaffen bewußt oder unbewußt regelt, zu ergründen und in einem System logisch zusammenhängender Lehrsätze darzulegen habe.'

[60] See Michael Arntz, *Hugo Riemann (1849–1919): Leben, Werk und Wirkung* (Cologne: Concerto-Verlag, 1998), pp. 136–62.

[61] Riemann's 'Die Natur der Harmonik' points towards his late work 'Ideen zu einer "Lehre von den Tonvorstellungen"' (1914/15), in the direction of a completely psychology-based music theory.

[62] See Schnädelbach, *Philosophy in Germany*, pp. 126–9. Lotze's important student Wilhelm Windelband, for one, regarded psychology as a natural science.

[63] Riemann, 'Natur der Harmonik', p. 185. 'Wenn es sich aus der Erfahrung erweist, daß wir ebenso im Stande sind, einen Ton als Vertreter eines Mollakkordes zu verstehen wie als Vertreter eines Durakkordes (ohne daß der eine oder der andere Klang wirklich erklingt), so ist das ein wissenschaftliches Faktum, auf welches so gut weiter aufgebaut werden kann, wie auf die akustischen Phänomene. Sind wir erst zu dieser Erkenntnis durchgedrungen, so kümmert uns die physikalische Begründung des Mollakkordes kaum noch.'

Here the importance of empirical psychology is made quite clear: it forms a suitable substitute for acoustical science on which to base a music theory. Sudden though it may seem, this leap between the disciplines of physics and psychology was not quite so strange as it may at first appear. In fact, it was a common assumption of scientific empiricism, known as 'psycho-physical parallelism', particularly of Theodor Fechner's psychology, that the processes of the mind correspond to those of physical nature.[64] In psychology, Riemann tells us, experience can replace a scientific fact – it is as good as one – and once this notion is accepted (that is to say, once psychology is granted the status of a science), psychology is even more useful than physics in founding a music theory.

In an example in which he demonstrated the superiority of psychological nature (to the extent that physical facts are rendered unnecessary) he drew on the discrepancy between physics and music theory in their approach to the six-four chord:

First it was necessary to concede that it was impossible for physics and physiology to get to the bottom of musical concepts before psychology could take up its rightful position. Nowadays we know that there is no such thing as an absolute consonance, that what would be according to physical and physiological explanations the sweetest sounding chord (such as the six-four) can musically be a dissonance.[65]

Psychology steps in where acoustical arguments fall short, Riemann suggested. (Note the emphasis on up-to-dateness and scientific progress conveyed in the opening tag of the last sentence.) This statement, however, presupposes a very particular relationship between musical theory and practice: the six-four *is* dissonant, because music theory treats it as such. When this 'fact' cannot be theoretically grasped by physics or physiology, this means, so Riemann concluded, that the explanatory devices are insufficient. Instead, psychology – presenting experience as 'hard facts' to work with – would form a working basis. Riemann's insistence on the truth discovered by psychological empiricism in this case underlines the problematic character of his idea of nature, particularly if one contrasts it with his rejection of the misguided 'conventions' that have led to a misunderstanding of the minor mode. It seems that for Riemann nature, as the object of scientific investigation, was a category

---

[64] As mentioned before, Riemann repeatedly drew on Fechner, particularly on his aesthetic writings. Note, however, that Lotze did not subscribe to psycho-physical parallelism. See Willey, *Back to Kant*, p. 43.

[65] Riemann, 'Natur der Harmonik', p. 186. 'Erst mußte die Unmöglichkeit eingesehen werden, daß Physik und Physiologie bis zur Begründung der musikalischen Begriffe gelangen, ehe die Psychologie in ihre Rechte eintreten konnte. Heute wissen wir, daß es absolute Konsonanzen überhaupt nicht giebt, daß auch der nach physikalischen und physiologischen Aufstellungen ungestörteste, wohlklingendste Akkord musikalisch eine Dissonanz sein kann (z.B. der Quartsextakkord).'

that required no further specification or explanation. This assumption allowed him to conflate the nature of human cognition with the nature of musical material – and both were invoked wherever necessary to support his views of the way music worked. To put it bluntly, nature is invoked as a category in Riemann's theoretical system because it invariably presents an argument that cannot be contradicted.

However, this casts the relationship between musical logic and the underlying natural laws in a different light. When Riemann stated initially that music theory presents the natural laws of music in the form of logical rules, he made a direct connection between nature and logic, which is exemplified by the $T – S – D – T$ cadence. This has indeed led one commentator to describe Riemann's concept of the nature of music as 'a *physis*, which is at the same time *logos* (reason)'.[66] In fact, it is best to reverse the relationship between nature and logic: Riemann's conception of the nature of music is based on a concept of 'logic' in the first place, to which the 'natural laws' do not form a foundation but rather ancillary devices. By defining the nature – whether it be psychological or physical – according to the needs of the rules of music theory, his 'logic' of music, Riemann effectively reverses the two components: his musical logic requires nature as a means of justification. His nature of music thus reveals itself as a *logos*, which at the same time seeks to be *physis* as well.

The premises of Riemann's theory, therefore, seem seriously flawed in their reliance on the portentous term of nature without giving it a firmly outlined basis. The dichotomy in the pair of *logos* and *physis*, however, can be reconciled. In fact, Riemann himself remedied the flaw by employing a third fundamental category: history. History is the controlling device for our experience; Riemann explained in his essay 'Die Natur der Harmonik' (1882) that 'a fact observed through experience over centuries, but which can also easily be substantiated through psychological experiments' is 'thus a law'.[67] History thus seems to occupy a position equivalent to the nature discovered in psychology.

History in Riemann's system of musical logic is, quite appropriately, borrowed from nineteenth-century science. He asserted in an oft-quoted statement:

But I think that the actual purpose of historical research is to make recognisable that which is a primordial law in all ages, governing all perception and artistic creation. There is still enough left to characterise specifically the age from which the works stem.[68]

[66] Anon. [C. Dahlhaus?], 'Riemann, Hugo', in Carl Dahlhaus, ed., *Riemanns Musiklexikon* (Mainz: B. Schotts Söhne, 1975), supplementary volume, p. 485.
[67] Riemann, 'Natur der Harmonik', p. 189.
[68] Hugo Riemann, *Musikgeschichte in Beispielen*, ed. Arnold Schering, 4th edn (Leipzig: Breitkopf & Härtel, 1929), p. 1. 'Aber ich denke, daß doch der eigentliche Zweck

History for Riemann is thus not the study of changes but that of consistency, in the manner of the universal history of progressive scientific discoveries. Within this model of history, he did acknowledge historical periods with a distinctly different outlook from the preceding age. As such, however, they were merely regarded as diversions straying from the path of truth.[69] For instance, the Baroque period – to which Riemann referred as the 'age of figured bass'[70] – was for him a period of aberration from the logical meaning of the chords themselves: not only does the practice of figured bass indiscriminately pile up major and minor chords alike over the triad's root, it also failed to recognise the inversional equivalence of chords – two elements that were irreconcilable with Riemann's own agenda.

Riemann's view of history, which looks for the same in different periods and musical styles, may appear static and atelic in its indifference to change and difference, but on closer inspection it reveals itself as its opposite: a clear teleology is discernible in the implicit assumption that there is one truth about music which is gradually unearthed. This truth itself is eternal but needs to be uncovered by music theory. In this conception, music theory is always concerned with the same problems because its object of investigation is forever true. It is in this spirit that Riemann 'is caused to imagine the difference between the way of hearing millennia ago and in our days to be as small as possible'.[71] That is to say, if the premises on which music is based are taken from pre-human, pre-historical nature, then music has only one ideal type, which is entirely in accordance with the natural principles.

Under this notion of history – as the progress of the unchangeable, to express it paradoxically – the question arises as to whether Riemann's monumental project of a 'history of music theory' is not a contradiction in terms. However, it is important to remember that it is only music that is conceived as eternal and universal, not music theory. This way, his *Geschichte der Musiktheorie* is not only possible but much rather indispensable. It serves, above all, as a device for the validation of his theory. In the final paragraph of the book he stated:

For twenty-five years I have worked diligently to develop the natural laws of harmonic succession . . . I have surveyed the theorists of all ages as far as they were available to me and have dug up many a grain of gold, which seemed to

der historischen Forschung, das allen Zeiten Urgesetzliche, das alles Empfinden und künstlerische Gestalten beherrscht, erkennbar zu machen. Es bleibt dabei immer noch genug übrig, was speziell dem Zeitalter, dem die Werke entstammen, charakterisiert.'

[69] Riemann, *Geschichte der Musiktheorie*, p. 473.

[70] Riemann, *Grundriß der Musikwissenschaft* (Leipzig: Quelle und Meyer, 1908), p. 135.

[71] Hugo Riemann, *Handbuch der Musikgeschichte* (Leipzig: Breitkopf und Härtel, 1904), vol. 1, p. vi. See also Riemann, *Die Elemente der musikalischen Aesthetik* (Stuttgart: W. Spemann, 1900), p. 122.

me worth the effort of recoining. In many cases I have also been pleased to find retrospectively that ideas which came to me independently had already been thought out by others before me (but again forgotten). It would be foolish to attach great significance to my independent reformulation in such cases, but I consider the proof highly significant that ideas which contain a truth flare up again and again until they can no longer be kept down.[72]

The truth that Riemann codified under the term 'musical logic' thus ultimately receives its weight from history – it is legitimised by the number of theorists saying similar things independently of each other. This mode of legitimation, building on a Whiggish model of history, is common among the natural sciences: predecessors are 'normalized' against one's own work, a genealogy is created.[73] Often the ancestry of scientists credited with adumbrations of one's own discovery is fabricated, since previous generations of scientists were ordinarily oblivious of the particular circumstance or premise that marks the new discovery. In Riemann's peroration this process of 'normalization', for which he used the euphemistic term 'recoining', was particularly crude: the thought at the basis of his statement equated truth with perseverance in a strange twist of Darwinism – the more often something is said the truer it becomes[74] – and gave Riemann the opportunity to misread earlier theorists with the aim of legitimising his own ideas.[75] Thus history as a category in the substructure of Riemann's music theory has the same validatory function to musical logic as nature does.

This particular relationship between logic and history is most prominently expressed in Riemann's reading of Rameau's harmonic theory.

---

[72] Riemann, *Geschichte der Musiktheorie*, p. 529. 'Da ich seit nunmehr 25 Jahren nach Kräften an dem Ausbau der Lehre von der natürlichen Gesetzmäßigkeit der Harmoniefolgen arbeite . . . so habe ich bei den Theoretikern aller Zeiten, soweit sie mir erreichbar waren, Umschau gehalten und dabei manches Goldkorn gegraben, welches umzumünzen mir der Mühe wert schien, mich auch in vielen Fällen gefreut, *nachträglich* Gedanken, auf die ich selbständig gekommen war, von anderen vorgedacht (aber wieder vergessen) zu finden. In solchen Fällen auf die selbständige Neuaufstellung Gewicht zu legen, wäre töricht; aber für höchst wichtig halte ich den Nachweis, daß Gedanken, denen eine Wahrheit innewohnt, immer wieder aufflammen, bis sie endlich nicht mehr niederzuhalten sind.'

[73] Thomas S. Kuhn discusses the strategy of crediting earlier scientists with partial discovery or adumbration of one's own results in Chapter 11, 'The Invisibility of Revolutions', of *The Structure of Scientific Revolutions*, 2nd edn (Chicago: University of Chicago Press, 1970), pp. 136–43. I take the term 'normalization' for this strategy from Nicholas Jardine, *The Scenes of Inquiry* (Oxford: Clarendon Press, 1991), pp. 121–45.

[74] As we shall see in Chapter 4 below, this is precisely the strategy Riemann employed in his canonisation of Johann Stamitz.

[75] This particular issue has already been the subject of some studies; see particularly Scott Burnham on Riemann's reading of Rameau in 'Method and Motivation in Hugo Riemann's History of Music Theory', *Music Theory Spectrum* 14 (1992), pp. 4–9, and Carl Dahlhaus, 'War Zarlino Dualist?', *Die Musikforschung* 10 (1957), pp. 286–90.

The basic concept of harmonic function, the existence of three primary harmonic pillars, is acknowledged by Riemann as an extension of Rameau's principle: 'There are only three fundamentals in the mode, the tonic, its dominant, which is the fifth above, and its subdominant, which is its fifth below, or simply its fourth.'[76] The latter two of these fundamentals, dominant and subdominant, are distinguished from the tonic by what Riemann was to call their 'characteristic dissonances'. In the case of the dominant, Rameau had explained, this dissonance was the minor seventh, while the subdominant obtained either an added sixth (*sixte ajoutée*) or a third below.[77]

Riemann praised Rameau for realising that the added sixth pertained to the major triad of the major subdominant, whereas the third below was added to the the minor subdominant. He quoted Rameau, apparently in support of this point:

But if the dissonance is added, to make the mode more definite, then instead of one sound, there will be three in common:

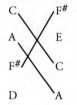

Thus D, as dominant of the major mode, receives the seventh, C; and A, as subdominant of the minor mode, receives the major sixth, F#.[78]

However, on closer inspection, it appears that Rameau's position does not at all support Riemann's point. First of all, in Rameau's example the difference between major and minor is relevant on the level of the *key*:

---

[76] Jean-Philippe Rameau, *Génération harmonique* (Paris, 1737), ed. E. Jacobi (reprint New York: American Institute of Musicology, 1968), p. 171 in Rameau's pagination. 'Il n'y a que trois Sons fondamentaux, la *Tonique*, sa *Dominante*, qui est sa Quinte au-dessus, & sa *Soudominante*, qui est sa Quinte au-dessous, ou simplement sa Quarte.'

[77] Ibid., pp. 111–13.

[78] Ibid., p. 142. 'mais si l'on y ajoute la Dissonnance nécessaire pour en rendre le Mode plus déterminé, au lieu d'un, on en trouvera trois communs

ainsi *re*, comme Dominante recevant la Septième *ut*; & *la* comme Sou-dominante, recevant la Sixte majeure *fa*$_x$'. Cited in Riemann, *Geschichte der Musiktheorie*, p. 511n.

he compared the dominant with the subdominant of the relative minor key. For Riemann this was of no interest: his sole interest concerned the difference of major and minor on the level of *function*, within the same key (or rather, irrespective of key altogether). He argued that the major subdominant differs markedly from the minor subdominant, namely in 'the $\frac{6}{4}$ of the fourth scale-degree in the major mode, and the sub-posed third for the triad of the fourth scale-degree in the minor mode'.[79] There is no indication in the example, however, that Rameau explained the 'characteristic' dissonance of the minor subdominant as the third below, as Riemann's explanation would demand. On the contrary, in the quoted excerpt Rameau explicitly referred to the characteristic dissonance of the minor subdominant as 'the major sixth'.

Riemann was at pains to argue that the minor subdominant possessed exactly the same qualities as the dominant in the major – it is probably for this reason that he drew on the above passage from Rameau, even though it only caused confusion in the immediate context. Although Rameau's theories – above all *Génération harmonique*[80] – lent themselves to some extent to this purpose, the correct position of the 'added dissonance' of the subdominant depends on factors other than its major or minor mode.[81] Riemann complained that Rameau, having identified the five-six position of the subdominant added-sixth as its root position, still 'kept peeking over to the seventh chord of the second scale degree as the "actual" basis'.[82] Where in Rameau's theory – which had no predetermined or paradigmatic course of harmonic motion – the structure of the subdominant was determined by the rule that the fundamental bass could not move stepwise, Riemann's musical logic, by contrast, demanded just that, namely in postulating the direct succession of the two dominants. The special means of employment of the subdominant chord, Rameau's concept of the *double emploi*, had to be misunderstood by Riemann, since it could not be reconciled with his own agenda.

---

[79] Riemann, *Geschichte der Musiktheorie*, p. 511.

[80] Thomas Christensen points out that in *Génération harmonique* Rameau came close to postulating the dominant and subdominant as poles within a Newtonian forcefield. See his *Rameau and Musical Thought in the Enlightenment* (Cambridge: Cambridge University Press, 1993), pp. 131–2 and 185–90. It is also the treatise that attempts an approach to the minor chord which resembles Riemann's undertones.

[81] Rameau explained earlier in *Génération harmonique*: 'La proportion harmonique nous apprend que le premier ordre, *la. ut. mi. sol*, est le plus parfait, d'autant plus encore qu'il est pareil à celui de l'Harmonie de la Dominante, dans sa division par Tierces' (pp. 113–14). Where the context – determined by *basse fondamentale* and *double emploi* – demanded it, the major subdominant could also be imagined with an added lower third.

[82] Riemann, *Geschichte der Musiktheorie*, p. 488. For an example of Rameau's 'peeks' see the previous footnote.

Example 3.9 'Characteristic dissonances' of Dominant and Subdominant.

$$D^7 \qquad S^{VII}$$

The doctrine of dualism not only motivated Riemann's thought but also proved extremely helpful in representing the equivalence between subdominant and dominant which Riemann postulated and hoped to find prefigured in Rameau. With minor chords being read top to bottom, the minor subdominant with its characteristic dissonance could, as Example 3.9 shows, become the exact complement of the major dominant seventh – the 'characteristic dissonances', the pointers to the respective other dominant are reciprocal in that they each refer to the fifth of the other dominant. (This is something that Rameau would have not considered relevant, since for him dominant and subdominant were primarily types of chords, which could potentially occur on any scale degree.) Because of the stringent demands of harmonic dualism, however, Riemann had to introduce one further pair of 'characteristic dissonances' that would account for the major subdominant added-sixth (S_3^6). The premises of Riemann's dualism demanded that there should be a dual opposite, which is identified in the – primarily theoretical – D_{VI}^V.

Since Riemann felt he was closer to the gradually unfolding 'truth' about harmony, he presumed to be in a position to improve upon the earlier theorist. He could pick out the 'correct' pieces and forget about the parts that Rameau 'got wrong', just as a natural scientist might improve on the ideas of his elders and refine them. There is, however, another dimension in this 'rereading' of Rameau: by interpreting Rameau in the light of the advanced knowledge of Riemann's own time, he also fashioned the eminent French theorist into one of his forebears. In appropriating a theory across history and culture, Riemann demonstrated his premise that music theory is indeed concerned with a matter that stands outside history and culture: it adds to the legitimation of both Riemann's method and the results it yields. It is ironic that where Rameau boasted that his theory was based on the principles of nature, Riemann made use of Rameau's authority in *history*.

However, history and logic stand in a more strongly reciprocal relationship than do logic and nature. For Riemann's Whiggish premise about the history of music theory – a consequence of the claim that music theory examines the same object at all times – also implies that the reverse is true: the music of all times must be subject to the selfsame theoretical rules. This is indeed the implicit premise of the quotation

Example 3.10 Riemann's conception of medieval modes as 'failed' incomplete tonal systems, from *Systematische Modulationslehre*.

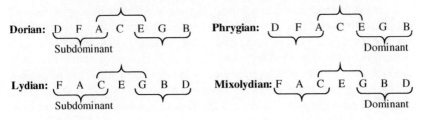

at the beginning of Riemann's chapter on 'Musikalische Logik' quoted above (see n. 59).

In fact, Rameau had been attacked by the *philosophes* for a similar premise a century previously: if indeed all music is based on the same natural principle, they argued, why does not all music sound like French music of the eighteenth century?[83] Riemann would have argued similar criticisms away by claiming that other types of music – pre-tonal and non-European music – had not attained the same level of perfection. To this end, Riemann had to indicate that, say, medieval modes were rudimentary diatonic scales. As Example 3.10 demonstrates, the modes were for him logically deficient, as they focus not on the tonic, but erroneously on one of the dominants – yet they were ultimately perceivable in a major or minor sense:

[The church modes] were a very peculiar dilemma, a struggle for clarity, a vain search. A D minor, which is actually a subdominant of A minor, and is transformed at the close into a real modern D minor; a G major, which is the dominant of C major, but turns into the real G major at closes. Who would see anything valuable in the attempt to revive this way of modulating, which is illogical from the viewpoint of advanced knowledge? In historical terms it is fully explicable, but it is nevertheless overcome by time.[84]

In brief, Riemann argued that medieval modes are useless because they do not reflect the current state of knowledge in the nineteenth century.

---

[83] Thomas Christensen shows how in his later years Rameau tried to argue his case historically. See *Rameau and Musical Thought*, pp. 294–8.

[84] Riemann, *Systematische Modulationslehre*, p. 63. 'Es war das gar ein merkwürdig Zwitterding, ein Ringen nach Klarheit, ein vergebliches Suchen. Ein D-moll, das eigentlich eine Unterdominante von A-moll ist und in den Schlüssen in ein wirkliches modernes D-moll verwandelt wird: ein G-dur, das Oberdominante von C-dur ist, aber in den Schlüssen jedesmal zum wirklichen G-dur wird – wer wollte etwas Werthvolles darin sehen, wenn man diese von Standpunkte einer vorgeschrittenen Erkenntniss aus unlogische Modulationsweise, die historisch sich vollkommen erklärt, aber eben durch die Zeit überwunden worden ist, wieder lebendig machen wollte?' Also see Riemann, *Studien zur Geschichte der Notenschrift* (Leipzig: Breitkopf und Härtel, 1878), pp. 86–102.

It is on account of their logical deficiency that they perished and were superseded by the diatonic scale.

Various critics have taken Riemann to task for attempting to view all kinds of music, irrespective of historical appropriateness, in the light of his harmonic system. One critic, for instance, has dismissed such attempts as an 'unnecessary complication'.[85] However, this criticism is wide of the mark: within Riemann's musical thought, this is neither a complication nor unnecessary, but no less than a prerequisite of his theory of harmony – to show that the system can be applied to any kind of music. Deviations from the logical ideal type necessarily disappear over time in this teleological framework, since nothing that is not in accordance with nature – perversions, deformities – can survive for long, and will be replaced by more complete types. Medieval modes are thus relegated to a place in pre-history, as an 'insufficiently developed art'.[86] The fact that they are outdated appears to prove to Riemann that the inevitability of historical logic is the final arbiter of harmony.

From this angle of the historical conception, it seems, then, that musical compositions are not the central object of Riemann's musical thought, but rather that they primarily fulfil a function as a component of the system, illustrating the state in which the immutable musical ideal had become manifest in reality. Compositions function, in other words, as documents of a particular historical constellation. This thought, however, is pregnant with consequences. For it implies, on one level, a portentous relationship between the (developmental) history of music and the (discovery) history of music theory. For one thing, it grants full independence to musical structures as an abstract category. That is to say, if none of the compositions that are generally regarded to mark the history of Western music had been written, it appears this would have made very little difference to the history of music theory – at best, Riemann might argue, music theory would perhaps have avoided a few aberrations, for instance in Baroque music. This theoretical independence of musical structures from actual compositions was amply demonstrated by Riemann's general habit of omitting consideration of pieces from the canonical repertoire in his theoretical works. In its abstract nature, the appearance of Riemann's theory underlined the alleged universality of its claims.

On a different level, however, musical compositions *do* play a vital part in the theory, again in connection with history, but forward-looking and

---

[85] Mickelsen, *Hugo Riemann's Theory of Harmony*, p. 40.

[86] In his *Die Elemente der musikalischen Aesthetik*, p. 6, Riemann expressly focuses on 'fully developed art'. See also Rudolf Heinz, *Geschichtsbegriff und Wissenschaftscharakter der Musikwissenschaft in der zweiten Hälfte des neunzehnten Jahrhunderts* (Regensburg: Gustav Bosse, 1968), p. 51.

utopian this time. For once the universality of the system was secured, once history had validated the eternal logic of Riemann's system, the roles of historical and logical elements could be reversed: harmonic logic became a postulate that *must* underlie all composition – otherwise the work in question would perish like the medieval modes. In other words, Riemann could use his theoretical system as an admission pass to the 'imaginary museum of musical works'; only those works that possess musical logic will be truly lasting, as Riemann's historical investigations had shown:

> Should not music, too, which doubtless came to technical mastery over its means later than other arts, have gradually come so far as to boast types of lasting value? Once this realisation has taken place, once it has become a matter of conviction, the desire for new forms seems just as nonsensical as the painter, the sculptor, the architect yearning for new forms.[87]

This strand first came to the fore in *Systematische Modulationslehre* of 1887, but was then a recurring feature in his pedagogical works. History thus reveals itself as both the validation and the motivation of Riemann's harmonic system.

One might remark that Riemann's use of history is absurd and that this particular view of history causes the whole system to collapse. No doubt there is a highly tendentious element to it, as has been criticised in Riemann repeatedly and will be reviewed below. However, if we accept Riemann's scientistic approach to history – defined as the study of continuity throughout the ages – then there is surprisingly little left that can be criticised. Indeed, the three categories that form the extra-musical foundation of Riemann's theory of harmony (and which are all located outside the human element) – logic, nature and history – are so well aligned that, albeit weak and impugnable separately, the structure on the whole successfully obscures the inherent tautology and is thus rather strong. Nature is that which is constant throughout history and which provides the unchanging rules for musical logic; history gradually reveals the nature of harmony in musical compositions and perpetuates the truth about musical logic; and logic itself, finally, can be traced in 'classical' pieces of music and is the living proof that reason manifests itself through nature and history. It is therefore this constellation of three elements – not just the two, *logos* and *physis* – that provides justification

---

[87] Riemann, 'Wohin steuern wir?', in *Präludien und Studien*, vol. 2, pp. 43–4. 'Sollte nicht doch auch die Musik, die ja allerdings unzweifelhaft später als andere Künste zur technischen Beherrschung ihrer Mittel gelangte, allmählich so weit gekommen sein, dass sie Typen von bleibendem Werthe aufzuweisen hätte?! Hat aber erst diese Erkenntnis einmal Platz gegriffen, ist sie Ueberzeugungssache geworden, so erscheint das Verlangen nach neuen Formen als eine ebenso grosse Ungereimtheit, als wenn der Maler, der Bildhauer, der Baumeister nach neuen Formen verlangen wollte.'

and would allow Riemann to fend off reproaches of tautological reasoning. Only on the conditions set up by the triumvirate of history, nature and logic can Riemann's theory of cadential order work.

IV

In the year after his theory of function was first published Riemann asked rhetorically: 'Do not the masterworks of past times exist in all the arts as templates and ideals for all times, incapable of ageing, let alone outdating?' He condemned the urge of progressive artists to find new models as 'utter nonsense' (*eine große Ungereimtheit*), since these would jettison the eternal values that the old types represent.[88] The double entity of the $T - S - D - T$ model and the eight-bar phrase of Riemann's metric theories clearly resonate in structures that are familiar from the classical repertoire, and that represent such tried and tested types. Or, to be more precise, the model fits in with nineteenth-century approaches to what Charles Rosen calls the 'mode of understanding'[89] that we have come to call the classical style. The view that Riemann promoted, of a symmetrical eight-bar structure together with the 'natural circular succession of harmonies', was in line with most theorists of the turn of the century, above all Schoenberg. Even Schenker in his early *Harmonielehre* was in rare unanimity with the 'Un-Ear' Riemann, when he regarded the $I - IV - V - I$ (and even its more controversial dual $I - V - IV - I$) model as the basis of the cadence:

In general, the character of the full close is defined merely by *V–I*; that of the plagal cadence by *IV–I*. However, I should warn the student not to forget the *IV* in the former case, and the *V* in the latter.[90]

Indeed, Riemann's *Große Kompositionslehre* lists numerous examples of the $T - S - D - T$ cadence put into practice, as reproduced in Example 3.11.

Various critics have pronounced that Riemann dogmatised the classical age.[91] And indeed, with structures as obviously modelled on late

---

[88] Ibid., p. 43.

[89] Charles Rosen, *The Classical Style*, revised edn (London: Faber and Faber, 1976), p. 19.

[90] Heinrich Schenker, *Harmonielehre* (reprint Vienna: Universal Edition, 1978), p. 297; trans. Elizabeth Mann Borgese as *Harmony* (Cambridge, Mass.: MIT Press, 1973), p. 224. 'Im allgemeinen wird zum Wesen des Ganzschlusses allerdings bloß V–I, und zum Wesen des Plagalschlusses nur IV–I gezählt, doch möchte ich davor warnen, im ersteren Falle an [sic] die vierte und im letzteren Falle an die fünfte Stufe zu vergessen.' The name *Un-Ohr* is found in Schenker's *Der Tonwille*, reprint with intro. by Hellmut Federhofer (Hildesheim: Georg Olms, 1990), vol. 1/1, p. 45.

[91] Heinz, *Geschichtsbegriff und Wissenschaftscharakter*, p. 55, and more generally, Carl Dahlhaus and Lars Ulrich Abraham, *Melodielehre* (Cologne: Heinz Gerig, 1972), pp. 10–20. For a recent reconsideration of Riemann and classicism, see also Rudolf

Example 3.11 Examples of 'double-sided cadences' in classical works by Haydn and Mozart, from *Große Kompositionslehre*, vol. 1.

eighteenth-century procedures as this, it seems hard to disagree. We must, however, remember Rosen's sagacious dictum about the fictional

Stephan, ' "Klassizismus" bei Hugo Riemann', in Tatjana Böhme-Mehner and Klaus Mehner, eds., *Hugo Riemann (1849–1919): Musikwissenschaftler mit Universalanspruch* (Cologne, Weimar, Vienna: Böhlau, 2001), pp. 131–7.

Example 3.12 Examples of inverted 'double-sided cadences' from nineteenth-century works (Hugo Wolf, 'Gesang Weylas', Franz Liszt, *Sposalizio* and Richard Wagner, *Tristan und Isolde*, end).

character of the classical style: Riemann's harmonic and metric prototypes are a nineteenth-century abstraction of the imaginary classical style. As such, they tell us more about Riemann than about the music they concern.

The criticism that Riemann dogmatises the classical style does not hit the nail squarely on the head in so far as it only accounts for one of the two models that Riemann suggested, in accordance with the doctrine of dualism. What about the second model, $T - D - S - T$? This model does not seem to have any prototypical validity in its own right, and is practically impossible in the classical repertoire.[92] Nonetheless, it plays a certain role in the nineteenth-century repertoire – as shown in Example 3.12;

---

[92] Dahlhaus resorts to a statistical survey of cadences in Beethoven's sonatas Op. 10 to prove empirically that there is only one example of a cadence that complies with Riemann's minor paradigm. See 'Über den Begriff der tonalen Funktion', pp. 96–101.

perhaps the most famous instance of this inverted cadential model is the end of *Tristan und Isolde*.[93] It is as such that it forms an indispensable part in Riemann's outlook on music.

Since the inverted model, as we have seen, receives its justification from nature directly via the inaudible undertone series, just as the 'classical' model does, it could – or rather, remembering Lotze's ethics, ought to – have been actualised in music. Only with the two cadences $T-S-D-T$ and $T-D-S-T$ together was Riemann in a position to encompass the whole of tonal music. If we read his theory of function closely, we find that the status of cadences did indeed differ slightly but significantly from the pre-function works: in *Vereinfachte Harmonielehre* (1893), which presented his first explicit theory of function, it was described as 'quite typical'.[94] Riemann did not – as a rule – say anything that suggested a binding, normative prototype, as most of his critics assume. On the contrary, what Riemann did state occasionally was that the successions $D-S$ in the major mode and $S-D$ in a minor context are 'neither illogical nor rare'.[95]

As a rule of thumb, Riemann was more emphatic about the validity of the cadential model in his pedagogical works, such as *Große Kompositionslehre*, while he was more cautious in his speculative works. (The difference between the 'practical' and the 'speculative' works of Riemann's theory, which he himself emphasised,[96] would, on this level, be primarily one of rhetoric: not surprisingly, the pedagogical works have a much stronger sense of the musical ought, since this imperative can best be actualised by means of teaching.) One consequence of this conflation of the two cadential models is that the difference between major and minor functions becomes irrelevant. This is the answer to the third question posed at the outset of this chapter, as to why Riemann chose not to introduce independent function symbols for major and minor; his talk about conventions (see n. 27) was mere prevarication.

Likewise, Riemann's notion of 'musical logic' is equally vague. A definition is lacking in his *Musik-Lexikon*. Since the *Musik-Lexikon* is usually the infallible compendium of Riemann's ideas, its absence is all the more conspicuous. The nearest we get to a definition is in the entry on *Kadenz*:

All musical logic resides in continual cadences, that is in movements away from the tonic (central harmony) towards closely related subsidiary harmonies (dominant and subdominant) and the return to the tonic.[97]

---

[93] I am grateful to Brian Hyer for bringing this passage to my attention.

[94] Riemann, *Vereinfachte Harmonielehre*, p. 30.

[95] Riemann, *Handbuch der Akustik*, p. 109.

[96] See for instance Riemann, 'Theorie', in *Musik-Lexikon*, 5th edn, p. 1131.

[97] Riemann, 'Kadenz', in *Musik-Lexikon*, 7th edn (Leipzig: Max Hesse, 1909), p. 674. 'alle musikalische Logik [beruht] auf fortgesetzten Kadenzierungen...d.h. auf

Example 3.13 Examples of 'double-sided' cadences with 'wrong'
Dominant or Subdominant, from *Vereinfachte Harmonielehre*.

In other words, $T - S - D - T$ is as good as $T - D - S - T$ in major or minor:
the order of function cannot be determined definitively or, at the very
least, does not matter. All we can say about cadential units is that they
should start and end in the tonic. An open admission of this, however,
could easily be read as 'there is no musical logic', a predicament that
Riemann's sense of responsibility sought to avert at all costs.

There is one last straw at which Riemann might clutch to save his
concept of tonal logic; it resides in the restriction of functions that
his concept of tonality imposes: in theory, as Riemann explained (see
Example 2.5), the major mode can never comprise the minor dominant, ^{o}D, while the minor mode can under no circumstance contain the
major subdominant S^{+}.[98] Riemann attempted to explain this by means
of his harmonic dualism: the principal tones of the chords that are characterised by the function symbols S^{+} (in A minor or ^{o}e: d^{+}) and ^{o}D (in
C major: ^{o}d) respectively, he argued, are more than one fifth removed
from the central tone of the key, and have no direct link with the tonal
centre.[99] They cannot, consequently, count as key-defining. But in practice, this last straw breaks: whenever the forbidden function occurred,
as in Example 3.13, Riemann merely circumscribed it as a chromatic
alteration, in the manner of $S^{III<}$ or $D^{3>}$.

Ultimately, Riemann must himself bow to his critique of Hauptmann:
his notion of 'musical logic' in practice merely requires that the tonic
should 'be shown from all sides', but cannot propose a succession. Why,
then, did Riemann insist on cadential models if the idea is deflated so
easily? We saw in Chapter 2 that the major stumbling block in Riemann's

Wegbewegungen von einer Tonika (Zentralharmonie) zu ihr näherstehenden Neben-
harmonien (Dominante und Subdominante) und der Zurückwendung zur Tonika'.
This definition is missing in earlier editions of the *Musik-Lexikon*.

[98] He first explored this rule in *Skizze einer neuen Methode der Harmonielehre* (Leipzig:
Breitkopf und Härtel, 1880), p. 18.

[99] Riemann, *Vereinfachte Harmonielehre*, p. 98. 'the chief pitches of the major tonic and the
minor dominant on the one hand, as well as the minor tonic and the major subdominant
on the other, would be two fifths apart . . . i.e. they appear only to be related in the second
degree'.

early dualist work, *Musikalische Syntaxis*, was its boundlessness. At the end of the book he circumscribed the need for order – or, to use the overstrained phrase that also forms the basis of Riemann's aesthetics: 'unity in diversity'[100] – in vivid imagery:

Thank God the combinations [of harmonies] are inexhaustible in number, and one cannot explore the area of harmony in its entirety by walking across it step by step but only by flying over it and surveying it from a bird's-eye view. It is sufficient, however, to recognise the chief paths through this magnificent Garden of Eden, which Heaven has left us after the Fall; everybody may then find new side paths for himself leading to ever new perspectives on regions never entered before. It all depends on [the teacher] stimulating [the student] in a quite comprehensible manner and pointing out the logical laws of musical listening and thinking; since modern practice has broken the old laws, the student of composition has to become aware of new and higher laws, according to which to create and to judge the creations of the masters: only in this way is it possible to counter the tendency of our modern theorists and practitioners towards formlessness and capriciousness.[101]

This last sentence provides the key to understanding Riemann's position. As he indicated, humankind, having suffered the biblical Fall from Grace, is confronted with another impending Fall: what is at stake this time is no less than the future of tonal harmony. The dangers which the harmonic Garden of Eden has to be defended against are not only the licentious harmonies of late-nineteenth-century music but also, more importantly, the support such composers find from critics and theorists. (Riemann was particularly thinking of theorists such as Laurencin and Weitzmann.)

Riemann assumed here an extraordinarily close dialogue of theory and practice; theory in its pedagogical aspect is the formative influence on composition: 'The theoretical system of a [given] age can, indeed,

---

[100] Riemann, *Die Elemente der musikalischen Aesthetik*, p. 170.

[101] Hugo Riemann, *Musikalische Syntaxis* (Leipzig: Breitkopf und Härtel, 1877; reprint Niederwalluf: Dr. Martin Sändig, 1971), p. 120. 'Die Kombinationen sind Gott sei Dank unerschöpflich an Zahl und man kann das Gebiet der Harmonik nicht Schritt für Schritt abgehen, sondern nur überfliegen, aus der Vogelperspektive überschauen. Es genügt aber, die Hauptwege durch diesen herrlichen Garten Eden, den uns der Himmel nach dem Falle gelassen, zu erkennen; jeder mag dann selbst weitere Seitenpfade zu immer neuen Durchblicken in nie betretene Reviere finden. Es kommt nur darauf an, in recht verständiger Weise anzuregen, auf die Natur der Harmonik und auf die logischen Gesetze des Musikhörens und Musikdenkens hinzuweisen; der Schüler der Komposition muß sich, nachdem die Praxis die Gesetzestafeln der alten Schulregeln zerbrochen hat, neuerer höherer Gesetze bewust [sic] werden, nach denen er schaffen, nach denen er die Schöpfungen der Meister beurtheilen kann: nur so ist es möglich, der Richtung unserer modernen Theoretiker und Praktiker auf Formlosigkeit und Willkür zu begegnen.'

must gain an influence over the compositional style.'[102] Combined with this is therefore an ethical postulate: the teacher has a responsibility to his student and the future of music at large. It would be rash to dismiss Riemann as reactionary – we have seen how Riemann's theory tried to come to terms with matters of contemporary compositional concern, and how the grid of harmonic relations allows considerable chromatic freedom.[103] Rather, he seems to be justifying and at the same time hypostatising certain nineteenth-century harmonic procedures. From one angle, it is fair to argue that Riemann provided a theoretical basis for certain progressive musical tendencies. However, it is the notion of progress itself that poses a problem to Riemann, namely when progressive music oversteps the borders of harmonic tonality, forsaking the Garden of Eden. The image of the paradise garden makes it clear that harmony is not itself subject to historical progress: the potential is always there; the notion of historical progress only applies to how far composers explore the possibilities at their disposal. The image spatialises progress in history, presenting it synchronically, just as his music theory spatialises harmony as a whole.[104] As a consequence, musical progress has fixed boundaries – and it seems, contemporary musical practice had reached them.

The metaphor of the Garden of Eden illustrates the dilemma of Riemann's position: on the one hand he believed there was – there must be – a musical logic, but on the other hand he was unable to codify it in a prescriptive fashion. As in the case of the undertone series, there is therefore a definite sense of ought. The means Riemann employed to tackle the problem was harmonic dualism. As we have seen, the dualistic idea of cadence encompasses virtually any succession of chords between two statements of the tonic. In this reading, then, dualism comes quite close to embracing the whole of the Garden of Eden. In this way Riemann created the best of both worlds: the cadential paradigms $T - S - D - T$ and $T - D - S - T$ are not actually normative prototypes but they are presented *as if* they were. The cadential models can then function as the 'chief paths' that allow the student to find 'side paths' on his own. But in actual fact, they are rhetorical devices that cover up the discrepancy between what *is* and what *ought* to be.

---

[102] Riemann, *Die Elemente der musikalischen Aesthetik*, p. 119.

[103] Crucial in this respect is a detail from *Handbuch der Akustik*: Riemann rejects just intonation because it would limit the harmonic freedom of his age (see Chapter 4 below, n. 40).

[104] The spatialisation of harmony in Riemann is an aspect that Burnham pursues in 'Method and Motivation in Riemann's History of Harmonic Theory', as well as in *Beethoven Hero* (Princeton: Princeton University Press, 1995), pp. 81–8.

V

Let us retrace our steps. We started with Riemann's notion of 'musical logic', which he considered to reside in cadential progressions. The logic of these cadential progressions we found to be predicated upon a concept of nature that vacillated between physics, physiology and psychology. This view of nature in turn legitimised a model of 'discovery history' of music theory which holds that all music is fundamentally based on the same natural principles, which are manifested in musical works to a greater or lesser degree. Musical styles that do not comply with Riemann's theoretical assertions (which, after all, have the legitimising power of nature behind them) are regarded as imperfect prototypes. On the basis of a neo-Kantian logic of history, these imperfect types are not viable, and give way to more complete types. Common to all three stations on our route from logic via nature to history is an element of Vaihinger's 'As if', which can be brought to bear on Riemann's concept of the undertone series. The 'As if' functions as an expedient, as a smooth link between these actually disparate moments. On the basis of the fictitious triumvirate of logic, nature and history, Riemann could fully establish the spatial nature of his theory of harmony: the utopian 'Garden of Eden', a paradisiacal space that exists outside history, is the ultimate consequence of Riemann's didactic concern.

Finally, we are in a position to understand fully why Riemann needed something like Vaihinger's concept of 'fiction' to salvage his undertone series. In this last instance, Riemann deviated from Vaihinger to a critical degree: although Riemann – at least from 1891 onwards – was aware of the fictional character of the undertone series (as Vaihinger's third category holds), he used it as more than what Vaihinger called in his fourth category a 'logical crutch'. The type of reality – Vaihinger would call this 'relative reality' – that Riemann constructed by virtue of the undertone series was virtual, yet tried to pass for absolute reality.[105] Riemann did not dream of putting the logical crutch aside. For it was only thanks to dualism that he could keep up the pretence that there is such a thing as a musical logic, which manifests itself in cadential statements. In Vaihinger's theory, this would come close to the case of the 'lie' – a fiction that deliberately arrives at a distorted view of reality for ulterior motives. However, before we rashly condemn Riemann as a liar, there are two additional factors that contribute to Riemann's case which must be considered. First and foremost, the problem might be located

---

[105] Even in his 1905 article 'Das Problem des Dualismus', where Riemann explicitly stated that he was deceived by the 'pseudo-logic' of the undertones, he immediately replaced it with physical relations, whose musical significance remains dubious. The category of nature may have been rethought, but it was not completely discarded.

in Vaihinger himself: if indeed 'ultimate reality' is unknowable and we can only approach it through a fictional hall of mirrors, how can we ever know that the reality we have arrived at, constructed through fiction, is Vaihinger's ultimate reality? One might say that the problematic concept of 'ultimate reality' that Vaihinger postulates is, in the final analysis, the only real fiction.[106]

Second, Riemann's aspiration to invest his theory with the status of natural science is misguided. He was interested not so much in the results of science as in the prestige that science enjoyed in his time; in this context it becomes clear why Riemann would take fiction for reality, why he attached so much importance to the overtone and undertone series, and most importantly, why he chose to ignore Helmholtz's much underrated warning 'that the construction of scales and harmonic tissues is a product of artistic invention and by no means furnished by the natural formation or natural function of our ear, as has been hitherto most generally asserted'.[107] Helmholtz effectively excluded music theory from the exact sciences: he separated physiology from aesthetics, and denied music a natural basis. However, if there were no natural basis to Riemann's Eden of tonality, then there would be no reason why the major and minor triads should be the only permissible harmonies. The admission would pull the rug from underneath Riemann's feet. Without the support of a scientific notion of nature, Riemann could not argue for the necessity of diatonic major–minor tonality, and claim that everything else is an imperfection. He needed the scientific expertise manifested in the overtone and the fictional undertone series alike in order to hammer his point home.

Indication of this necessity for the certainty that science provides can be found in Riemann's critiques of Stumpf. In the course of their debate about the concept of 'tonal fusion', Riemann attacked the psychologist's notion of consonance, arguing that in proposing four levels of 'fusion', Stumpf had, like Helmholtz before him, introduced a relativised notion of dissonance.[108] Riemann argued instead that consonance and dissonance are absolute phenomena, and that the basic unit of consonance

---

[106] It is noteworthy that the debate about scientific reality is ongoing: Richard Boyd, on the one hand, is a prominent advocate of the 'Truth Realism' position in science (see his article 'Realism, Approximate Truth and Philosophical Method', in David Papineau, ed., *The Philosophy of Science* (Oxford: Oxford University Press, 1996), pp. 215–55). However, his main argument, namely that the success of science would be an incredible coincidence if science did not provide us with a truthful representation of reality, leaves something to be desired. A further topical discussion, which holds absolute reality to be impossible, but replaces it with pragmatic local and temporal realities, is led by Nicholas Jardine in *The Scenes of Inquiry* (see n. 73 above).

[107] Helmholtz, *On the Sensations of Tone*, trans. Alexander J. Ellis (London, 1885; reprint New York: Norton, 1954), p. 365.

[108] See Chapter 2, n. 41.

is inextricably bound up with triadic shapes. The psychologist partly conceded this point, and proposed the concept of 'concordance' (and 'discordance') as an additional category designating consonance and dissonance respectively on a chordal level, whilst reserving the conventional terms for intervals. This was a reconciliatory gesture to Riemann's appropriation of his ideas, since, Stumpf explained, 'the contemporary musician thinks... in triads and thus perceives every dyad as part of a triad'.[109] This argument, however, was not good enough for Riemann: he rejected Stumpf's concept on the basis that ultimately, the perception of triads as entities was reduced to a matter of habituation and convention. Hence he regarded concordance as a prevarication – the historically contingent basis that Stumpf's notion implied was not 'scientific' enough for Riemann.[110] In this light, however, Riemann's initial comment that Stumpf had uttered the 'redeeming word' assumes a different meaning: given that from very early on, Riemann himself had based his theory on the notion of chordal fusion[111] without defining what exactly he meant by it, let alone how it came about, Stumpf seemed, at least initially, to offer the timeless certainty that only scientific knowledge could provide.

Riemann's theory is not a scientific concept, although it borrows the status of science to give credence to its speculative nature; nor does it falsify reality in an absolute sense, since harmony has no hard-and-fast relation to the nature of scientific investigation. Riemann's theory, however, relies on forging this relation, as it attributes a heightened importance to pedagogy: the 'dualistic reality' it invokes is thus primarily of practical concern. As we noted in the rupture between rhetoric and content apropos the passage about the harmonic paradise: if the teacher shows the pupil the main paths, the chief harmonic progressions, then the student will get an idea of how far to go without transgressing the borders of tonality. The Hegelian slant in Riemann's notion of history, regarding world history as a kind of 'court of judgement' (which, incidentally, is not opposed to Lotze's critique of Hegel) complements the didactic necessity of his theory. Riemann warned:

One cannot meander planlessly and heedlessly between harmonic areas with impunity. If inner unity and logical necessity are lacking, the infallible artistic

---

[109] Carl Stumpf, 'Konsonanz und Konkordanz', in *Zeitschrift für Psychologie und Physiologie der Sinnesorgane. I. Abt.: Zeitschrift für Sinnesforschung* 58 (1911), p. 346n.

[110] Hugo Riemann, 'Zur Theorie der Konsonanz und Dissonanz', in *Präludien und Studien*, vol. 3, p. 45.

[111] Riemann had used the term *Verschmelzung* in 'Die objective Existenz der Untertöne in der Schallwelle', *Allgemeine deutsche Musikzeitung* 2 (1875), p. 214; *Musikalische Syntaxis*, p. 7; and *Skizze einer neuen Methode der Harmonielehre*, p. 1. All these precede Stumpf's work.

judgement of the world spirit will cause the death warrant of the work to be signed.[112]

Riemann's theory of harmony, the notion of a systematic logic in music, is thus a bastion against historical change. We have noted how in the way the theory is laid out – as supported by the spatial image of a paradise impervious to historical changes – harmony is depicted as a force independent of history, as a timeless, unchanging structure. Yet his theory is not only made resilient to the forces of history in both form and content, but in its didactic nature it must also be seen as an attempt to ban the Hegelian 'Furies of Disappearance', to guarantee an everlasting future of music. The internal logic of the theory, its abstract, formal status, removed from musical reality, and most importantly, its alleged adherence to the perennial principles of nature are all devices of banishing the detrimental forces of history. This ideological task of the theory finally provides an answer to the question with which we were left at the end of Chapter 2, as to why Riemann was reluctant to develop the relational character of the theory beyond the fairly narrow concept of the apparent consonance: he could not give too much leeway to harmonies deflecting from the tonic, lest the evasive tonal order should be endangered.[113] A single modification of the harmonic function (parallel, leading-tone change or variant) apparently presented no danger, whereas two or more applied simultaneously would easily obfuscate the underlying harmonic function and hence the musical logic.

The first victory against history which Riemann could claim for his theory is of course related to the period of the Viennese School: the music between Haydn and Beethoven, on whose harmonic language his theory is cast, is the manifestation of logic in the phenomenal world. As such, it has beaten history and proved imperishable. Such a victory over history, however, is nothing but the condition of classicism itself. While prior to his theory of function, Riemann had defined classicism in formalist terms (as 'a work of art whose form is congruent with its content'[114]) the very next edition of the *Musik-Lexikon*

---

[112] Riemann, *Systematische Modulationslehre*, p. 167. 'Kein plan- und gedankenloses Herumirren in fremden Tonarten bleibt ungestraft; fehlt die innere Einheit und logische Nothwendigkeit, so wird das unfehlbare Kunsturtheil des Gesammtgeistes den Stab über das Werk brechen.' Note how the metaphor of meandering invokes a spatial imagery again.

[113] This is not to say that his theories cannot be used in relation to music that does 'endanger' the tonal order. On the contrary, in musical analysis his system allowed him to reduce very complex passages to very plain processes. This will be examined in some detail, for instance on Riemann's analysis of Liszt's *Faust Symphony*, in Chapter 4.

[114] Riemann, 'Klassisch', in *Musik-Lexikon*, 3rd edn (Leipzig: Max Hesse, 1887), p. 494. On the distinction between 'Classicism' and 'Romanticism' see Boris von Haken, 'Brahms und Bruckner', *Musiktheorie* 10 (1995), pp. 150–2.

after the paradigm change in which functions were introduced defined 'classical' as:

a work of art which is resistant to the destructive power of time. Since this characteristic can only become evident over the course of time, there are no living composers who are 'classic', and all real classics counted as Romantics in their own time, i.e. as minds that transcended the scheme, the template [of their own age].[115]

Although a 'classic' composer is only recognised retrospectively, Riemann's system could help him on the way. The music of the nineteenth century to which we would conventionally refer as romantic has technically the same claim to classicism in Riemann's definition as that of the eighteenth, provided it adhered to the timeless – classicising – 'musical logic' that Riemann described in his harmonic theory.

The reproach that Riemann dogmatised classicism now gains a new meaning: the theory is geared towards the tonality of Viennese (and Mannheim[116]) classicism, the *point de la perfection* of Western music. It uses harmonic dualism in order to capture in equivalent terms music that falls outside this period. As soon as the music is systematised, however, classicism becomes an abstract concept in which the aspect of perfection is idolised at the expense of its historical position. The underlying syntactical model is elevated into the sphere of eternal truth.[117]

Riemann's dilemma, the rupture between the rhetoric and content of his 'musical logic', can thus be seen as symptomatic of the dialectic of progressivism and classicism in late-nineteenth-century German thought. His theory is an attempt at synthesising the two. The spatialisation of progressive harmony that we encounter in the harmonic 'Garden of Eden' is thus part and parcel of Riemann's conception of music: ahistoricity is turned into a weapon to combat history. Whilst the imposition of a new classicism denies the historical contingency of the notion of harmonic tonality, it implies at the same time a premonition – conscious or not – of its actual, contingent nature. The preservationist view that Riemann exhibits is particularly pregnant at a time when tonality is palpably at stake: the whole theory is built on a feeling of

---

[115] Riemann, 'Klassisch', in *Musik-Lexikon*, 4th edn (Leipzig: Max Hesse, 1894), p. 540. 'Klassisch heißt ein Kunstwerk, dem die vernichtende Macht der Zeit nichts anhaben kann; da der Beweis für diese Eigenschaft er[st] durch den Verlauf der Zeit geführt werden kann, so giebt es keine lebenden Klassiker und alle echten Klassiker galten in ihrer Zeit als Romantiker, d.h. als Geister, die aus dem Schema, der Schablone herausstrebten.'

[116] On Riemann's canonisation of Johann Stamitz see Example 4.3 below.

[117] James Webster, *Haydn's 'Farewell' Symphony and the Idea of Classical Style* (Cambridge: Cambridge University Press, 1991), pp. 319–20, offers seven different definitions for the various aspects of 'classicism' and recommends careful distinction in the usage of them. In Riemann's case, however, the conflated ambiguity of the term is crucial.

angst, a Spenglerian feeling that the end of an age – the end of German music – is imminent. To invoke Hegel once again, Riemann's classicising harmonic theory is the owl of Minerva, setting out at the dusk of harmonic tonality. The ahistoricity that the dualistic view made possible was thus extremely timely: it not only enabled Riemann to treat nineteenth-century harmony *as if* it were classical music, but also to transfer the implications of classicism to his own age.

4

Musical syntax, nationhood and universality

Besides the metaphor of musical logic, as discussed in the previous chapter, the metaphor of a syntax of music was prominently employed by Riemann to describe his idea of how music works. Again, its precise meaning and the interrelation between the two metaphors are anything but clear.[1] It is noticeable that Riemann's early works are oriented by various aspects of language: after his dissertation, *Musikalische Logik*, he embarked on two projects entitled *Musikalische Syntaxis* (1877) and *Musikalische Grammatik*, though the latter manuscript remained unpublished and was destroyed when he could not find a publisher.[2] In some ways, the early works would have appeared like a kind of 'musicological trivium', in which linguistic aspects of music are determined. The relation between logic and syntax is addressed in *Musikalische Syntaxis*:

If one insists on drawing analogies, one could roughly compare the...simple [cadential] thesis with the sentence of the simple judgement in language. The subject would be the tonic and the predicate the confirmation through *Quintklänge, Terzklänge*, etc.[3]

The relationship between language and logic that Riemann presents here is marked by a certain uneasiness: although he seems to be talking about language, the 'simple judgement' that he mentioned would suggest that he is primarily thinking about logic. Under this ambivalent notion it becomes impossible to tell whether the 'subject' and 'predicate' which he defined in the sentence that follows are supposed to be

---

[1] M. Kevin Mooney offers a comparison between the notions of 'Syntax' and 'Logic' in early Riemann in his The "Table of Relations" and Music Psychology in Hugo Riemann's Harmonic Theory', Ph.D. dissertation (Columbia University, 1996), pp. 178–81.

[2] He referred to musical grammar once again in his *Neue Schule der Melodik* (Hamburg: Karl Gradener und J. F. Richter, 1883), p. 156.

[3] Riemann, *Musikalische Syntaxis* (Leipzig: Breitkopf und Härtel, 1877; reprint Niederwalluf: Dr. Martin Sändig, 1971), p. 23. 'Wollte man durchaus Analogien, so könnte man die...einfachen Thesen etwa der sprachlichen Satzbildungsform des einfachen Urtheils vergleichen. Das Subject würde die Tonika sein und das Prädikat die Bestätigung durch den Quint-, Terz- etc. Klang.'

logical or linguistic terms – or rather, Riemann appeared to underline that he considered the two to be indistinguishable. As logical terms, we have seen, the analogy would be possible, in the sense that the musical cadence, the 'simple judgement' of music, is circumscribed by both the tonic and its related sounds. A tonic can only be the 'subject' of the cadence if it is confirmed by kindred *Klänge*, the 'predicates' that are only understood in relation to the central tonic.

However, if we compare *Musikalische Syntaxis* with Riemann's previous publication, the article 'Musikalische Logik' (1872), whose dialectical conception we encountered at the outset of Chapter 3, then we find crass conceptual differences: in many ways, *Musikalische Syntaxis* exhibits the least 'logical' approach of all of Riemann's harmony treatises – its theoretical concern about cadential order is reduced to a bare minimum. We seem to fare better, then, if we reinterpret the terms 'subject' and 'predicate' from the above quotation linguistically. In *Musikalische Syntaxis* Riemann was obviously not interested so much in developing further the 'logic' as in exploring the multifarious possibilities of chord relations. Riemann's logic and syntax, albeit closely linked in his rhetoric, are conceptually contrasted.

And yet, Riemann underlined precisely the very same conflation of logic and language when in 1888 he opened his aesthetics lectures *Wie hören wir Musik?* with a quotation from Moritz Hauptmann:

Music is in its expression universally intelligible, not only to the musician but to men in general. Nor is music essentially different in the folk song and the Bach fugue or the Beethoven symphony. Though the complicated character of a work of art may render it hard to be understood, yet the same means, which when taken separately, are intelligible to all, are used in the largest as well as the smallest composition; music speaks to us in a language the words and grammar of which we need not first learn ... What is musically inadmissible is so not because it is contrary to a rule established by the musician, but because it is contrary to a natural law imposed on the musician by his human sentiment – because it is logically untrue and self-contradictory.[4]

---

[4] Hugo Riemann, *Catechism of Musical Aesthetics*, trans. and ed. Hans Bewerunge (London: Augener, 1895), p. 1. He quotes from Moritz Hauptmann, *The Nature of Harmony and Metre*, trans. William E. Heathcote (London: Swan Sonnenschein, 1893; reprint New York: Da Capo Press, 1991), pp. xxxix–xl; elision in Riemann's quotation. 'Die Musik ist in ihrem Ausdruck allgemein verständlich. Sie ist es nicht für den Musiker allein, sie ist es für den menschalichen Gemeinsinn. Auch ist die Musik nicht von grundverschiedener Beschaffenheit im Volkslied und in der Bach'schen Fuge, oder Beethoven'schen Symphonie. Wenn der Inhalt des complicirteren Kunstwerkes sein Verständniss erschweren kann, so sind es doch immer dieselben im Einzelnen allgemein verständlichen Ausdrucksmittel, durch welche das grösste, wie das kleinste Musikstück zu uns spricht, in einer Sprache sich uns mittheilt, zu der wir die Worte und die Grammatik nicht erst zu lernen nöthig haben ... Was musikalisch unzulässig ist, das ist es nicht aus dem Grunde, weil es einer vom Musiker bestimmten Regel entgegen, sondern weil es einem,

Music, Riemann agreed with Hauptmann, is essentially understood as a language. The words and grammar of this language, Hauptmann assured us, we understand intuitively. Riemann tried to develop this thought by exploring the grammar of music and locating it in nature. Like Hauptmann before him, Riemann saw the nature of music in logic. Whilst from this statement we must assume that the two theorists are in perfect agreement, a small but significant detail, the elision in the middle of the quotation, suggests otherwise. With the omission of more than one paragraph from Hauptmann's original, Riemann acted as a ventriloquist: he contrived a link in Hauptmann – his dummy, as it were – that Hauptmann had in fact not made in that way. Thanks to the omission, language and logic could be smoothly and explicitly connected; one seems to be the direct equivalent of the other.

In the paragraph omitted, Hauptmann had elaborated his idea that music is immediately and universally intelligible. For him, this intelligibility is granted by pure intonation: 'To pronounce upon the purity of musical intervals requires no technical skill; the feeling for it is innate and is given in the nature of human-rational existence.'[5] However, this was not the basis on which Riemann hoped to make the connection between language and logic. On the contrary, it was precisely this question of pure intervals and tuning that sharply separated Riemann from Hauptmann. On the basis of tuning impurities Hauptmann had declared that the *Klang* D–F–A in C major had to be considered a diminished triad, as its fifth is too small by 27/40.[6] Riemann's concept of a musical language, by contrast, dwelt precisely on the ambiguity that, on the one hand, the chord D–F–A in itself could be perceived as a pure triad, but on the other hand, received its status as an 'apparent consonance' within the tonal framework of C major. In a later article he took issue with Hauptmann's distinction: showing in Example 4.1 that D minor could well be heard as a pure triad, namely when preceded by an applied dominant, he concluded, 'our musical practice does not know two kinds of D in C major'.[7]

---

dem Musiker vom Menschen gegebenen, natürlichen Gesetz zuwider, weil es logisch unwahr, von innerem Widerspruche ist.'

[5] Hauptmann, *Nature of Harmony and Metre*, p. xl (translation modified).

[6] To understand the technical side of this argument more fully, one must remember that Hauptmann tuned fifths in the ratio of 2:3 and major thirds as 4:5. To note this difference, he employed both upper and lower-case letters: F a C e G b D. The diminished triad b D|F (derived by joining the extremes of the model) thus does not comply with the usual triadic structure. Analogously, the formation D|F a, which in Hauptmann's representation is the symmetrically opposite extreme to b D|F, is also declared diminished (*Nature of Harmony and Metre*, pp. 23–7).

[7] Hugo Riemann, 'Ideen zu einer "Lehre zu den Tonvorstellungen"', *Jahrbuch der Musik-bibliothek Peters* 21/22 (1914/15), p. 18.

Example 4.1 Riemann's attempt to refute Hauptmann, who had declared the triad on D in the context of C major to be 'diminished'. In Riemann's concept of tonality, by contrast, there can be no 'two kinds of D'.

T   (D)   Sp   D   T

Compared with the essentially acoustical conception on which much of the conception of musical logic hinged, as we saw in Chapter 3 above, this attitude, which emphasises the flexibility of tonal relations in musical syntax, would seem surprising. As we shall see later in this chapter, issues of tuning not only divided Hauptmann's approach from Riemann's, but also caused the tension between the language trope and the notion of logic within Riemann's approach.

Why did Riemann insist on a connection between language and logic, in the face of the difficulties that have just been indicated? One possible answer would hold that there was a tradition which would make this link between grammatical and logical categories in composition. A century previously, both Johann Nikolaus Forkel and Heinrich Christoph Koch had independently developed the idea of a musical logic which in both cases was inextricably bound up with language.[8] Koch started by interpreting melody in terms of subject and predicate, but soon abandoned it, apologising for not developing his thought fully, as most students would not have a sufficient grasp of general grammar and logic.[9] Forkel explained the relationship on the basis of an analogy, arguing that if language (*Sprache*) is the dress of thoughts, then melody is the dress of harmony.[10] Harmony is thus, he proceeded to say, a kind of logic in music, since 'it corrects and determines a melody [*melodischen Satz*] such that for the sentiments it seems to turn into actual truth'.[11]

The position of language in Riemann's work, however, shows slight but significant deviations from the two earlier music theorists. Unlike Koch, who was primarily concerned with melody, Riemann's

[8] See also Carl Dahlhaus, *Die Musiktheorie im 18. und 19. Jahrhundert; Zweiter Teil: Deutschland*, ed. Ruth E. Müller (Darmstadt: Wissenschaftliche Buchgesellschaft, 1989), p. 90.

[9] Heinrich Christoph Koch, *Versuch einer Anleitung zur Composition* (Leipzig: Adam Friedrich Böhme, 1787–93; reprint Hildesheim: Georg Olms, 1969), vol. 2, pp. 350–6.

[10] Johann Nikolaus Forkel, *Allgemeine Geschichte der Musik* (Leipzig: Schwickert, 1788), vol. 1, p. 24.

[11] Ibid.

grammatical analogy was pitched at harmonic successions. Forkel, on the other hand, remained on the level of analogy; the language trope of thought and speech had been an opportune simile to explain the inextricable connection between melody and harmony, but there had been no true crossover between language and music for him. Ultimately, Forkel was only interested in the notion of a musical grammar as far as it forms a corrective for melodies, to prevent them from being wrong and illogical.[12] As for the crucial question of what it is that constitutes these grammatical rules, he cavalierly referred to Kirnberger's treatise *Die Kunst des reinen Satzes* (1771–9).

In brief, the tension between the notions of logic and language that we found in Riemann had not been present in either Koch or Forkel a century earlier. It is no coincidence that the rift between logic and language in Riemann was paralleled by a similar move in the philosophical discourse of his age, where the position of logic was increasingly threatened by language.

I

After Johann Gottlieb Herder's critique of the Enlightenment discourse on language, stressing its importance to cultural and national identity, language came to be seen in Germany no longer as merely a means of communication, but rather as representative of a *Weltanschauung*.[13] Indeed, language was seen by Herder as no less than the cornerstone of the community in which it is spoken. He asked rhetorically: 'Is not the language of each country the clay out of which the ideas of its people are formed, preserved and transmitted?'[14] Although Herder tended to suppress the chauvinism that characterised nationalism in later years, he could nonetheless be called the father of nationalism.[15] Since for him every nation was unique, it was most important for a nation to remain authentic to itself. In this sense, he professed against the absolute standards that French thought assumed, in favour of historical and cultural relativism: an indigenous tradition is always more valuable to its own people than a foreign one, even if it were possible to prove, by some absolute standard, that this culture is inferior to the foreign one. For Herder, spiritual renewal of a nation can only occur from within; true

---

[12] Ibid., p. 25.

[13] The best English-language introduction to Herder remains Isaiah Berlin, *Vico and Herder: Two Essays in the History of Ideas* (London: Hogarth Press, 1976).

[14] Johann Gottfried Herder, *Sämmtliche Werke*, ed. B. Suphan (Berlin: n.p., 1877–1913), vol. 14, p. 13; cited in Maurice Olender, *The Languages of Paradise*, trans. Arthur Goldhammer (Cambridge, Mass.: Harvard University Press, 1992), p. 46.

[15] Berlin attributes the coinage of the term nationalism to Herder in *Vico and Herder*, p. 181.

creativity must be devoid of the influence of foreign elements because any such element is meaningless outside its original sphere.[16]

In the new framework in which language was treated as the basis of national culture, logicians found themselves in a cul-de-sac. Traditionally, logicians had assumed that logic corresponded to the abstract principles of thought in its pure, unadulterated form, being autonomous and in the first place independent of the specificities of languages.[17] Formal logic rested essentially on the principle, formulated succinctly by Leibniz, that all true statements should be expressible in the form 'Subject = Predicate'. In the example, 'A horse is a four-legged mammal', the subject 'horse' is an element defined by the two predicates 'four-leggedness' and 'mammal'. (It was not until George Boole's *Algebra* (1847), which was regarded with great suspicion in Germany, that a mathematical element to rival the pre-eminence of language found a place in logic.[18]) The central terms of logic, 'subject' and 'predicate', were of course identical with those of grammar – as is indeed suggested by the combination of the two subjects in the medieval trivium. They were often used in suggestive ambiguity. The logician Gottlob Frege, who created a symbolic language of logic in his *Begriffsschrift* of 1879, complained about the careless, indifferent conflation of logical and linguistic terms.[19]

Indeed, the new meaning language had assumed in the course of the nineteenth century, especially its new significance for national culture, made such sleight of hand inexcusable. For if the relation between language and thought is reversed such that language is no longer an immediate representation of thought (no matter how incomplete), but rather becomes instrumental in *constituting* thought specific to a nation, then logic is in turn dependent on language. It is perhaps understandable that most logicians in the late nineteenth century shied away from the conclusion that logic must consequently also be subject to the nationality principle. Too much would be at stake: no less than the asserted purity and universality of logic would have to be jettisoned. This problem, as we shall see later, surfaces in Riemann's stances on nationality and the universal.

The way out of the deadlock for the logicians came with the new discipline of comparative linguistics. The interest in language as a decisive factor in the determination of nationhood had triggered a series of important research in linguistics and philology. Of particular interest in that respect was the revival of the question concerning the origin of language. (This topic, incidentally, had been banned from academic debate in the mid-eighteenth century, because it was deemed futile.) German

---

[16] Ibid., pp. 186–94.
[17] See Verena Mayer, *Gottlob Frege* (Munich: C. H. Beck, 1996), pp. 41–2.
[18] Ibid., p. 17.   [19] Ibid., p. 41.

linguists carried out ambitious linguistic enterprises – witness Wilhelm von Humboldt's monumental study of the Kawi language (published posthumously, 1836–40) and Friedrich Schlegel's *Language and Wisdom of the Indians* (*Sprache und Weisheit der Indier*, 1808). Following Herder, both Schlegel and Humboldt placed language at the top of the scale of national characteristics: language constituted thought – or rather, language and wisdom of the Indians were one and the same thing in Schlegel's work. The beauty of Sanskrit grammar reflected the wisdom of the Indians or, to put it more accurately, the Indians possessed wisdom *because* their language was close to perfection. Due to its great age, Sanskrit became so popular as the candidate for the original language that it even threatened to supplant Hebrew, which had been favoured by theologians. A historian of language explains:

It is easy to understand, then, that Sanskrit became the lodestar of early comparative linguistics; without it the right path could not have been found. And it is easy to understand, also, that the first students of comparative linguistics were inclined to follow this lodestar blindly, so much so that they did not sufficiently keep in view the fact that Sanskrit itself deviates from the original language, and they often forgot to inquire whether the other languages had not here and there preserved older forms.[20]

The interest in language was bound up with the search for pure origins; the age and purity of a language always implied a judgement on its quality. Put differently, the frenetic search for the original language was always at the same time an implicit examination of the originality of German as well. It is not by coincidence that the term 'Indo-Germanic' was only too happily adopted by German philologists after it was coined by French colleagues in 1810,[21] as it signified a closer relation to the *Ursprache*, and hence greater authenticity, than any other European language could claim. (Indeed, the term 'Indo-Germanic' enjoyed such popularity, even among linguists who should have known better, that the German philologist Franz Bopp had to warn repeatedly that German was not the sole representative of a language of Indian descent.[22] To this day the term is used alongside the more accurate 'Indo-European'.)

In spite of this more or less covert national bias, comparative linguistics helped reintroduce the autonomy of thought so crucial to logicians.[23]

---

[20] Holger Pedersen, *Linguistic Science in the Nineteenth Century*, trans. John W. Spargo (Cambridge, Mass.: Harvard University Press, 1931), p. 22.

[21] Olender, *The Languages of Paradise*, p. 151n.

[22] Ibid., p. 13.

[23] Mayer, *Gottlob Frege*, p. 42, mentions particularly Wilhelm von Humboldt. Humboldt's significance is hard to overestimate. Even in the work of the late neo-Kantian Ernst Cassirer, Humboldt still occupies a significant place, although Cassirer critically points out the dichotomy between the discipline of logic and Humboldt's linguistics. See Ernst Cassirer, *Geist und Leben* (Leipzig: Reclam Leipzig, 1993), p. 293.

Although the aims of their research projects were vastly different, it seems that logicians and linguists had a common problem to solve: to be able to compare languages, it was necessary to find the common denominator at the base of all languages. A central feature of German linguistics in particular was to place grammar, rather than vocabulary, at the core of comparative linguistics. Eminent philologists such as Franz Bopp, Wilhelm von Humboldt and Friedrich Schlegel insisted that the grammatical structure of a language was a better yardstick than the richness and sound of words.[24] They placed at the top of the scale 'organic' inflecting languages, paradigmatically represented by Sanskrit, and its filial languages Greek, Latin and – perhaps not surprisingly – German.

While Schlegel simply differentiated between two distinct categories, 'organic' inflecting languages on the one hand, and 'mechanical' or 'dead' non-inflecting ones on the other,[25] Humboldt introduced four language classes in his *Kawi Introduction*: isolating (e.g. Chinese), agglutinating (e.g. Hungarian), inflective (Indo-European) and incorporating (e.g. Native American). The classes are discrete, but are ordered as a continuum: isolating languages, which according to Humboldt only possessed a rudimentary grammatical structure and a 'unisyllabic nature',[26] are at one end of the scale, while the incorporating form of American languages, at the other end of the continuum, is so compact and abundant that it shoots over the goal and obscures the grammatical structure. Agglutinating and inflective languages are somewhere in between these extremes, though agglutinating languages strive for the principle of inflection, but fall short of attaining it.

In this continuum of language types it is obvious (though never made clear why) that the 'wealth of forms in India'[27] – that is, inflection – is the highest principle and as such, desired by all language forms, the fixed point of reference:

Since the natural disposition to language is universal in man and everyone must possess the key to the understanding of all languages, it follows automatically

---

[24] In fact, the emphasis on grammar was prevalent well into the 1870s and beyond. Only then was a method of systematic lexical comparison sufficiently developed so that vocabulary and phonology could be considered scientifically as well. See Pedersen, *Linguistic Science in the Nineteenth Century*, p. 245.

[25] Friedrich Schlegel, *Sprache und Weisheit der Indier*, ed. E. F. K. Koerner, introd. and trans. J. Peter Maher (Amsterdam: John Benjamins, 1977), p. xx.

[26] Wilhelm von Humboldt, *Über die Verschiedenheit der menschlichen Sprachbaues und ihren Einfluss auf die geistige Entwicklung des Menschengeschlechts*, ed. Andreas Flintner and Klaus Giel, 8th edn (Darmstadt: Wissenschaftliche Buchgesellschaft, 1996); trans. into English as *On Language* by Peter Heath, intro. Hans Aarsleff (Cambridge: Cambridge University Press, 1988), p. 22. This text is commonly referred to as 'Kawi Introduction'.

[27] Ibid.

that the form of all languages must be essentially the same, and always achieve the universal purpose. The difference can lie only in the means, and only within the limits permitted by attainment of the goal.[28]

This goal was of course the inflectional principle found in Sanskrit. At the heart of this ultimately aesthetic classification into more and less perfect languages was, by necessity, the idea of a universal grammar, as was perhaps most famously postulated by the grammar of Port-Royal (1660) and which has recently been revived – to very different ends – by Noam Chomsky and Michel Foucault. By introducing the idea that a timeless, universal structure was at the core of all languages, Humboldt attempted to maintain an Idealist distinction between language (in the singular) and languages (in the plural). Language, on the one hand, as the universal core, transcends nationhood; it is 'no work of nations, but a gift fallen to them by their inner destiny'.[29] On the other hand, the individual languages that fall into one of Humboldt's four categories are relegated to the surface, below which the universal grammar is at work at the deep structural level:[30] 'It is no empty play upon words if we speak of language as arising in autonomy solely from itself and divinely free, but of languages as bound and dependent on the nations to which they belong.'[31] Thanks to Humboldt's theory of language, the logicians could finally recover the autonomy of language so dear to them, but they could only do so by ignoring Humboldt's aesthetic treatment of languages as well as the national bias with which Humboldt assessed the surface structure of the different languages. The link that Humboldt had contrived between language and languages was thus effectively severed by the logicians. This mode of reception, however, had its price: the purported universality of the 'deep structure' harboured some grave problems.

Riemann remarked in retrospect about his completed theories of harmony and metre that they constituted 'a kind of musical grammar'.[32] Based on three natural *Klänge*, the central one a fifth apart from the other two, this arrangement is the foundation of Riemann's musical equivalent to what Humboldt had called mankind's 'natural disposition' to language. Consequently, the basic form of all music must be the same. For Riemann, this basic form can best be expressed in the diatonic scale,

---

[28] Ibid., p. 215.   [29] Ibid., p. 24.

[30] It is only too obvious that Humboldt's model of language could be related also to Schenker's concept of a background structure. As far as I am aware this has never been attempted. It might prove an interesting point of comparison between Riemann and Schenker.

[31] Humboldt, *On Language*, p. 24.

[32] Riemann, 'Ideen zu einer "Lehre von den Tonvorstellungen"', p. 1.

Example 4.2 Riemann explains the link between the 'primary pillars' of functional harmony and the diatonic scale by means of a chain of thirds.

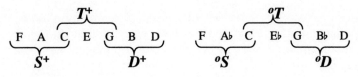

which he, following Hauptmann, related to the chordal configurations as shown in Example 4.2.

The diatonic scale – which Riemann described poetically (but judiciously) as the 'river bed', supporting the stream of functional harmonies – is inextricably connected with the 'natural *Klänge*' and is in his view itself a consequence of them:

> Harmony is the primordial source from which all music flows, but the diatonic scale is the primeval river bed. The stream may overflow its bed, but it is always dammed back inside it.[33]

On the one hand, the diatonic scale is for Riemann inconceivable without harmony: it would dry up without harmonic support. On the other hand, the diatonic scale is seen as a corrective for harmony, which would otherwise go hopelessly astray. Both forces require one another and appear to work in perfect symbiosis: the river bed is shaped by the flow of water, but then acts as a conduit to the stream. As such, the diatonic scale finds a place which corresponds to Humboldt's aestheticised grammar: the diatonic scale, like the Indo-Germanic language family, has made the most out of mankind's 'natural disposition' to (musical) language and represents the highest developed form, closest to the ideal.

While the link between harmonies and the scale was presented as virtually self-evident by Riemann, the Viennese musicologist Guido Adler described this relation as 'one of the most complex problems, perhaps even the fundamental and principal problem of musicology'.[34] One complication right at the core of this great problem of musicology arises from the circumstance that the ideal relation between triads and scale is not quite attainable, not even by the diatonic scale: in the form

---

[33] Riemann, *Vereinfachte Harmonielehre* (London: Augener, 1893), p. 182. 'Die Harmonie ist allerdings der Urquell[,] aus dem alle Musik fliesst, aber die diatonische Skala ist das uralte Strombett, über welches der Strom wohl überschäumen kann, in das er aber immer wieder zurückgedämmt wird.'

[34] Guido Adler, *Handbuch der Musikgeschichte* (Frankfurt: Frankfurter Verlagsanstalt, 1924), p. 8.

in which it has been used in the nineteenth and twentieth centuries, the diatonic scale is not exactly the correlate of the natural *Klänge*. For the sake of greater harmonic and modulatory freedom, the intonation of the diatonic scale has to be adjusted. The principle of equal temperament, although commonly used in practice, was not universally accepted the-oretically in the nineteenth century. In the climate of empiricism, the study of intonation was therefore an important aspect of music theory.[35] Purists in harmonic matters attached more importance to devising sys-tems that would enable the player to play justly tuned harmonies, ideally in as many chords as possible. Often these efforts were at the expense of practicability, such as a fifty-three-step scale that would permit a wide range of near-approximations to pure intervals but which would require an unwieldy and extraordinarily complex instrument.[36]

Riemann discussed these various possibilities of intonation in his *Handbuch der Akustik*. Among these, an Indian scale proved interesting: with its division into twenty-two steps, he considered the resulting val-ues 'not bad', describing the scale as a 'usable diatonic scale with good chromatic intervals'.[37] Indeed, it would seem that its finer pitch varia-tion makes it superior to the twelve-step Western scale, as it achieves good approximations of multiple justly intoned triads at once. However, Riemann still found one snag in his assessment of the scale: the problem for him was its impracticability, since, as he contended, 'the ear lacks any yardstick for the twenty-two-step octave'.[38] As the premises of the Indian scale do not conform with nature (in this case, the physiological aspect of nature), he considered it unusable. Later in the same book he elaborated on what he meant:

The ear judges, today as in the distant past and future, in the sense of pure har-monies, and the fact that it has made progress in this is proved in the tremendous development of the harmony of the last two hundred years.[39]

Under these circumstances it is hardly surprising that Riemann opted against the Indian scale.

---

[35] Witness especially the fervour with which Helmholtz's English translator, Alexander Ellis, advocated just intonation in his copious annotations.

[36] See Riemann, *Handbuch der Akustik (Musikwissenschaft)*, 3rd edn (Berlin: Max Hesse, 1921), pp. 58–65.

[37] Riemann seems to take the idea of a twenty-two-step scale of Indian music from the work of Rajah Sourindro Mohun Tagore, *Hindu Music From Various Authors*, 2nd edn (Calcutta, 1882), the authoritative source of Indian music in the latter half of the nine-teenth century.

[38] Riemann, *Handbuch der Akustik*, p. 34.

[39] Ibid., p. 88. 'das Ohr urteilt, heute ganz wie in aller Vergangenheit und Zukunft im Sinne reiner Harmonien, und daß es darin Fortschritte gemacht hat, beweist doch wohl die gewaltige Entwicklung der Harmonik in den letzten 200 Jahren.'

If the properties of the scale (as a linear construct composed of intervals, not simply as an ordered group of triads) are also to be considered – which cannot mean anything other than the postulation of the semitone as the smallest intelligible interval – then the combination of diatonic scale, built on the reservoir of twelve semitones, and triadic harmony is the only admissible one. Riemann said as much in the 'river bed' metaphor, which links natural chords and diatonic scales inextricably. As a second consequence, then, it follows from Riemann's position that the ear perceives only pure harmonies, irrespective of the tuning system, that one might as well opt for the greatest harmonic range and ignore the intricacies of accurate intonation.

For this reason Riemann decided on equi-tempered intonation as the ideal tuning system, over just intonation:

Just intonation would, if it should not fail due to its practical unfeasibility, entail a tremendous restriction in chordal and modulatory processes. And what would be gained from it: some slight sensual euphonious quality of the individual harmonies – at the expense of more profound expression, seizing and captivating the soul![40]

It should not surprise us that Riemann savoured harmonic connection over the sensual pleasure derived from the individual chord; in fact, this is precisely what one should expect from a theorist of harmony. One is reminded of the paradise image, which we encountered in the previous chapter. However, there are far-reaching consequences arising from this position. On the one hand, this statement implies no less than a confession to a belief in the nineteenth-century harmonic sublime and musical progress. For the sake of innovative harmonic connections he accepted the equi-tempered scale in spite of its acoustical impurities. On the other hand, with this admission he severed the correlation between triadic harmony and external nature. He irrevocably left the realm of physical nature and had to retreat into the much shadier area of psychological nature, as indicated in his lecture 'Die Natur der Harmonik', given three years previously.

From this psychological stance Riemann found it much harder to argue for the universal conformity to the natural law of the diatonic scale. When at the beginning of the twentieth century comparative (ethno-)musicologists considered alternative musical systems in their own right, Riemann insisted defiantly on the diatonic scale as the universal basis of all music:

[40] Ibid. 'Die reine Stimmung würde, wenn sie nicht an der praktischen Undurchführbarkeit scheitern soll, eine gewaltige Einschränkung im Akkord- und Modulationswesen bedingen. Und was wäre dabei gewonnen: etwas sinnlicher Wohlklang der Einzelharmonien – auf Kosten tieferen, die Seele gewaltig packenden Ausdrucks!'

The striking congruences of the division of the octave into twelve semitones, which completes the seven-step scale interspersing a semitone between alternately two and three tones [i.e. the diatonic scale], found likewise by the Chinese, Greeks and the nations of the European West in the space of many centuries, is a historical fact, which cannot simply be overthrown by a couple of pipes with faulty bores from Polynesia or by some coloured women's singing of questionable quality.[41]

It is notable that Riemann here no longer referred to the scientific truth of his concept, but appealed to history as a legitimising authority. Yet the claim that the diatonic scale could not be an eternal truth but should rather be viewed as a cultural construct, as ethnomusicology posited, was inconceivable to Riemann. Consequently, in his estimation it is not the universal principle of diatonicism that is tainted by the findings of ethnomusicology. Rather, in his eyes the fault remained with the researchers and the inadequate methodology employed by them.

Interpreting this in Humboldt's sense, it appears that every nation has the potential to develop the diatonic scale as a basis of triadic, functional harmony. While all nations possess the potential for the diatonic scale in one form or another – some, such as the pentatonic scale of ancient music, are presented by Riemann as rudimentary forms of diatonicism, lacking semitone steps[42] – it is not up to the whole of humanity to realise the potential to the full. This comes very close to Humboldt's basic conception that languages are a manifestation of the mental capacity of the nation:

In pondering on language in general, and analysing the individual tongues that are clearly distinct from one another, two principles come to light: the sound-form and the use made of it to designate objects and connect thoughts. The latter is based on the requirement that thinking imposes on language, from which the general laws of language arise; and this part, in its original tendency, is therefore the same in all men, as such, until we come to the individuality of their mental endowments or subsequent developments.[43]

---

[41] Riemann, *Handbuch der Musikgeschichte* (Leipzig: Breitkopf und Härtel, 1904), vol. 1, p. vi. 'Die frappante Übereinstimmung der in Zeitabständen von vielen Jahrhunderten gleichermaßen von den Chinesen, Griechen und den Völkern des europäischen Westens gefundene Teilung der Oktave in zwölf Halbtöne als letzte Vervollkommnung der wechselnd nach zwei und drei Ganztönen einen Halbton einschaltenden siebenstufigen Skala ist denn doch ein historisches Faktum, das man mit ein paar mangelhaft gebohrten Pfeifen aus Polynesien oder mit fragwürdigen Gesangsleistungen farbiger Weiber nicht über den Haufen rennt.'

[42] See Riemann, 'Tonart', in *Musik-Lexikon*, 5th edn (Leipzig: Max Hesse, 1900), pp. 1143–4. Also see the diagram included in the entry 'Geschichte der Musik', p. 382. 'The oldest guise in which tonal systems appear among all peoples is that of strict diatonicism, originally with the omission of semitone relations (five-step scale).'

[43] Humboldt, *On Language*, p. 54.

Riemann never spelled out a link between the intellectual capacity of a nation and its musical language as Humboldt did, though the above comments about non-Western music would strongly suggest that this idea is not alien to his musical thought: Riemann's comments are based on the belief that everybody is originally endowed with the same potential to develop the diatonic scale out of the natural, universal triads. However, it takes a certain mental capacity to succeed in the flexibility and coherence that, according to Riemann, only the equi-tempered diatonic scale possesses. The West possessed this mental capacity to form the diatonic scale to the full, while other nations attained it only imperfectly. According to this universality principle, any deviation from the ideal type is not an indication of the limitations of the principle itself, but rather a sign of the nation's incapability of attaining it in pure form.

While Humboldt's principle of language may go a long way to uncover the thinly veiled cultural bias in Riemann's 'musical grammar', this is, historically speaking, nothing remarkable: in the colonial age around the turn of the century, when Riemann was writing, it was self-evident, and almost considered good form, to emphasise one's own natural superiority over primitive peoples.[44] Indeed, it might be argued – and has been[45] – that this position was but an inevitable consequence of Riemann's historical model, whose single grand trajectory makes it necessary to distinguish between 'essential' and 'inessential' events. Primitive peoples were confined to the status of 'natural reserves'[46] (Lévi-Strauss) and thus excluded from history.

To understand the broader systematic way in which the language trope functions in Riemann's thought, and how it is entangled with Riemann's view of history, the first point to clarify is the concept of universality, which stands in stark opposition to the post-Herderian national appropriation of language. Even if Riemann, following the Humboldian argument, made a claim for the West's full understanding of the potential of harmony, it still remains a universal concept – with its (albeit dwindling) roots in nature – which lacks the particularity that Herder ascribed to languages. Or, to use Humboldt's distinction, Riemann's 'musical grammar' has been shown so far to function as 'language', the abstract concept of grammatical and lexical rules. But can it also be

---

[44] I have explored this cultural context in greater depth in my 'The Quest for the Origins of Music in Germany circa 1900', *Journal of the American Musicological Society* 53 (2000), pp. 356–60.

[45] Carl Dahlhaus, *Geschichte der Musiktheorie im 18. und 19. Jahrhundert; Erster Teil: Grundzüge einer Systematik* (Darmstadt: Wissenschaftliche Buchgesellschaft, 1984), pp. 58–60.

[46] This is discussed by Albrecht Schneider in *Analogie und Rekonstruktion* (Bonn: Verlag für systematische Musikwissenschaft, 1984), p. 47.

understood as one of Humboldt's 'languages' in the plural, that is to say, as one particular national language?

II

'The German nation is assigned a universal vocation', proclaimed Constantin Frantz, who could stand for any number of mid-nineteenth-century German historians.[47] Universality itself was claimed as the inalienable trait of the Germans. This was due to the peculiar situation in which Germany found herself for most of the nineteenth century, as a non-existent political entity split up into thirty-nine small states. The German nation understood itself to be a *Kulturnation*, not a politically based *Staatsvolk*. Ernst Moritz Arndt expressed this when he asked 'What is the German's fatherland?' and answered with an expansive patriotic poem. Conventional geographical boundaries, he concluded, are insufficient to demarcate Germany; wherever the German language is spoken, there is the German's fatherland:

> What is the German's fatherland?
> O name the great country!
> As far as the German tongue sounds
> And sings songs to God in heaven,
> There it shall be!
> That, brave German, shall be yours.[48]

While the song itself lost part of its appeal after 1849 (when it was superseded by the patriotic song *Die Wacht am Rhein*), the language trope itself did not cease to be relevant: for want of other, more material ties, language became the supreme factor in German nationalism. This did not even change substantially after 1871, when Germany was unified under Bismarck. Although the political reality posed some awkward problems to the continuation of the discourse, given that parts of the German-speaking population were excluded from the state while some non-German minorities were part of it, ideologues were unimpressed by this change. As late as 1869, writers still insisted that language was the sole adequate indicator of nationality, even though the political and geographical situation in Europe no longer supported this view.[49] German nationhood remained an idea, even when the state suggested otherwise.

[47] Constantin Frantz, *Die Wiederherstellung Deutschlands* (Berlin: Ferdinand Schneider, 1865), p. 415.

[48] Ernst Moritz Arndt, 'Des Deutschen Vaterland', in *Werke*, ed. Heinrich Meisner (Leipzig: Karl Fr. Pfau, 1892–1909), vol. 4, p. 20. 'Was ist des Deutschen Vaterland? / So nenne mir das große Land! / So weit die Deutsche Zunge klingt, / Und Gott im Himmel Lieder singt. / Da soll es sein! / Das, wackrer Deutscher, nenne Dein!'

[49] See Eric J. Hobsbawm, *Nations and Nationalism since 1780*, 2nd edn (Cambridge: Cambridge University Press, 1990), pp. 98–9.

We must not be deluded into believing that the position language occupied was ever anything other than ideological. In fact, the German language was as little unified as the state itself.[50] Local dialects prevailed, making communication between different regions difficult. (An example of the preponderance of dialects can even be found in Goethe's *Faust*. Gretchen's lines '*Ach neige, / du Schmerzensreiche*'[51] do not rhyme, unless they are pronounced in the broad dialect of Goethe's native Frankfurt.) Unity of language, like nationhood on the whole, was an idea rather than a fact.

The philosopher Johann Gottlieb Fichte, arguably the most influential among the German nationalist thinkers,[52] employed language in this manner at the centre of his *Reden an die deutsche Nation* (*Addresses to the German Nation*, 1808). In Fichte's conception, language was assigned a position which went far beyond a mere means of communication: it is not man that forms language, but rather language that forms man. Fichte took this Herderian thought back to an original language, which once, he supposed, embraced the whole of mankind:

It is not actually man who speaks, but human nature speaking within him and announcing itself to his fellows. And so one should have to say: there is only one language, and this language is a necessary one.[53]

This original human language is lost to most nations; instead, national languages have taken its place. Only when both language and the fatherland are congruent and remain unadulterated, Fichte argued, can a people attain the status of a nation. The only *Ursprache* – the remaining primordial language, rooted in nature – that Fichte accepted, was, needless to say, German. Germans alone – or so Fichte claimed, at least – have without fail remained true to their nature on their home soil, and equally, their language has withstood all foreign, impure influences. It is impossible to disentangle a cause-and-effect relationship between language and national identity, because one is representative of the other.

---

50 See Hobsbawm, *Nations and Nationalism*, pp. 51–4. Most of the recent social theories of nationalism – Benedict Anderson, *Imagined Communities*, revised edn (New York and London: Verso, 1991); Ernest Gellner, *Nations and Nationalism* (Oxford: Blackwell, 1983); Hobsbawm, *Nations and Nationalism* – stress that the discourse about language is common to nationalist ideology, and is in dire need of deconstruction.

51 Johann Wolfgang von Goethe, *Faust*, ed. Albrecht Schöne (Frankfurt am Main: Deutscher Klassiker Verlag, 1994), vv. 3587–8.

52 For a narrative, carrying through several elements found in Fichte's nationalist discourse across the ages with particular emphasis on their relation to nature, see Simon Schama, *Landscape and Memory* (London: Fontana, 1996), pp. 75–134.

53 Johann Gottlieb Fichte, *Reden an die deutsche Nation*, intro. Reinhardt Lauth (reprint Hamburg: Felix Meiner, 1978), p. 61. 'Nicht eigentlich redet der Mensch, sondern in ihm redet die menschliche Natur, und verkündigt sich andern seinesgleichen. Und so müßte man sagen: die Sprache ist eine einzige, und durchaus notwendige.'

The *Ursprache* German is an outward manifestation of the spiritual conception of German nationhood.

Fichte demonstrated with a rather disconcerting argument how the purity of the language is indicative of the purity of the nation: the ancient Germans, he explained, were destined to destroy Rome, in spite of her superior civilisation. For Rome's civilisation was not Germany's, so the Germans' enjoyment of Roman civilisation would necessarily have been at the expense of the autonomy and integrity of the German nation. In this way, the defeat of the Romans by the Germans was predestined, for 'they were enthralled by the eternal'.[54] This aspect of the eternal, the perpetual renewal of the people as a whole, is at the core of Fichte's conception of the nation. The German nation, Fichte explained at the outset of the Addresses, is an a priori category: no other communal band has ever had genuine validity.[55] In his idealist framework, Germanness is a natural, eternal, and above all noumenal category; the non-existence of a unified state of Germany does not mean that the nation does not exist. On the contrary, it could be argued that the absence of a German state heightens the significance of the concept of the nation, since it makes this 'myth of ethnic election'[56] all the more potent. Fichte's Germans, who have survived as a nation where the state has declined, are the 'Urvolk, das Volk schlechtweg, Deutsche'[57] – the 'primordial people, the people as such, Germans'. Only an original people like the German nation is capable of true patriotic love.

This is proof enough for Fichte for the noumenal existence of German nationhood. Yet, as Fichte firmly believed, it still needed to be communicated to his compatriots, who were oblivious of their eternal but dormant nationhood: they needed to be taught it. (This aspect of teaching was of particular relevance to Riemann, as we shall explore below.) To this end, Fichte formulated Germanness as a moral postulate: 'Therefore we have called for the need to create internally and fundamentally good humans, since only in such [humans] can the German nation persist. In bad ones, however, it necessarily merges with foreign nations.'[58] To be German is synonymous with being good. And conversely, as I

---

[54] Ibid., p. 137.   [55] Ibid., p. 13.

[56] Anthony D. Smith, 'Chosen Peoples: Why Ethnic Groups Survive', in J. Hutchinson and A. D. Smith, eds., *Ethnicity* (Oxford: Oxford University Press, 1996), p. 189.

[57] Fichte, *Reden an die deutsche Nation*, p. 121. Also see Hans Kohn, *Prelude to the Nation States* (Princeton: D. van Nostrand, 1967), p. 241.

[58] Fichte, *Reden an die deutsche Nation*, p. 30. 'Wir sind daher sogar durch die Not gedrungen, innerlich, und im Grunde gute Menschen bilden zu wollen, indem nur in solchen die deutsche Nation noch fortdauern kann, durch schlechte aber notwendig mit dem Auslande zusammenfließt.' For a corresponding concept of Germanness in the musical sphere, basing nationhood on qualitative judgments, see Franz Brendel's 'Zur Anbahnung einer Verständigung', *Neue Zeitschrift für Musik* 50 (1859), pp. 265–73.

shall explore in greater detail below, one's nationality becomes a quality judgement. This moral concept of Germanness, however, moves beyond the merely nationalistic: German now becomes a universal category, a way of life. As a transcendental, moral concept, Germanness is no longer confined to the boundaries of Germany.

One historian remarks on Fichte: 'The great idealist, who always sought for the eternal in the temporal, was delighted to discover the national spirit, which simply was not backed by history, and [to work on] the task of contributing to the creation of a national spirit that was altogether the work of conscious reason and of freedom.'[59] However, this observation concerning the lack of history is not quite correct – the comment that Fichte 'discovered' the national spirit, like a natural phenomenon, suggests that deliberate myth-making is going on. Fichte did indeed make use of history, namely by referring to the ancient Germans. He initially rested his judgement of German superiority, ironically enough, on the verdict of the Roman historian Tacitus, who wrote favourably about them in his *De Germania*. What is conspicuous in Fichte's argument, rather, is the conflation of transcendental arguments and primordial history. The same strategy, as we saw in Chapter 3, is also at work in Riemann's approach. The roots of nationhood – as well as those of tonality – in reason and nature exist outside of any historical development, but the simultaneous emphasis of their *Urnatur*, their primordial nature, strains history to support the claim to eternity.

It was in this cultural context, in the increasingly xenophobic climate of the 1890s, that the meaning of 'musical language' changed for Riemann, and took a temporary nationalist turn. What changed was not his belief in the universality of the principles of his musical system – he continued to maintain that 'the foundations of musical hearing are stable, unchangeable and not dependent on arbitrary regulations and familiarities',[60] in other words, beyond historical and cultural differences – but rather he added a new layer to his argument, particularly in his works of the 1890s and 1900s: he tried to prove that these principles originated with and therefore belonged to the German nation. In this spirit, in his *Geschichte der Musiktheorie* of 1898, the summation of his theoretical ideas, he included an extraordinary account of the purported origin of music, which amounts to no less than a musicological 'myth of ethnic election'.

It is hardly a coincidence that, as historical research keeps bringing to light, Germanic nations brought the raw beginnings [of simultaneous singing] to a certain artistic height, and that England of all places became the actual cradle

---

[59] Friedrich Meinecke, *Weltbürgertum und Nationalstaat* (Munich: R. Oldenburg, 1962), pp. 108–9.

[60] Riemann, *Handbuch der Musikgeschichte*, vol. 1, p. vii.

of fully developed counterpoint. The third as the foundation of harmony is something remote, something completely unthinkable for the peoples educated in the theories of the ancients. This healthy core of harmonic music could not be found through speculation, rather it was the vocation of the nations to whom this notion was self-evident, familiar for centuries, to bring order and meaning at once into the theory and practice of an art, which the heirs of an ancient culture had fundamentally ruined in their attempt to assimilate an element foreign to them.[61]

It is worth pondering the references and allusions of this statement in some detail, not least since Riemann's argument rests on a number of conflations and apparently self-evident truths that need to be reconstructed to understand the passage fully. First of all, the two groups that are contrasted here rest on an implicit bipolar distinction: the 'theories of the ancients' are associated with 'the European south'[62] and are set against the 'Germanic people', who gave rise to modern music. These Northerners seem to follow the idea of a pan-Germanic nation, which includes Germans, Scandinavians and Celts. Again, this is nothing out of the ordinary in this cultural context: Houston Stewart Chamberlain, for one, would further include the Slav people under this pan-Germanic umbrella in his influential *Grundlagen des neunzehnten Jahrhunderts*.[63]

This broad, inclusive nature of German nationhood is crucial, since Riemann's argument that 'England became the actual cradle of fully developed counterpoint' rests significantly on a tendentious interpretation of *Descriptio Cambriae* by the twelfth-century archdeacon Giraldus Cambrensis (Gerald of Wales), who explained that three-part singing was second nature to the Welsh people and that this practice might have come from Scandinavia.[64]

---

[61] Riemann, *Geschichte der Musiktheorie*, 2nd edn (Berlin: Max Hesse, 1920; reprint Hildesheim: Georg Olms, 1990), p. 3. 'Es ist auch schwerlich zufällig, daß, wie die Geschichtsforschung mehr und mehr ans Licht bringt, germanische Nationen zuerst die rohen Anfänge zu einer gewissen künstlerischen Höhe brachten, und daß gerade England die eigentliche Wiege des vollausgebildeten Kontrapunkts wurde. Die Terz als Grundlage der Mehrstimmigkeit ist für die in den Anschauungen der antiken Theorie aufgewachsenen Völker etwas fern Abliegendes, völlig Undenkbares; dieser gesunde Kern der harmonischen Musik konnte nicht auf dem Wege der Spekulation gefunden werden, vielmehr mußten die Völker, denen dieser Begriff ein selbstverständlicher, seit Jahrhunderten geläufiger war, berufen sein, mit einem Schlage Ordnung und Sinn in die Theorie und Praxis einer Kunstübung zu bringen, welche die Erben der antiken Kultur in dem Bestreben, ein ihnen fremdes Element zu assimilieren, zunächst gründlich verfahren hatten.'

[62] Ibid., p. 2.

[63] Houston Stewart Chamberlain, *Die Grundlagen des neunzehnten Jahrhunderts*, 3rd edn (Munich: Bruckmann, 1901), vol. 1, p. 466.

[64] Riemann discusses Gerald's work in his *Geschichte der Musiktheorie*, pp. 2 and 25. It is noteworthy that Riemann was by no means the only musicologist who used Gerald in such an evolutionary account of music. See, for instance, Victor Lederer, *Über Heimat*

Although Gerald spoke explicitly of Welsh three-part singing, as distinct from the English practice of only two parts, Riemann ignored this distinction and ascribed the origin of counterpoint – and implicitly harmony – to England. Furthermore, Gerald's account does not offer anything to indicate that this three-part singing – be it Welsh or English – was in thirds. (The practice to which Gerald referred is now assumed to be heterophony.[65])

Riemann was strengthened in his belief by the circumstance that fauxbourdon, the singing of three-part triadic harmony (in characteristic first-inversion sound) – and as such, for Riemann, the first practice of modern harmony – first occurred in England in the fifteenth century. Like other theorists at the time, Riemann was at pains to find the earliest possible origin of fauxbourdon. (At one point, for instance, he wishfully suggested the possibility that a reference in the English medieval source, known as 'Anonymous 4', might be related to fauxbourdon – in which case, he argued, the practice could be dated back to 1250.[66])

This argument, which tries to locate the origins of harmonic music among the Germanic peoples, gives a different twist to Riemann's previous musical thought. While time and again Riemann emphasised in his works the roots of harmony in nature and, consequently, the strictly scientific side of his theory, this was not to say that harmony is common to the whole of mankind. On the contrary, it is – according to this text – only truly at home among the Germanic peoples. The 'southern cultures of antiquity', which Riemann opposed to the all-embracing 'Germanic peoples of the North', by contrast, did not crack the secret of polyphony and harmony; their music was supposed to be entirely monophonic. Riemann made no effort to explain the cause of this provenance of harmony any further. Instead, he took it for granted: the interval of the third is the 'healthy core' of harmonic music, and it is no coincidence that the Germanic people should be familiar with it.

It may seem odd at first that the third should be a carrier of ethnic identity, but it has to be remembered that the third held a pivotal position in Riemann's musical thought. The third was not merely an element of the triad, but its recognition revolutionised the order of harmonic relations. For in a (non-dualistic) system that reckons on the basis of fifth relations, the third would be a complex ratio and must hence be a distant harmonic relation: $(2:3)^4$ or $(64:81)$. In this sense, Riemann pointed

und Ursprung der mehrstimmigen Tonkunst (Leipzig: C. F. W. Siegel, 1906), and Otto Fleischer, 'Ein Kapitel vergleichender Musikwissenschaft', *Sammelbände der Internationalen Musikgesellschaft* 1 (1899/1900), p. 18.

[65] For a modern interpretation of Gerald, see Shai Burstayn, 'Gerald of Wales and the Sumer Canon', *Journal of Musicology* 2 (1983), pp. 135–50.

[66] See *Geschichte der Musiktheorie*, p. 109.

out, before Hauptmann's dualistic conception, third relations were a big theoretical problem:

Even a theorist of Marx's stature is surprised that the keys of E major and A major are immediately intelligible in the key of C major, while D major and B major sound strange, incoherent against C major; since Marx had no idea of third relations, he had to be surprised indeed that the key four fifths away seemed better mediated than that two fifths away.[67]

The view of third relations as a direct link that the dualists endorsed does not merely result in the simpler acoustical and mathematical ratio of 4:5. What is more important is that the third relation opens a second harmonic dimension which enlarges the harmonic range tremendously. It must be remembered that the major third was the quintessentially dualistic interval: its theoretical relevance in music was discovered by the dualists, because in their approach the major third was fundamental to both major and minor triads. In its wider-ranging consequences the introduction of the third as a harmonic relation, then, is the precondition of the harmonic grid that we encountered in Chapter 2. In brief, the discovery of the third was to Riemann the musical equivalent of the discovery of the wheel: in its double significance as the foundation of triadic harmony (as a simultaneous interval) and the facilitator of a flexible modulatory range (as a harmonic relation) it is the third that makes progress possible.

Just as Fichte's ancient Germans were destined to conquer Rome and to spread their Germanness there, so Riemann's musical Germans conquered ancient music by bringing their intuitive knowledge of harmony to the south, where they instilled new life in the ancient theories that had reached their limits. However, not everybody was entitled to make use of this knowledge. Among the Roman peoples, as Riemann went on to explain in his 'myth of ethnic election', the innovation of harmony first resulted in the 'reactionary' form of *déchant*. (It seems that Riemann used the French form instead of the more common *discantus* in order to stress the Romance origin of this musical style. Elsewhere he uses the Latin form.[68]) *Déchant* is particularly distinguished, in Riemann's view, by misunderstanding the idea of harmony: what should correctly be harmony in thirds and sixths, Riemann explained, was wrongly replaced

[67] Riemann, 'Die Natur der Harmonik', in *Waldersees Sammlung musikalischer Vorträge* 4 (1882), pp. 183–4. 'Noch ein Marx wundert sich, daß die Tonarten e-Dur und a-Dur nach c-Dur sofort verständlich sind, während d-Dur und b-Dur fremdartig, zusammenhangslos gegen c-Dur klingen; da Marx von der Terzverwandtschaft noch keine Erkenntnis hatte, mußte er sich allerdings wundern, daß die Tonart der vierten Quint besser vermittelt erschien als die der zweiten Quinte.'

[68] The *Musik-Lexikon* defines the term under its Latin name, and he offers *discantus* as an alternative later in his *Geschichte der Musiktheorie*, p. 97.

in *déchant* by fourths and fifths, the nearest approximation available in the limited musical theoretical concepts of the ancient and Southern cultures.[69]

In his rhetoric Riemann left no doubt that the French *déchant* is the musical equivalent of what Fichte called dismissively a 'neo-Latin' language. Isolated and disconnected from the native soil and origins out of which their language grew, both neo-Latin languages and *déchant* are inauthentic, adulterated and bereft of life: 'Although such a [neo-Latin] language may be stirred on the surface by the breeze of life, and that way emit the semblance of life, it has a dead element somewhat deeper and is, by entering in the new circumstance and the interruption of the old one, cut off from the living root.'[70] (It goes without saying that Fichte had primarily the French language in mind, given that at the time he wrote his *Addresses* Napoleon still occupied large parts of German territory.) Fichte went so far as to deny the French a true mother tongue, just as they did not know in music, according to Riemann, how to employ the third properly. Their attempt to assimilate this foreign element spoilt the heirloom. Although fauxbourdon – the northern triadic answer – came later than *déchant*, Riemann regarded it as superior, namely as 'a correction in the sense of the musical feeling of the northern nations'.[71] This was because it realised the importance of the third as a 'natural fact' and put it into practice. Fauxbourdon is the correct way forward, as it builds on the cultural roots of the nation.

In the 1890s, when Francophobia in Germany reached new heights – and Fichte's *Addresses to the German Nation* were eagerly read again – such statements were nothing out of the ordinary.[72] Because German music remained true to itself, Riemann contended, it gained a central

---

[69] Riemann, *Geschichte der Musiktheorie*, pp. 25–6.

[70] Fichte, *Reden an die deutsche Nation*, p. 68. 'Obwohl eine solche Sprache auf der Oberfläche durch den Wind des Lebens bewegt werden, und so den Schein eines Lebens von sich geben mag, so hat sie doch tiefer einen toten Bestandteil, und ist, durch den Eintritt des neuen Anschauungskreises, und die Abbrechung des alten, abgeschnitten von der lebendigen Wurzel.'

[71] Riemann, *Geschichte der Musiktheorie*, p. 4. At the same time, it is worth remembering his efforts to backdate fauxbourdon, to bring it closer to *déchant*. A similar strategy can also be observed in Guido Adler's *Studie zum Ursprung der Harmonie*, in *Sitzungsberichte der (kaiserlichen) Akademie der Wissenschaften in Wien, philosophisch-historische Klasse* 98 (1886), pp. 781–830, a book that Riemann praised for its insights into the Germanic origins of harmony. See also the entry on Adler in Riemann's *Musiklexikon*, p. 10, where Riemann draws particular attention to Adler's work on the emergence of harmony and counterpoint from secular song.

[72] See Paul Hayes, 'France and Germany: Belle Epoque and Kaiserzeit,' in Paul Hayes, ed., *Themes in Modern European History 1890–1914* (London: Routledge, 1992), p. 26; and Fritz Stern, *The Politics of Cultural Despair* (Berkeley and Los Angeles: University of California Press, 1961), pp. 279–80.

position over the centuries as 'the current main representative of musical high culture'.[73] His explanation, quoted here at length, followed closely the Fichtean argument:

It is of great interest to music historiography to demonstrate that the peoples currently striving to participate in the struggle for future hegemony in the field of music possessed a plain folk music, which already exhibited the same traits that are now identified as national ones, long before the emergence of such particular tendencies. However, this pre-existence of folk music is actually self-evident and forms, as it were, merely the legal title, on the basis of which such pretensions are made...Only nations which have, more or less in isolation, in themselves withstood foreign influences can give a new signature to art music by manifesting a strong characteristic [of their national identity], rather than simply adopting art music as it has been brought to its current height by other nations.[74]

It took a long time, Riemann concluded in his deliberations concerning the origin of harmony, to bring a theoretical hegemony (to match their musical hegemony) home to Germany – and here Riemann alluded to modern Germany, the nation of 'thinkers and poets',[75] not the ethnic group of Germanic people of the north:

But with the same toughness with which they at first knew to keep away from theory, they retained it once they had given admission to it, and thus they became carriers of the last great progress in the developmental history of music theory, of the complete penetration of the nature of harmony and the full exploitation of its effects.[76]

---

[73] Riemann, *Geschichte der Musik seit Beethoven (1800–1900)* (Stuttgart: W. Spemann, 1901), p. 547.

[74] Ibid., pp. 501–2. 'Es ist für die musikalische Geschichtsschreibung zwar von hohem Interesse, nachzuweisen, daß lange vor dem Hervortreten dieser Spezialtendenzen die Völker, welche neuerdings sich anschicken, an dem Kampfe um eine künftige Hegemonie auf musikalischem Gebiete teil zu nehmen, eine schlichte Volksmusik gehabt haben, die bereits ebenso diejenigen Merkmale zeigte, welche heute als national herausgestellt werden, aber diese Präexistenz ist an sich selbstverständlich und bildet sozusagen nur den Rechtstitel, auf welchen hin die Prätensionen erhoben werden... Nur Nationen, welche an sich mehr oder minder abgeschlossen gegen fremdländische Einflüsse bestanden haben, können, anstatt einfach die durch andere Nationen auf die gegenwärtige Höhe gebrachte Kunstmusik zu übernehmen, wie sie ist, durch Offenbarung einer kräftigen Eigenart derselben eine neue Signatur geben.'

[75] Riemann, *Geschichte der Musiktheorie*, p. 4. 'It took a long time to turn our forebears into the quintessential thinkers.'

[76] Ibid. 'Aber mit derselben Zähigkeit, mit welcher dieselben sich zunächst das Theoretische fernzuhalten wußten, hielten sie dasselbe fest, nachdem sie ihm einmal Eingang gestattet hatten und wurden damit Träger des letzten großen Fortschrittes, den die Entwicklungsgeschichte der Musiktheorie aufzuweisen hat, der völligen Durchdringung des Wesens der Harmonie und der vollen Ausbeutung ihrer Wirkungsmittel.'

Here, surely, Riemann was flattering himself (and his colleagues Hauptmann and Oettingen). However, there is more to this statement than a mere moment of personal vanity. Riemann was obviously at pains to score this point, otherwise there would be no need for the bizarre claim that the Germans first willed not to have music theory and then suddenly they willed with equal determination to possess it. De Staël's dictum of the nation of 'thinkers and poets' is not in itself a strong enough incentive for this move. Rather, I believe we can turn to Fichte again for an answer.

Fichte emphasised the element of pedagogy in his writings, particularly drawing attention to Pestalozzi, the educator.[77] The German nation must be educated towards its nationality, as it must be educated towards tonality according to Riemann. As we saw in the previous chapter, Riemann stressed time and time again the importance of internalising the rules on which his musical thought was based: the rules of functional tonality as well as the moral concept of Germanness must be instilled in the pupil until he can no longer act but in accordance with the laws. In Fichte's words:

If you wish to have any influence over your pupil, then you must do more than merely admonish him: you must remake him, and make him in such a fashion that it will be quite impossible for him to will anything but what you wish him to will.[78]

Riemann placed such importance upon theory in order to ensure that the future of German music remain governed by functions: theory may be a didactic tool, but in this case it was clearly more than that. Theory, once it has 'come home' to be wed to practice, will flourish to result in the harmonic garden of paradise that Riemann envisaged at the end of *Musikalische Syntaxis*, as we saw in the previous chapter.

It is here that the forward-looking utopian element shines forth in Riemann's search for the origins of music. The didactic element of his musical thought is the essential characteristic; it is here that the cultural import resides. It shows Riemann's concern with 'the moral regeneration of the national community' that characterises cultural nationalism.[79] The timing of Riemann's nationalist turn – which only came to the fore in the 1890s – is telling. Like other thinkers participating in the nationalist

---

[77] For a more contemporary example of this trend, which was still prevalent eighty years after Fichte, see Julius Langbehn's notorious *Rembrandt als Erzieher*, 42nd edn (Leipzig: n.p., 1893).

[78] Fichte, *Reden an die deutsche Nation*; cited in Hans Kohn, *Prelude to the Nation States*, p. 240.

[79] John Hutchinson, *The Dynamics of Cultural Nationalism* (London: Allen and Unwin, 1987), p. 9.

discourse, Riemann raised his moral rhetoric at a time of social disorder, and drew on the past in order to construct from the historical imagination a brighter future. Riemann's exploration of the origins of harmony among the Northern nations is thus an extension of his earlier utopian vision of harmony as a paradisiacal space: the golden age of fauxbourdon links up apparently seamlessly in this utopian vision, in order to materialise in a new, or rather renewed, spiritual progress. Riemann's concept of everlasting classicism, which we explored in Chapter 3, is thus not a backward-looking ossified tradition, but the way into an everlasting – spatialised – future. The teaching of harmony in an ever-renewing classical tradition is Riemann's most important didactic tool.

In this sense, the warning that a theorist of nationalism issues, that the 'invocation of the past...must be seen in a positive light, for the cultural nationalist seeks not to "regress" into an arcadia but rather to inspire his community to ever higher stages of development',[80] applies to Riemann in full: he saw the future of German music in an eternal regeneration of triadically based music of harmonic function. It is thus understandable that Riemann praised *Die Meistersinger* among contemporary compositions, leading the way into the future: 'Wagner himself showed with his *Meistersinger* a path that makes artistic creation of no lesser value still possible.'[81] The process of nation-building thematised in this opera is clearly in accordance with Riemann's ideas, as is, on the musical level, the diatonic triadic surface that exploits far-reaching harmonic relations.

It is in this sense that Riemann's musical thought, in both its theoretical and historical aspects, took a turn towards cultural nationalism. As was common in the 1890s and 1900s, this was coupled with a particular brand of cultural pessimism, which became prevalent after the new national art – expected to flourish in the wake of the *Reichsgründung* of 1871 – had hardly come to fruition.[82] Just how much was was at stake became particularly clear in Felix Draeseke's polemic of 1906

[80] Ibid.

[81] Riemann, *Geschichte der Musik seit Beethoven*, p. 492. More commonly, however, Riemann had very little interest in opera.

[82] On what the music aesthetician Paul Moos called 'Aesthetic Pessimism' in music (*Moderne Musikästhetik in Deutschland* [Leipzig: Horst Seemann Nachfolger, 1902], pp. 327–44), see Arthur Seidl, *Das Erhabene in der Musik: Prolegomena zu einer Ästhetik der Tonkunst*, Inaugural Dissertation (Regensburg: M. Warner, 1887), and Rudolf Louis, *Der Widerspruch in der Musik* (Leipzig: Breitkopf und Härtel, 1893). For a parallel in literary history see Andreas Schumann, 'Glorifizierung und Enttäuschung: Die Reichsgründung in der Bewertung der Literaturgeschichtsschreibung', in Klaus Amann and Karl Wagner, eds., *Literatur und Nation: Die Gründung des Deutschen Reiches 1871 in der deutschsprachigen Literatur* (Vienna: Böhlau, 1996), pp. 31–43. For Riemann's own

against the state of composition, in which Riemann was to side with Draeseke (and thus unwittingly contribute to his break with Max Reger):

Musical art has been and remains incontestably the most prized possession of the German people, for even when the atrocities of the Thirty Years War had turned Germany into a desert, and had eroded almost all culture, music emerged unharmed, as one of our greatest composers, Heinrich Schütz, unflaggingly carried its banner and did it honour. Preserve your most precious possession, O German nation, and do not be blinded by agitators, who do not wish to see your progress but only your surrender.[83]

When two years later Riemann added the catchphrase of 'degeneration' to the debate – which at that time was a ubiquitous battle cry of cultural pessimists – the tasks for cultural nationalists were clear. 'Healthy' classicism, Riemann argued alongside many like-minded cultural critics at the time, is the best safeguard against degeneration, and a source for spiritual – musical – renewal.[84]

III

The cultural nationalism of the 1890s not only embraced the systemic character of Riemann's theoretical work; it is also the point at which his historical and theoretical interests come together. We saw in Chapter 3 that the apparently ahistorical treatment of harmony was on the contrary marked by highly historical interests. We can now go a step further. For whilst Riemann used his concept of history as an incentive, indeed a categorical order, for his students to write ever-lasting works, the obverse was also possible and indeed necessary: a composition which complied with Riemann's eternal musical values ought to survive history and be assigned its rightful state in classicism.

cultural pessimism see particularly his article 'Die Musik seit Wagners Heimgang', in *Präludien und Studien* (reprint Hildesheim: Georg Olms, 1967), vol. 2, pp. 33–41, with the ominous subtitle 'A Dance of Death (1897)'.

[83] Susanne Shigihara, *'Die Konfusion in der Musik': Felix Draesekes Streitschrift und die Folgen* (Bonn: Gudrun Schröder, 1990), p. 61. 'Die Tonkunst ist das unbestrittenste Gut des deutschen Volkes gewesen und geblieben; denn selbst als die Greuel des Dreißigjährigen Krieges aus Deutschland eine Wüste gemacht und fast alle Kultur weggeschwemmt hatten, war sie unversehrt aus derselben hervorgegangen und einer unserer größten Tonsetzer, Heinrich Schütz, hat unentwegt ihre Fahne hochgehalten und zu Ehren gebracht. Wahre dir dein teuerstes Gut, deutsches Volk, und laß dich nicht verblenden von Umstürzlern, die dir nicht den Fortschritt wollen, sondern nur den Umsturz!'

[84] See particularly Riemann's article 'Degeneration und Regeneration in der Musik', *Max Hesses deutscher Musikerkalender* 23 (1908), pp. 136–8.

Riemann's interest in the composer Johann Stamitz and the whole of the Mannheim School can be viewed in this light: according to Riemann, Stamitz is a figure who has been unfairly neglected in music history. One aspect of Stamitz's style that mattered above all in Riemann's conception of history was the circumstance that his textures were no longer governed by figured bass (which was viewed by Riemann as an aberration of history, as seen in Chapter 3) but instead gave way to the functional harmonies and clearly structured eight-bar phrases that Riemann associated with the classical style. He explained:

> There can be no doubt that the gradual overcoming of figured bass first took place in Germany and that German composers were the first to grasp the greater artistic value in thoroughly prepared keyboard parts as opposed to the improvisations of the accompanists, which frequently enough were at odds with the composer's intentions.[85]

The importance Riemann attached to Stamitz is further testified by the numerous examples of his music in *Große Kompositionslehre*.[86] Yet, despite exuding what Riemann saw as eternal musical value, Stamitz's music was not assigned the place among the classics that it deserved.

Riemann never tired of putting history right. In fact, Riemann was the first person to underline systematically the historical importance of Stamitz and the whole Mannheim School and to promote it as a musical centre of equal standing with Vienna.[87] In his first publication on the Mannheim School he proclaimed grandiosely:

> The refined expression of the whole movement is characterised by a truly classical distinction, noblesse and compelling logic which does not permit one to change even a single note. These features endow it with perennial value...No further doubt: *Johann Stamitz is the long sought-after forebear of Haydn!*...We shall therefore not bear a grudge against the fact that it is a Bohemian and not a German to whom we have to give the laurel. Such primeval roots were required to counter the dry formalism which tended to prevail especially in the Berlin School.[88]

---

[85] Riemann, ed., *Sinfonien der Pfalzbayerischen Schule (Mannheimer Schule)* (Leipzig: Breitkopf und Härtel, 1902–7), vol. 1, pp. xvii–xviii. 'Es unterliegt wohl keinem Zweifel, dass die allmähliche Antiquierung des Generalbasses sich zuerst in Deutschland vollzogen hat und dass deutsche Komponisten zuerst den höheren Kunstwert sorgfältig ausgearbeiteter Klavierparte gegenüber den oft genug ihre Intentionen kreuzenden Improvisationen der Akkompagnisten begriffen haben.'

[86] Volume 1, incidentally, is a rare example among Riemann's numerous tutors on harmony that extensively uses examples from composers' works rather than specially composed exercises.

[87] Riemann, *Sinfonien der Pfalzbayerischen Schule*, vol. 1, p. xxi.

[88] Stamitz had been 'discovered' in 1898 by Friedrich Walter in *Geschichte des Theaters und der Musik am kurpfälzischen Hofe*; see Eugene K. Wolff, *The Symphonies of Johann*

The essential features of classicism are easily recognisable in this pane-gyric; Riemann followed the attributes of Winckelmann's description of classicism as 'noble simplicity, quiet greatness' very closely. He stressed the compelling logic, the primordial originality and above all the eternal quality of Stamitz's work.

Stamitz is presented not merely as a predecessor of classicism in the sense of an incomplete prototype that was later discarded by history. Rather, Riemann was making an argument on the lines of the philosophy of origins here. Stamitz preceded the canonical classics, and therefore his contribution to the perfection that classical music was to attain must be recognised. This he made quite clear in a related article entitled 'Ein vergessener Großmeister'[89] (A forgotten Great Master): Stamitz was, in Riemann's eyes, not simply a *Kleinmeister*, a minor master. Stamitz's rightful place is among the great composers.

So hard did Riemann try to link Stamitz with the Viennese School that he even claimed it was an innovation of Mannheim to expand the three-movement 'old Viennese' symphony to include a minuet, which was then readily taken up by Viennese composers such as Haydn, Dittersdorf and Leopold Hoffmann.[90] In fact, as the editor-in-chief re-marked in a footnote, the examples of Wagenseil and Leopold Mozart on which Riemann built his contention about the 'old Viennese' sym-phony must count as exceptional; Riemann's conclusion concerning Stamitz's spiritual parentage of Haydn is built on extremely fragile evidence.[91] Yet Riemann so insistently emphasised Stamitz's influence

---

Stamitz (Utrecht: Bohn, Scheltema & Holkema/The Hague: Martinus Nijhoff, 1981), p. 11. Riemann, *Symphonien der Pfalzbayerischen Schule*, vol. 1, p. xxiv. 'Die feine Abtönung des Ausdrucks des ganzen Satzes, der von einer wahrhaft klassischen Gewähltheit und Noblesse und von einer bezwingenden Logik ist, die auch nicht eine Note ohne Schaden zu ändern gestattet, verleihen demselben dauernden Wert... Kein Zweifel mehr: *Johann Stamitz ist der so lange gesuchte Vorgänger Haydns!*... Wir wollen uns nicht darum grämen, dass es ein Böhme und nicht ein Deutscher ist, dem wir diesen Lorbeer reichen müssen. Es bedurfte eines solchen urwüchsigen Elements, um dem trockenen Formalismus zu begegnen, welcher besonders in der Berliner Schule überhand zu nehmen begann.' Emphasis in original.

[89] Riemann in *Max Hesses deutscher Musikerkalender* 18 (1903), pp. 139–41. In this article Riemann points out that among the forgotten composers whom he exhumed, Stamitz is the most important, as 'he speaks our language' (p. 141).

[90] Riemann, *Sinfonien der Pfalzbayerischen Schule*, vol. 1, p. xiv.

[91] The debate about the contribution of Mannheim to the classical style continues to this day. The generally well-disposed critic Alfred Heuß noted that the influential position Riemann attributes to the Mannheim School is simply exaggerated. See Alfred Heuß, 'Zum Thema "Mannheimer Vorhalt"', *Zeitschrift der Internationalen Musikgesellschaft* 8 (1908), pp. 273–80. While Jens Peter Larsen dismisses Mannheim entirely ('On the Importance of the "Mannheim School"', in *Handel, Haydn and the Viennese Classical Style* (Ann Arbor, London: University of Michigan Press, 1988), pp. 263–8), Eugene K. Wolff

that the composer, as well as the Mannheim School, is now a stock-in-trade figure of music history textbooks.[92] Indeed, this case would make for a model example of how to establish a 'fact' of music history – it is an ossified hypothesis, stated with the purpose of illustrating or supporting a particular historical narrative.[93]

It transpires that Riemann was driven by an interest that lay even outside his urge to promote his system of harmonic function and the stature of Johann Stamitz. This additional interest, which points towards nationalism, became particularly pronounced in the ensuing debate between Riemann and Guido Adler: who was the true precursor of the Viennese School? Adler vehemently dismissed Stamitz and the Mannheim School as the spiritual ancestors of the Viennese School – largely on account of geographical improbability – and instead posited the Viennese composer Georg Monn, who had written a four-movement symphony in 1740.[94] Adler's approach to the subject was at first glance subtler and more circumspect than Riemann's. Yet the debate soon degraded into pedantic bickering: Adler claimed superiority for Monn partly on statistical grounds, since out of eleven symphonic works by Stamitz only seven contain four movements, while eight out of the ten symphonies in the Monn volume show the typical four-movement form.[95] Riemann, on the other hand, fought fervently for chronological priority; he insisted on Stamitz's pre-eminence as the inventor of the classical symphony solely on the basis of lack of evidence to the contrary: 'The fact that the autograph of a symphony by Monn dating from 1740 exists would only give way to claims of priority over Stamitz if it were proven that [Monn's] exact contemporary Stamitz had not written a symphony at that age

has reviewed Stamitz's symphonies, particularly the claim to four-movement form, in *The Symphonies of Johann Stamitz*, pp. 354–61. This book also contains an extended bibliography on the debate, including French and Italian music which subsequently made claims for their own national priority in the classical style.

[92] See among numerous others Gerald Abraham, *The Concise Oxford History of Music* (Oxford: Oxford University Press, 1979), p. 492; Hugo Leichtentritt, *Music, History and Ideas* (Cambridge, Mass.: Harvard University Press, 1947), p. 165; Alec Robertson and Denis Stevens, eds., *The Pelican History of Music* (Harmondsworth: Penguin, 1960–8), vol. 3, pp. 52–5; and Stanley Sadie and Alison Latham, eds., *The Cambridge Music Guide* (Cambridge: Cambridge University Press, 1990), p. 225.

[93] See Carl Dahlhaus, *Foundations of Music History*, trans. J. Bradford Robinson (Cambridge: Cambridge University Press, 1983), p. 43.

[94] Later other musicologists such as the Italian Fausto Torrefranca joined in the debate to propose their national champions – in Torrefranca's case the little-known composer Giovanni Platti – as the true initiators of Viennese classicism.

[95] Guido Adler et al., eds., *Wiener Instrumentalmusik vor und um 1750. Vorläufer der Wiener Klassiker* (Vienna: Artaria, 1908), p. xi; Riemann, *Sinfonien der Pfalzbayerischen Schule*, vol. 2/2, p. xi.

(he was no less than twenty-three years old!).'[96] Questions concerning dissemination or detailed modes of influence were largely ignored by Riemann; the quarrel about the origin of the symphony turned out to be one of copyright and intellectual property.

In short, Riemann was trying to fashion Stamitz into a national icon. By the 1900s, when the Adler–Riemann controversy took place, Austria was separated from *Kleindeutschland* (lesser Germany) – by then, the German Empire – and Mozart and Haydn had been established as genuinely Austrian composers. To pronounce the Mannheim School the spiritual forebear, the mentor of the Viennese School would therefore be a shrewd move to retrieve the cradle of musical classicism for Germany. Indeed, following Fichte, such a move would even be imperative, since all traditions on which nationhood is built must be autochthonous. In this context it is anything but incidental that Riemann published his editions of works by the Mannheim School in the Bavarian branch of the series *Denkmäler deutscher Tonkunst* (Monuments of German Musical Art), a series launched in 1892 whose task was the promotion of an explicitly national musical canon. Adler, on the other hand, was the founding editor (1894) of the equivalent series in Austria, *Denkmäler der Tonkunst in Österreich*. The jealous rivalry between the two foundations was considerable: in a somewhat pedantic footnote – before the quibbles with Adler began – Riemann had already complained that the editor of the *Denkmäler der Tonkunst in Österreich* volume on Michael Haydn (vol. 14/2) failed to acknowledge the contribution of the Mannheim School.[97]

It may be objected that any national appropriation of Stamitz was undermined by Riemann himself: did he not make it quite clear in the above quotation that Stamitz was in fact not German but Bohemian? On the contrary, it seems to me that this concession is a red herring; in designating Stamitz a Bohemian, Riemann underlined the circumstance

---

[96] Riemann, *Sinfonien der Pfalzbayerischen Schule*, vol. 2/2, p. xiii. 'Daß von Monn eine autographe Sinfonie vom Jahre 1740 existiert, würde jedoch Monn gegenüber Stamitz Prioritätsansprüche nur dann geben, wenn erweislich wäre, daß der ihm völlig gleichalterige Stamitz so früh (mit immerhin 23 Jahren!) noch keine Sinfonie geschrieben hätte.' See also Riemann's retort to Adler, 'Stamitz – oder Monn?', *Blätter für Haus- und Kirchenmusik* 9 (1907/08), pp. 97, 113.

[97] Riemann, *Sinfonien der Pfalzbayerischen Schule*, vol. 2/1, p. ix n. As for the tension between the two 'Monument' collections in general, it is enlightening to follow particularly the letters to the editor in *Zeitschrift der Internationalen Musikgesellschaft* of 1908. It is noteworthy that this debate was a strictly public and professional affair. As Michael Arntz notes in *Hugo Riemann (1849–1919): Leben, Werk und Wirkung* (Cologne: Concerto-Verlag, 1999), pp. 111–19, Adler remained Riemann's loyal and supportive friend throughout, and subsequently made him an editorial member of the *Denkmäler der Tonkunst in Österreich*.

that Stamitz is *not Austrian*. Adler's prompt reply makes the surreptitious *tertium comparationis* quite obvious: he stressed in turn that the Mannheim School was merely a group of native Austrian composers that 'were called to Mannheim', a 'seedling of Austrian musical culture, shifted West'.[98] It is striking how oblivious to historical accuracy both scholars appear to be. During his lifetime, Stamitz's nationality would have been neither Austrian nor Bohemian. Bohemia – as well as Vienna and Mannheim – was then still part of a murky entity called the Holy Roman Empire of the German Nation. (The division between Czechs and Germans is one dating from after 1848, whilst a historically more sensitive distinction would have been between *Deutschböhmen* and *Stockböhmen*.[99]) Riemann thus insisted on the German affinity of Stamitz's works when he noted: 'The *Sinfonies d'Allemagne* [of Stamitz], which enraptured the world abroad around 1750, are not Viennese but Mannheim symphonies.'[100]

The remarkably unscrupulous scholarship that Riemann delivered in these volumes of *Denkmäler der deutschen Tonkunst*, distorting much historical evidence for the sake of the argument, was not uncommon in this and comparable series.[101] Selective argumentation, it seems, is a virtually inevitable feature of persuasion in any nationalistic enterprise. The writer must not only create a glorious past for the national community but also make the nationality principle appear an inevitable, natural consequence. The reinterpretation of history that nationalism is invariably based on makes it necessary to block out those parts that are irreconcilable with the ends of the reinterpretation. Ernest Renan recognised one of the cornerstones of nationalism in his seminal lecture *Qu'est-ce qu'une nation?* (*What is a nation?*, 1882), when he pointed out that an essential premise of the process of nation-building is 'that everyone must already have forgotten many things'.[102] The theorist of nationalism Benedict Anderson, who draws attention to this passage, notes that it is not enough for the nation simply to forget historical events, but rather it is, to put it paradoxically, the act of

---

[98] Adler, *Wiener Instrumentalmusik vor und um 1750*, pp. x–xi, see also p. xxv.

[99] Ernst Bruckmüller, 'The National Identity of the Austrians', trans. Nicholas T. Parsons, in Mikuláš Teich and Roy Porter, eds., *The National Question in Europe in Historical Context* (Cambridge: Cambridge University Press, 1993), p. 215.

[100] Riemann, *Handbuch der Musikgeschichte*, vol. 2/3, p. 150.

[101] See John Deathridge, 'Germany: the Special Path', in Jim Samson, ed., *The Late Romantic Era from the Mid-Nineteenth Century to World War I* (London: Macmillan, 1991), p. 60.

[102] Ernest Renan, *Qu'est-ce qu'une nation?* (Paris: Ancienne Maison Michel Lévy Frères, 1882), p. 9. '[il faut] que tous aient oublié bien de choses.' Also: 'L'oubli, et je dirai même l'erreur historique, sont un factor essentiel de la formation d'une nation, et c'est aussi que le progrès d'études historiques est souvent pour la nationalité un danger' (p. 7).

already-having-forgotten that is essential in forging a viable concept of nationhood.[103] One of the first things that must have been forgotten, of course, is the imaginative power of nationalism itself.

Riemann and Adler had both 'forgotten' Stamitz's historically authentic national affiliation. But in doing so, they 'remembered' – dialectically entangled in the act of forgetting – a different national identity for Stamitz. That, too, is a familiar strategy in defining nationhood. It is also a direct consequence of Renan's state of 'having forgotten': a nation 'imagines' itself through the selective memory of its historical past. Riemann and Adler placed Stamitz in a framework that accorded with the state boundaries of their own time but not his. In their historical forgetfulness, they both reinforced the notion that the concepts of the states of Austria and Germany are somehow transcendent, existing outside history.

On one level, the strategies employed by Riemann and Adler appear similar. Above all, both emphasised the *genius loci* of Vienna and Mannheim respectively to insist on the primacy of their school. Adler maintained that 'the common bond of a group of artists is above all dependent on the locality in which these masters find themselves united. It is from the soil of folk music of this place, or this territory, that the school, merged into unity, draws its natural nourishment.'[104] The Viennese School thus epitomises classicism because it draws on its indigenous traditions:

During their lifetime there was little opportunity for the Viennese masters of the transitional years to present their works, which themselves cannot historically be praised highly enough, to more remote countries – in this their compatriots working in Mannheim were obviously at an advantage; the masters working in Vienna were for the large part restricted to their closer home region. However, here of all places they could work fruitfully and auspiciously for the future, so that already Joseph Haydn found in this locality the soil on which his genius could flourish and influence Mozart, twenty-four years his junior. So the third great man could join the art of the pair of *dioskures* and could find his artistic home in the same place.[105]

[103] Benedict Anderson, *Imagined Communities*, pp. 199–201.

[104] Adler, *Wiener Instrumentalmusik vor und um 1750*, p. ix. 'Die Zusammengehörigkeit einer Reihe von Künstlern hängt vor allem mit der Örtlichkeit zusammen, auf oder in der diese Meister sich vereint finden. Von dem Boden der Volksmusik dieses Ortes oder dieses Territoriums zieht die zur Einheit verschmolzene Schule ihre natürliche Nahrung.'

[105] Adler, *Wiener Instrumentalmusik vor und um 1750*, p. xii. 'Zu ihren Lebzeiten war wenig Möglichkeit geboten, daß die Wiener Meister des Überganges ihren historisch nicht hoch genug zu schätzenden Werken Eingang verschaffen konnten in ferner gelegene Länder und Kunststätten – darin waren ihre in Mannheim wirkenden Landsleute augenscheinlich im Vorteil –; die in Wien wirkenden Meister blieben zum großen

Note especially Adler's subtle rhetoric, which craftily avoids mentioning Beethoven's name or provenance while pointedly including him among the Viennese composers. He could have only flourished on Viennese, that is Austrian, soil. Austria, as a multi-nation state, was well defined by its geographical boundaries, but had no lingual or ethnic unity.[106] Adler's insistence on the influence that locality has is thus in accordance with this approach: for him, the cultural community was a consequence of the *genius loci*, not vice versa. The cause and origin of the *genius loci*, however, remain mysterious.

The figure of Beethoven is of course the bone of contention in the nationalist appropriation of composers. Riemann voiced his opinion on this topic elsewhere:

> Pedantically, the question has been raised of whether to count Beethoven among the North or South Germans. Would we regard Mozart as a North German composer if his prospects of appointment in Bonn of 1781 had become reality? Would little Bonn, instead of Vienna, have become the central point and chief place of action of musical life around the turn of the century, if political events had not obliterated Electoral Cologne? All these are surely futile questions; but we still have to point out that Bonn was on its way to becoming a musical Weimar at the time Beethoven was still an adolescent.[107]

Although Riemann prevaricated, refusing to give an answer to the questions he raised, the questions themselves are in fact not quite as futile as he claimed: the 'what if?' scenario that Riemann conjured up reveals that for him, too, locality was of central importance, as he insists on the

Teil auf ihren engeren Heimatsdistrikt beschränkt, allein gerade hier vermochten sie fruchtbringend und für die Zukunft verheißungsvoll zu wirken, so daß schon Josef Haydn an dieser Stätte den Boden gefunden hat, auf dem sich sein Genie entfalten und auf den um vierundzwanzig Jahre jüngeren Mozart so einwirken konnte, daß an die Kunst dieses Dioskurenpaares sich auch der Drittgroße im Bunde anschließen und an gleichem Orte seine künstlerische Heimat finden konnte.'

[106] On the failure of language-based concepts of nationhood in Austria and the problems arising from this, see Bruckmüller, 'The National Identity of the Austrians', pp. 216–17. For the most fascinating exploration of a separate non-German Austrian identity, see Robert Musil's *The Man Without Qualities*.

[107] Riemann, *Geschichte der Musik seit Beethoven*, p. 48. 'Allzukleinlich hat man die Frage aufgeworfen, ob Beethoven den Norddeutschen oder den Süddeutschen zuzurechnen sei? Würden wir in Mozart einen norddeutschen Komponisten sehen, wenn sich seine Bonner Aussichten i[m]J[ahre] 1781 verwirklicht hätten? Würde nicht anstatt Wien das kleine Bonn der Centralpunkt und Hauptschauplatz der Musiklebens um die Jahrhundertwende geworden sein, wenn nicht die politischen Ereignisse das Kurfürstentum Köln beseitigt hätten? Das alles sind gewiß müßige Fragen; aber daß Bonn auf dem besten Wege war, ein musikalisches Weimar zu werden, zu der Zeit, wo Beethoven noch ein Jüngling war, müssen wir doch konstatieren.' For a more contemporary account of the musical history of Bonn, which broadly supports Riemann's observations, see Theodor A. Henseler, *Das musikalische Bonn* (Bonn: n.p., 1959).

formative influence of Beethoven's upbringing in Bonn. It could even be imagined that Adler's appropriation of Beethoven as an out-and-out Viennese was a direct reaction to this or similar statements which tried to root Beethoven firmly and inevitably in Bonn.

By the same token, the principle of *genius loci* was also at work in Riemann's evaluation of Stamitz's position. It is true, Riemann emphasised, that personality, not location, was the central category in determining the Mannheim school: Stamitz's stature and influence was unequivocally attributed by Riemann to his outstanding personality.[108] At the same time, however, the inclusion of the 'Mannheim School' in the Bavarian series of 'Monuments of German Musical Art' is evidently based on a principle of locality. It is conspicuous, though – and this is the decisive difference from Adler's approach – that Riemann never managed to distinguish clearly between Stamitz and the Mannheim School in his writings. Stamitz, as the 'spiritual head',[109] is synecdochic with the school in its entirety. Place and person are not differentiated.

While one might dismiss this as a confused and therefore dubious basis for an argument, it seems that for Riemann the difference between the two was simply not significant: Stamitz's personality, which he overtly emphasised, was for him inextricably bound up with the covert principle of locality. The place of birth becomes a negligible category in this conception. As Fichte explained, Germanness is not strictly confined to the territory of Germany. His moral principle of nationhood is open to anyone who shares the belief in the eternal laws in which it is grounded:

The principle according to which it [i.e. the nation] has to agree on this [covenant with nature in order to form a state] is pre-given; whosoever believes in the spiritual concept, and the liberty of this spiritual concept, and [whosoever] wills the perpetual continuance of this spiritual concept through liberty, belongs to us. He is of our kin and will be part of us, wherever he may be born and whichever language he may speak.[110]

This outburst of cosmopolitan generosity seems unusual in a nationalistic document. It is, however, inextricably connected with the fundamental conception of language as identical with thought: whosoever agrees

---

[108] Riemann, *Sinfonien der Pfalzbayerischen Schule*, vol. 2/2, p. xiii.

[109] Riemann, *Sinfonien der Pfalzbayerischen Schule*, vol. 1, p. xxii.

[110] Fichte, *Reden an die deutsche Nation*, p. 122. 'Der Grundsatz, nach dem sie diesen zu schließen hat, ist ihr vorgelegt; was an Geistigkeit und Freiheit dieser Geistigkeit glaubt, und die ewige Fortbildung dieser Geistigkeit durch Freiheit will, das, wo es auch geboren sei, und in welcher Sprache es rede, ist unsers Geschlechts, es gehört uns an und es wird sich zu uns tun.'

with this German thought must think 'in' German; the actual mother tongue fades into insignificance.[111]

In a similar vein, he argued that the inner, spiritual boundaries demarcate the utopian state of the Germans. As it happens, however, these coincide with the geographical boundaries:

From these internal borders, drawn by the spiritual nature of the human himself, the external demarcation of the dwellings results only as a consequence of the former. And in the natural view of things, it is by no means thanks to the latter that those humans who dwell within the confines of certain mountains and rivers form a people. On the contrary, people live together, grouped together – as if by chance – by rivers and mountains, because they had already been one people before, by grace of a supreme natural law.[112]

Like their language, the nationhood of the Germans is original and eternal. Germans are destined to be members of their nation – their nationhood is a transcendent, natural law. It was on this basis that Riemann could state that Stamitz was Bohemian while still appropriating him for the nationalist project of erecting German monuments. Stamitz's spiritual nature was German, and Mannheim was the congenial place where his art could bear fruit.

The subsequent history of Stamitz's position underlines his importance in the establishment of a *'kleindeutsch'* classicism. In fact, the canonical position of Stamitz shifted slightly but significantly. Particularly in his late Beethoven analyses, Riemann came to stress perpetually the influence Stamitz had on Beethoven, for instance by suggesting 'that [Beethoven] went to Vienna in 1792 as Haydn's pupil' – not because of

---

[111] Fichte, *Reden an die deutsche Nation*, p. 139. Strictly speaking, this concession to likeminded people of all nations contains a twist of sophistry: besides the nineteenth-century Germans, only the ancient Greeks had a comparable status among the nations, as Fichte complained at the end of the following section. This comparison with ancient Greece was popular, not only because of the classicist ideals prevalent in Germany, but also because of the alleged political parallels between the Greek *polis* and the small German states. During the Austro–Prussian war, for instance, it was common to assign 'Spartan' and 'Attic' attributes to the quarrelling states. Yet it was far from self-evident that Prussia was likened to Sparta. The *éminence grise* amongst nationalist historians, the Prussian Heinrich von Treitschke, for instance, attributed the loveliness of Athens to Prussia, whilst leaving the brutality associated with Sparta to the Austrians. See Harold James, *A German Identity 1770–1990*, revised edn (London: Weidenfeld and Nicolson, 1990), p. 21.

[112] Fichte, *Reden an die deutsche Nation*, p. 207. 'Aus dieser innern, durch die geistige Natur des Menschen selbst gezogenen Grenze ergibt sich erst die äußere Begrenzung der Wohnsitze, als die Folge von jener, und in der natürlichen Ansicht der Dinge sind keineswegs die Menschen, welche innerhalb gewisser Berge und Flüsse wohnen, um deswillen Ein Volk, sondern umgekehrt wohnen die Menschen beisammen, und wenn ihr Glück es so gefügt hat, durch Flüsse und Berge gedeckt, weil sie schon früher durch ein weit höheres Naturgesetz Ein Volk waren.'

Haydn's intrinsic qualities as a composer but rather because 'he had understood early on that the continuation of the paths of the Mannheim School led into the direction which Haydn and Mozart had followed'.[113] To misquote a well-known dictum, Beethoven went to Vienna to receive the spirit of Stamitz from Haydn's hands.[114] In his insistent references to Mannheim throughout the three volumes of analyses, Riemann created the impression that even in the late period Beethoven did not manage to wrestle free from Stamitz's all-pervasive influence. Beethoven's Op. 109, for example, is characterised by Riemann as 'the final consummation of the stylistic reform of Mannheim (Johann Stamitz)'.[115]

While Riemann had initially introduced Stamitz as the 'missing link' before Haydn in the developmental history of the classical style, he became increasingly interested in forging a direct link between Stamitz and Beethoven. He credited the music historian Heuß with the observation that 'Beethoven is directly connected in more than one respect with the Mannheim School, i.e. Johann Stamitz, without actual mediation of Mozart or Haydn.'[116] By creating a direct link between Stamitz and Beethoven, Riemann would marginalise Mozart and Haydn. The Austrian composers would, in this way, be relegated to a mere sideline of pure German music.

The Adler–Riemann debate happened at a time when the classical core of the musical canon had been consolidated: nobody would doubt the towering preponderance of Beethoven, with Haydn and Mozart on either side of him.[117] However, shifts of emphasis did indeed take place within the established demarcations.[118] In Stamitz's case the validity of the established canon is not questioned; instead it is added to. Indeed,

---

[113] Hugo Riemann, *Ludwig van Beethovens sämtliche Klavier-Solosonaten*, 2nd edn (Berlin: Max Hesse, 1919), vol. 1, p. 84.

[114] The original is quoted for instance in Charles Rosen, *The Classical Style*, revised edn (London: Faber and Faber, 1976), p. 19.

[115] Riemann, *Ludwig van Beethovens sämtliche Klavier-Solosonaten*, vol. 3, p. 383.

[116] Riemann, *Handbuch der Musikgeschichte*, vol. 2/3, p. 147. See Alfred Heuß, 'Über die Dynamik der Mannheimer Schule', in Carl Mennicke, ed., *Riemann-Festschrift* (Leipzig: Max Hesse, 1909), pp. 433–55. In the article he claims that 'it is impossible to explain Beethoven without the Mannheimers' (p. 448), and concludes that of the Viennese classics Haydn is the 'healthiest', as his national pedigree is the purest (p. 455).

[117] Leo Treitler produces a fascinating document in 'Gender and Other Dualities in Music History', in Ruth A. Solie, ed., *Musicology and Difference* (Berkeley: University of California Press, 1993), p. 32, representing the reified musical canon, a 'Hall of Fame' of the great composers (dating from 1911) with Beethoven sitting regally on the central throne. In prominent positions around him, among the dozens of composers in this family portrait, are Wagner and Bach.

[118] In literature, too, the years around the turn of the century witnessed the placement of Hölderlin and particularly Kleist into the central canon. See Peter Uwe Hohendahl, *Literarische Kultur im Zeitalter des Liberalismus 1830–1870* (Munich: C. H. Beck, 1985), p. 220.

in stressing the direct influence of Stamitz on Beethoven, particularly in later years, Riemann testified to the pivotal position of Beethoven while canonising the Mannheim composer.

It is easy to lose sight of the point of Riemann's interest in Stamitz, given that the debate with Adler sidetracks the argument: Stamitz is incorporated on the basis of his musical classicism. While classicism itself was not a historical period but a historical condition for Riemann, the closely related classical style included for him a range of diverse features – from the basics of his musical language, the eight-bar period and the harmonic prototype, to global concepts such as thematic work, sonata form and symphonic writing. The backbone of his fascination with Stamitz was not so much the composer's role as a figure of chronological priority as his compliance with Riemann's idea of the classical style. Stamitz was a figure who in Fichte's terms would make an exemplary German composer, as through him the musical *ur*-language is combined with the soil from which it allegedly originated. The position of Stamitz underlines clearly the role that the musical canon came to play in the late nineteenth century. The idea of German classicism – in literary studies just as much as in musical[119] – was more than a tradition; it was a national heritage that had to be cultivated, protected and perpetuated.

Riemann's train of thought seems to be guided in a rather direct way by a concern for the contemporaneous political situation, which he grafted onto his conception of music history. This is at least in part the result of the peculiar situation in which Germany found herself after 1871, when the *kleindeutsch* state of Germany no longer corresponded to the ideals of the German nationalist discourse. Focusing on a spiritual unity through culture, the nationalists had promoted a pan-German concept of the nation. But while this had contributed to the unification in 1871, it could not possibly have accounted for the separation of Austria: linguo-cultural and political unities drifted apart, and needed to be reconsidered. That is to say, music history had to be amended to match the recent political events and retrospectively legitimate the cultural consequences that had arisen from it. Riemann's canonisation of Stamitz is perhaps the most striking example of this. On the establishment of this 'kleindeutsch' classicism, genuine German art could flourish and Riemann's utopia, conjuring up a renewed, contemporary classicism, could finally be achieved.

---

[119] See Hohendahl's study of the construction of a German literature around the two poets Goethe (the universal) and Schiller (the German), and the forever changing constellations in which they were found up until and beyond the unification of 1871, in ibid., pp. 194–271. The changing function of the 'classics' is further underlined by a change of terminology in Germany in the 1880s: the new term *Klassik* becomes prevalent rather than *Klassizismus*, which merely describes a style or an epoch.

IV

As we saw in Chapter 3 above, Riemann's musical 'grammar' was built on a vague, practically unrestricted logic. Under these circumstances, the use of the harmonic system as a key to founding a national canon becomes – as in all nationalist arguments – a rather non-rational, that is emotional and personal, affair. In its application, the dual reference to universal nature on the one hand, and (universal) German nationhood on the other, seems to prove a problem: the rules of Riemann's harmonic theory seem strangely ill suited to discern anything that might be characteristic of German music. Put differently, the concept of the 'other' appears not pronounced enough in Riemann's theory to demarcate the particularity of Germanness against that which it is not. It is typical of modern nationalism that 'cultural symbols are proposed... not to express a commitment to fundamental values, but rather to effect a differentiation of the group from others'.[120] If harmonic function is indeed so all-embracing that anything may happen between the initial and the final statement of the tonic, what is there left to differentiate?

As a matter of principle, this differentiation is often achieved in nationalist discourses by the most astonishing twists. The concept of 'humanity', as perhaps the most potent of these, features strongly in nationalism: although it should comprise the whole of mankind, leaving no space for the required opposite which is to be excluded, it is employed as an 'asymmetrical opposite'.[121] An 'asymmetrical opposite' is defined as a term that determines its complement only negatively, such as 'Greek' – 'Barbarian' (i.e. non-Greek), 'Christian' – 'Heathen' (i.e. unbeliever in the sense of non-Christian). In this sense, 'humanity' excludes its asymmetrical opposite 'non-human', often in the sense of inhuman and subhuman, occasionally even as superhuman. With the powerful principle of asymmetrical opposites, even apparently universal standards can be bent so as pointedly to exclude a certain group.

In Riemann's own writings, the analysis of the mysterious opening of Liszt's *Faust Symphony* and his analytical observations regarding Berlioz's overture to *Benvenuto Cellini* are a case in point of such asymmetrical opposites. In his *Faust* analysis, which shows a remarkable degree of interpretative freedom, reproduced here as Example 4.3, Riemann suggested that the panchromatic succession of augmented triads is actually a very simple progression. He interpreted them as a series

---

[120] Hutchinson, *Modern Nationalism*, p. 20.

[121] Reinhart Koselleck, 'Zur historisch-politischen Semantik asymmetrischer Gegenbegriffe', in Harald Weinrich, ed., *Positionen der Negativität* (Munich: Wilhelm Fink, 1975), pp. 65–105; reprinted (in excerpts) in Michael Jeismann and Henning Ritter, eds., *Grenzfälle: Über alten und neuen Nationalismus* (Leipzig: Reclam Leipzig, 1993), pp. 174–93.

Example 4.3 Riemann's analysis of Liszt's *Faust Symphony* (opening), from *Geschichte der Musik seit Beethoven*.

C minor   G minor   B♭ minor   F minor

of elided changing notes (which affects in each case the 'under-fifth' of the minor chord) that obscure the 'simple and indeed logical core' of the passage, to form C minor – G minor – B♭ minor – F minor, which may be translated into functions as $°T – °D – °\overset{S}{\underset{}{}} – °S$, an altogether satisfying example of what Riemann would call an 'open-ended minor cadence'. He concluded that this is 'a progression against which there are fundamentally no objections to be raised, [a progression] that is enharmonically veiled to the eye by changing notes. These changing notes coincide with chromatic changes leading ahead, so that one has to admire the ability of the ear to find a path through this labyrinth without serious confusion.'[122]

However, this defeats the object entirely: Riemann's analysis, which seeks to bring out the underlying logic, demystifies the sublimity of the moment. The passage is deliberately labyrinthine; the ear is, contrary to Riemann's assertion, asked and forced to be confused. Furthermore, some features of his analysis beg a few questions: why, for instance, is the A♭ at the beginning of the passage ignored? It is not difficult to imagine various alternative interpretations, making use of similar tricks and devices, aimed to push the pointedly non-functional music into cadential models. For it is the essence of augmented triads, as Riemann knew well, not to be determinable in one definitive way. No harmonic guidance is given to the ear in this context, there is no way it can know that the first chord is supposed to be perceived as a C minor triad.

Looking ahead in the movement, it transpires that Riemann's interpretation is never explicated harmonically, whereas the opening material

---

[122] Riemann, *Geschichte der Musik seit Beethoven*, p. 421. 'Eine Folge, gegen die nichts einzuwenden ist, die aber freilich durch die enharmonisch mit den weiterführenden chromatischen Veränderungen zusammenfallenden Wechselnoten für das Auge derart verschleiert ist, daß man die Fähigkeit des Ohres bewundern muß, sich ohne ernstliche Verwirrung durch dieses Labyrinth zu finden.'

Example 4.4 Alternative, non-functional harmonisation of the same passage, as suggested by a later occurrence in the movement.

does return later in the movement with a harmonic accompaniment, as indicated in Example 4.4. Following Liszt's own harmonic suggestion – which of course cannot be seen as definitive for the monophonic opening – a harmonisation in major thirds, rising themselves in minor-third steps, would have been a viable, if non-functional, alternative.[123] In short, it is evident that Riemann went to some lengths to justify Liszt's bold musical structures as agreeable and inoffensive – that is to say, as possessing musical logic.

However, Riemann's theoretical system can also swing the other way, to unmask a composer who apparently threatens tonality. Riemann employed his theory of function in exactly this way, namely when he discussed the overture to *Benvenuto Cellini* by Hector Berlioz. Significantly, this is one of the very few occasions on which he employed taxonomy of harmonic function outside his harmony treatises and analytical studies of Bach and Beethoven. As a rule, Riemann preferred the *Klang* shorthand notation for such more general occasions, as for instance in the Liszt comment discussed above. It is therefore all the more conspicuous when he turns to function analysis. Indeed, it seems that he was trying to prove a point in this particular case. After his analysis, reproduced in Example 4.5, he commented, not without a hint of sarcasm:

The gravest danger concerning the intentions of the composer is the possibility that the listener might lose [track of] the special significance of the individual configurations [of leitmotives] and begin to follow purely musical connections. In Berlioz ... the obvious aim of avoiding a healthy, purely musical development of the sounded themes becomes unpleasantly palpable. Hence, then, [stems] a progressive negation – purely musically speaking – of the familiar and expected, a forever new forceful turning and interrupting, which led people of healthy musical instincts such as Mendelssohn and Wagner to the same judgement, in spite of their fundamental personal differences, namely that Berlioz is not actually musical.[124]

---

[123] Richard Taruskin explores these relations and their inherent octatonicism in 'Chernomor to Kashchei: Harmonic Sorcery; or Stravinsky's "Angle"', in *Journal of the American Musicological Society* 38 (1985), p. 108.

[124] Riemann, *Handbuch der Musikgeschichte*, vol. 2/3, p. 248. 'Die schlimmste Gefahr für die Absichten des Komponisten bildet aber die Möglichkeit, daß der Hörer die

Example 4.5 Riemann's analysis of Berlioz's *Benvenuto Cellini* (opening), from *Handbuch der Musikgeschichte*, vol. 2/3.

In brief, Berlioz had committed the cardinal sin of leaving the realm of musical logic, for the sake of extraneous, leitmotivic effects. In his search for novel harmonic connections he failed to establish the cadential patterns that Riemann had prescribed in his theory.

It is noticeable that Berlioz's phrase rhythm consists of quite regular four-bar units. However, this regularity is deceptive: within the phrase, the metre is very hard to follow due to liberally syncopated rhythms – Riemann surely took exception to this feature. The harmonic order is similarly askew: not a single phrase begins and ends in the same functional framework. While the first phrase outlines the tonality of G major with its *T* and *S*, it closes unexpectedly in the *Tp* – unexpected because the shape of the melody would suggest a conventional *D – T* ending

besondere Bedeutsamkeit der Einzelbildungen [in der Leitmotivik] aus dem Auge verliert und anfängt, rein musikalische Zusammenhänge zu verfolgen. Bei Berlioz . . . wird darum das sichtliche Bestreben, eine gesunde, rein musikalische Entwickelung der angeschlagenen Themen zu vermeiden, unangenehm fühlbar. Daher denn eine – rein musikalisch gesprochen – fortgesetzte Negation des Gewohnten und Erwarteten, ein immer neues gewaltsames Umbiegen und Abbrechen, das Leute von gesunden musikalischen Instinkten wie Mendelssohn und Wagner trotz ihrer persönlichen Grundverschiedenheit doch zu dem gleichen Urteil führte, daß Berlioz doch eigentlich nicht musikalisch sei . . .'

in the same key. This is the 'progressive negation of the familiar and expected' that Riemann lamented. The second phrase has even more function-harmonic horrors to offer: ostensibly beginning in D major, the phrase employs the *minor* dominant (A minor), which in Riemann's concept of tonality – in theory if not in practice – is considered illogical. (It goes without saying that in this case Riemann would show little theoretical lenience here: he did not hear A minor as a local dominant to D major at all, but rather opted for the label *Sp*, relating the chord to the overall key of G major.) Like the first phrase, the second phrase swerves to an unexpected end, here in B minor, which Riemann heard as $\mathcal{F}$. The last two phrases follow a similar pattern to the previous ones: a C major triad is sounded at bar 12, where an A minor harmony would have been expected (Riemann's label *S* is not as suitable as $\mathcal{F}p$ would have been in its local context, but in the functional disorder that he intended to show up this would have been of little difference to him), and the final phrase could have been a model cadence if it had not suddenly swerved away from the $D_4^6 - ..._3^5$ pattern to close on its own dominant. Riemann could only add multiple exclamation marks to give expression to his outrage.

Taken in themselves, the swerving four-bar phrases are perhaps not quite as illogical as Riemann would have us believe: on a slightly more removed level it appears that the first two phrases both move from the main function, *T* and *D* respectively, to their parallels. The third phrase does not follow this pattern, but provides in its last chord the C major harmony that had been missing from the full cadence, and may on this level indeed be seen to assume *S* function, as Riemann wrote. Together with the last phrase, which then modulates, the sixteen bars could, assuming this different perspective on the composition in question, be regarded as a full (if inverted) cadence that 'shows the tonic from all sides'. However, this was not an option for Riemann, in whose aesthetic the surface detail had to be in place – as in his initial comparison with the contemplation of Cologne Cathedral – before the larger proportions could be considered.[125] If the details were askew, the large-scale plan was automatically marred. For this reason, Riemann explained elsewhere, Liszt's strong 'immanent logic' leaves Berlioz far behind;[126] Berlioz's innovations had to be mediated by the sagacious Liszt, to soften the peril of the Frenchman's 'destructive, anti-formal tendencies'.[127] In this situation, Riemann concluded, French music does

---

[125] Riemann, *Systematische Modulationslehre* (Hamburg: J. F. Richter, 1887), pp. 1–8.

[126] Riemann, *Geschichte der Musik seit Beethoven*, p. 759. It goes without saying at this stage that Liszt, albeit Hungarian by birth, is also at home in Germany. Riemann spells this out on p. 406.

[127] Ibid., p. 548.

not pose a threat, since Berlioz could not seriously challenge Germany's vanguard position as the musical 'standard bearer'.[128]

Nevertheless, the danger of Berlioz's pernicious influence made itself felt shortly afterwards, in Riemann's *Handbuch der Musikgeschichte* (1913). According to Riemann's historical trajectory here, Berlioz was instrumental in the decline and fall of harmonic tonality. Thus Richard Strauss's later works from *Also sprach Zarathustra* onwards (but above all *Salome* and *Elektra*) were to be considered a 'failure', beginning at precisely the moment when 'he was converted to Berlioz's ideas'.[129] Similarly, when discussing Schoenberg's non-tonal hexachordal constructions, which Riemann was at pains to explain as harmonic functions (namely as $D_{5>}^{9<}$ – which can in principle be resolved into T),[130] he concluded: 'That Hector Berlioz has given the first initiative to the antiformalist tendencies of the post-Beethovenian age, seeking novelties *à tout prix*, is beyond dispute.'[131]

When examining Riemann's argument in somewhat greater detail, however, it transpires that his accusation is unfounded. Berlioz's fault, as Riemann remarked earlier, was the evasion of familiar cadential patterns; his conception of the threatening end of harmonic tonality is thus located on a syntactical – 'middle-ground' – level. In Riemann's interpretation Berlioz sought to destroy the fundamental unit of functional harmony, the cadence, by substituting 'false' functions. Schoenberg's narrative about the end of harmonic tonality, on the other hand, is conceived in the first place on the surface, as a foreground phenomenon: the way into atonality led via the emancipation of the dissonance. In other words, Schoenberg's concern was initially on the level of chord formation, as indeed his search of alternative structures such as hexachords or his notion of 'vagrant chords' demonstrates.[132] The loosening of the apron strings of the tonic is only a consequence of the multifarious

---

[128] Ibid., pp. 547–8.

[129] Riemann, *Handbuch der Musikgeschichte*, vol. 2/3, pp. 257 and 269.

[130] Ibid., pp. 254–5. Here Riemann seems to contradict himself: if Schoenberg's hexachords can still be analysed as harmonic functions, what exactly is Riemann's concern? It is likely, however, that this analysis, pointless in itself, is rather theoretical muscle-flexing: in *Harmonielehre*, Schoenberg mocks 'Riemann, who is proud that his theory succeeds in sharper and stricter formulation of the rules, and who has no inkling that, for this reason, he will very swiftly be left behind'. See Arnold Schoenberg, *Theory of Harmony*, trans. Roy E. Carter (London: Faber and Faber, 1978), p. 409. By subjecting Schoenberg's 'unfunctional' passage to functional analysis, Riemann proves that he is not old hat yet.

[131] Riemann, *Handbuch der Musikgeschichte*, vol. 2/3, p. 256. 'Daß Hector Berlioz den ersten Anstoß gegeben hat zu den antiformalistischen und Neues à tout prix aufsuchenden Strebungen der Zeit nach Beethoven, ist nicht wohl in Abrede zu stellen.'

[132] See Arnold Schoenberg, *Theory of Harmony*, pp. 411–22; also Robert Falck, 'Emancipation of the Dissonance', *Journal of the Arnold Schoenberg Institute* 6 (1982), pp. 106–11.

possibilities opened up by these new chords. In Schoenberg's own words: 'the proportion of elements pointing to the tonic became ever smaller, as against those pointing away from it; the "natural preponderance of the tonic" was henceforth out of the question'.[133] The connection that Riemann sought to establish between Berlioz and Schoenberg is not watertight. Schoenberg's and Riemann's conceptions of the end of harmonic tonality differ in their approach. They only converge in the final analysis, in the sense that in Schoenberg's music functional tonality is overcome.

In 1913, when Schoenberg had crossed the harmonic boundaries of tonality, Riemann held Berlioz responsible for the ultimate loss of the Garden of Eden. It is not without irony that with this connection Riemann's historical narrative fulfilled the Fichtean prophecy: the decline of German tonality was caused, according to Riemann, from without, by French influence. The instant German music was not true to itself, allowing an alien element to exert an influence, it ceased to be alive.

V

If a nation is an 'imagined community', to use Anderson's felicitous term, a sizeable group of people who feel they belong together despite the fact that its members have no personal connection, then they need a vehicle that triggers the imagination at the basis of the community. Language, supposedly at the basis of any national community, could be a powerful vehicle of national identity. In the particular case of Germany, music was perceived as a prime carrier of a national identity in the general consciousness. Riemann, in the nexus between his music theory and his historical views, may have helped this communal imagination on its way by firmly relating music to the national consciousness. The then recently established academic discipline of musicology could lend this enterprise the institutional power it required.

At the same time, it is a truism that the conceptual link between music and language was inextricably bound up with the rise of absolute music. In this position, the relation between music and language became so malleable that it was not difficult for music theorists like Riemann to appropriate the term.[134] As a technical category, the notion of music as language is just as ambiguous as was that of logic, as we saw in Chapter 3. In Riemann's aesthetics, however, the idea of a musical language had

---

[133] Arnold Schoenberg, 'Opinion or Insight', in *Style and Idea*, ed. Leonard Stein, trans. Leo Black (London: Faber and Faber, 1975), p. 260.

[134] On language in instrumental music see, for instance, Carl Dahlhaus, *The Idea of Absolute Music* trans. Roger Lustig (Chicago and London: University of Chicago Press, 1989), pp. 103–16, and Daniel K. L. Chua, *Absolute Music and the Construction of Meaning* (Cambridge: Cambridge University Press, 1999).

validity primarily as a metaphor, a concept that would have readily been understood by his contemporary readership. For Riemann, the explicit language element of vocal music was replaced by a language inherent in instrumental music. He regarded the break away from the predominance of vocal music, following Herder, as an act of liberation and – *pace* Wagner – as music's greatest achievement:

Herder brilliantly pinpointed the essence of absolute music a hundred years ago, at a time when the free instrumental style had only developed into an eloquent means of expression of individual sensation a few decades previously . . . Is it not strange that this emerging self-consciousness of music's own power, this complete emancipation of all support of the sister arts [dance, song, gesture] could be so fundamentally misunderstood, barely half a century later, that one attempted to read the end of absolute music into Beethoven and depicted her as extending her arms in supplication towards word and gesture?[135]

Only in instrumental music, for Riemann, does the true and pure character of music come to the fore. Music drama was in his estimation not the music of the future: rather, vocal music would mean a step back. (Riemann in fact once suggested that Wagner should write a symphony to prove that he was a master of form: Riemann contended that the overtures of *Tannhäuser* and *Meistersinger* showed that Wagner had potential in the field of instrumental music.[136]) The achievements of absolute, instrumental music, inextricably connected with Riemann's notion of classicism, must be preserved at all costs; Riemann's utopia of music envisaged an instrumental future.

For this reason, it was important for Riemann to view Stamitz's 'invention' of the symphony purely from the angle of instrumental music. He drew up a stylistic table of 'Mannheim mannerisms',[137] whose partly anthropomorphic labels (such as the 'Mannheim sigh') make it difficult – at

---

[135] See Riemann, *Die Elemente der musikalischen Aesthetik* (Berlin and Stuttgart: W. Spemann, 1900), pp. 204–5. 'So kennzeichnete treffend Herder (*Kalligone*, I., 169ff.) das Wesen der absoluten Musik vor hundert Jahren, also zu einer Zeit wo der reine Instrumentalstil sich erst seit einigen Jahrzehnten zum beredten Ausdrucksmittel individuellen Empfindens entwickelt hatte . . . Ist es nicht merkwürdig, daß man kaum ein halbes Jahrhundert später dieses erstmalige Bewußtwerden der eigenen Kraft der Musik, diese vollständige Emanzipation von aller Mithilfe der Schwesterkünste so verkennen konnte, daß man versuchte, mit Beethoven das Ende der absoluten Musik als gekommen hinzustellen und sie hilfeflehend ihre Arme nach Wort und Geste ausstrecken ließ?'

[136] Hugo Riemann, 'Hie Wagner! Hie Schumann!', in *Präludien und Studien* (reprint Nendeln/Liechtenstein: Kraus, 1976), vol. 3, p. 211. It is worth remembering, however, that in early life Riemann had a somewhat notorious reputation as a Wagnerian. See footnote 10 of the Introduction.

[137] Riemann, 'Der Stil und die Manieren der Mannheimer', in *Sinfonien der Pfalzbayerischen Schule*, vol. 2/1, pp. xv–xxv. Heuß, by contrast, traces the 'Mannheim sigh' back to cantatas of Buxtehude and Bach ('Zum Thema "Mannheimer Vorhalt"', p. 274).

least from our present perspective, shaped by Rosen and Ratner – not to search for links to operatic conventions. Yet Riemann completely omitted vocal models from consideration in his discussion of style. For him, an adherent of the philosophy of origins, it seems, the Mannheim symphony had to be derived from pure, instrumental origins. Language could not be added to the musical genre from outside, but rather inhered in its harmonic structures.

The idea of an inherent language in instrumental music was part and parcel of Riemann's 'myth of ethnic election': he contrived a link between the predominantly German preoccupation with instrumental music, particularly sonata-form compositions, and language.[138] Although he attached this 'myth of ethnic election' to the vocal form of fauxbourdon, it is obvious that he appreciated it for its essentially harmonic (that is to say instrumental) qualities – in that it made use of the third and thus paved the way to an independent harmonic language. Through the link between language and instrumental music, he opened a door for the aesthetic appropriation of music – in its double meaning as specific musical works, and as the abstract principle, the parameters underlying compositions – to fashion it into a vehicle of national identity. It may indeed appear as if music, following Riemann's aesthetic, was not merely 'second nature' to the Germans but also 'second language'.

Assigning the language trope and its accompanying aspect of cultural nationalism a position in Riemann's work is a tall order. On the one hand, we have seen how swiftly all the constitutive elements – scale and harmony, classicism and progress, universality and uniqueness, nature and nation – can all be arranged without any effort so as to change the supposed universality into the nationality principle. Nationalism would then be, latently perhaps, at the heart of Riemann's musical thought. This idea is particularly supported by his non-rational application of the function labels in the cases of Liszt and Berlioz: Liszt is lauded, even though in fact his symmetrical harmonisation in chains of thirds in his *Faust Symphony* is hardly analysable in terms of harmonic function. Strictly speaking, Liszt's harmony is more adventurous than Berlioz's, for while Riemann applied function labels that admittedly made little sense in Berlioz's case, even the mere application of such labels would have been impossible in Liszt's case. This kind of non-rational decision, the idiosyncratic interpretation of the rules, is, as we have seen,

---

[138] Although comparatively little space is given to the explanation of musical forms in Riemann's handbooks and harmonic tutors, chapter headings such as 'Modulation into the Second-Subject Area' (*Systematische Modulationslehre*, pp. 111–56) clearly have sonata-form principles in mind. By contrast, there is almost no mention made of vocal music.

indicative of nationalism at work. On the other hand, it is conspicuous that the overt nationalist claims in Riemann's writings are limited to one period in his life, the 1890s and 1900s, broadly corresponding to the increasing aggression and militarism of Wilhelmine culture at large. This circumstance would lead one to conclude, by contrast, that the nationalist element of Riemann's theories was not endemic, but merely a superficial layer, partaking of a rhetoric that was in vogue at the time. Perhaps because of their partly non-rational character, it was then comparatively easy to remove all references to nationalist ideas after these years.

Compare, for instance, the following passage, taken from the *Handbuch der Musikgeschichte* of 1913, with the *Geschichte der Musiktheorie* discussed above. Here, once again, Riemann went over some aspects of his primordial history of music, but he noticeably re-evaluated the significance of fauxbourdon:

In any case, the somewhat mechanical restrictions of strict fauxbourdon assign it a significantly lower aesthetic rank than the free flexibility of the actual organum, and the melodic losses are not necessarily compensated for by the harmonic gain. The eminent historical significance of fauxbourdon rather resides in the fact that it adds harmonic movement to the inner shaping of the melodic parts – even though for now this lacks artistic imagination. For even if these chains of triads are not heard harmonically – even with modern ears – but rather perceived for the most part as simultaneous passing harmonies, some of them stand out nonetheless with compelling harmonic power.[139]

This statement effectively amounts to an undoing of Riemann's earlier 'myth of ethnic election': fauxbourdon remains distinguished by representing the emergence of harmony itself, but its aesthetic and cultural implications are significantly lessened. (In fact, Riemann even seems to concede the possibility here – 'even with modern ears' – that hearing might be historically variable.) And finally, Riemann untied the knot that held everything together when he admitted in the same discussion that 'the assumption that from the very beginning organum in its original

---

[139] Riemann, *Handbuch der Musikgeschichte*, vol. 1/2, p. 164. 'Jedenfalls steht der mechanische Zwang des strengen Fauxbourdon zunächst ästhetisch erheblich tiefer als die freie Beweglichkeit des eigentlichen Organums, und die melodischen Verluste werden durch den harmonischen Gewinn nicht unbedingt aufgewogen. Die eminent historische Bedeutung des Fauxbourdon liegt aber darin, daß derselbe, wenn auch einstweilen ohne Zutun der künstlerischen Phantasie, Harmoniebewegung in den inneren Verlauf der Melodieglieder bringt. Denn wenn man auch keineswegs alle diese gehäuften Dreiklänge selbst mit modernen Ohren harmonisch hört, vielmehr einen großen Teil derselben als gleichzeitige Durchgänge versteht, so treten doch einzelne mit zwingender harmonischer Kraft heraus.'

home (England) was on the interval of the third, is perhaps too bold'.[140] The 'myth of ethnic election' can be jettisoned; by 1913 it seemed no longer necessary.

Riemann gives us no clue whether his volte-face on the origins of harmony was caused by changes in his musical or his political convictions: the political situation in the years before the First World War would certainly have encouraged a more extreme version of nationalism. The difficulty of locating the nationalistic elements of Riemann's theories, however, can be pinpointed if one looks for their deeper roots: nationalism arises as a problem because of the volatile nature of his harmonic dualism. It must be remembered that Riemann's 'myth of ethnic election' could not have functioned without his dualistic outlook on harmony in the first place: the defining features not only of Germanness in music, but of the entire notion of musical progress from the very inception of harmony in fauxbourdon onwards, were based on the discovery of the potential inherent in the interval of the major third, the dualistic interval par excellence. Ultimately, it was the certainty of absolute theoretical knowledge about harmony, which the dualistic view could offer Riemann but which we have identified as fictitious, that allowed him in the first place to erect these bold nationalistic constructs.

Just as Riemann's musical thought took a 'psychological turn' in his later years, which relocated harmonic dualism in the cognitive realm, so did his views of national identity and music. During the years of the First World War, Riemann became an outspoken supporter of international collaboration, and in particular drew attention to the importance of the International Musicological Society.[141] Nevertheless, he introduced the second edition of his Beethoven analyses of 1918 on a patriotic note:

> The fact that our soldiers in their grey uniforms analyse Beethoven in their shelters in the field is a considerable contribution to the psychology of the Germans. May the second edition be in the sign of world peace![142]

While the statement begs some questions that are likely to remain unanswered, this simultaneous display of national specificity and internationalist pacifism harboured no contradiction – Beethoven's name seems to be invoked here in the spirit of humanism beyond national differences. This comment is perhaps best understood as a reflection of the

---

[140] Ibid., p. 161. 'der Gedanke, für das Organum in seiner Urheimat (England) von Anfang an die Terz anzunehmen, [ist] vielleicht allzu kühn'.

[141] See, for instance, Riemann's *Handbuch der Musikgeschichte*, 2nd edn (Leipzig: Breitkopf und Härtel, 1919), vol. 1/1, p. xi.

[142] Riemann, *Ludwig van Beethovens Sämtliche Klavier-Solosonaten*, vol. 1, no page number. 'Daß unsere Feldgrauen in den Unterständen Beethovens Klaviersonaten analysieren, ist ein nicht zu verachtender Beitrag zur Psychologie der Deutschen. Möge die zweite Auflage im Zeichen des Weltfriedens stehen!'

internalisation of his musical thought under the notion of *Tonvorstel-lungen*. Wilhelm Wundt's *Völkerpsychologie* seems to speak out of such sentiments; the national character of the Germans here remains a spiritual phenomenon beyond the temporary political situation. The link between musical language and national identity is still operative but now constitutes a psychological factor, not one of national chauvinism. In the realm of mental representations musical structures could finally remain a language without words.

5

Beethoven's deafness, exotic harmonies and tone imaginations

Among Riemann's analyses of Beethoven's piano sonatas, one has come under particular criticism, and often serves as an example of the musicologist's insensitivity to music: the Sonata 'quasi una fantasia' in E♭ major, Op. 27, no. 1.[1] In this analysis, Riemann decided to rebar the first movement, almost in its entirety. On the face of it, there is of course something very blunt about this single-handed intrusion into the score. In fact, however, his decision to change the score is nothing but an expression of his 'psychological turn', and the changes that this initiated in Riemann's later musical thought.

Riemann's meddling with the score may have roused the critics, since most analysts have traditionally taken the score as the starting point for their analytical observations, on the assumption that it forms the most manifest link to the composer's thought. Witness, for instance, Heinrich Schenker's deep involvement with manuscripts, which is also expressed in his meticulous editions (which are in stark contrast to Riemann's own *Phrasierungsausgaben*, his edition with phrasing annotations, where editorial fidelity became subservient to pedagogical concerns). In *Five Graphic Analyses*, for instance, Schenker noted that in the autograph of Bach's C major prelude from the *Well-Tempered Clavier*, the stems of the bass line in one bar point up rather than down. He interpreted that as justification – derived from no less a figure than Bach himself – for his decision to omit this bar from his analysis. It is not at all surprising that Schenker would claim for himself 'the honour of being the true founder of manuscript studies'.[2]

---

[1] See for instance, Helga de la Motte-Haber and Carl Dahlhaus, *Systematische Musikwissenschaft* (Wiesbaden: Akademische Verlagsgesellschaft Athenaion, 1982), p. 68; Harald Krebs, *Fantasy Pieces: Metric Dissonance in the Music of Robert Schumann* (New York: Oxford University Press, 1999), p. 10, and Hartmut Krones, 'Hugo Riemanns Überlegungen zu Phrasierung und Artikulation', in Tatjana Böhme-Mehner and Klaus Mehner, eds., *Hugo Riemann (1849–1919): Musikwissenschaftler mit Universalanspruch* (Cologne, Weimar, Vienna: Böhlau, 2001), p. 106.

[2] Heinrich Schenker, *Der freie Satz*, 2nd edn (Vienna: Universal Edition, 1956), p. 33. I am grateful to Suzannah Clark for pointing this quotation out to me.

Example 5.1a Riemann's analysis of Beethoven's Sonata in Eb major, Op. 27, no. 1, from *L. van Beethovens sämtliche Klavier-Solosonaten*, vol. 2. The whole first movement is rebarred to comply with Riemann's principle of *Auftaktigkeit*.

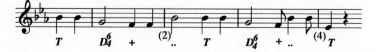

For Riemann, by contrast, such authorial intention as could be derived from the score was rather irrelevant. As we have seen before, the everlasting logic that forms the core of Riemann's musical thought does not necessarily reside with the composer, nor can it necessarily be found in the score. The score was for him a mere vehicle by which the composer conveyed his thoughts to the listener. As such, he assumed that notation could well be defective or wanting. When viewed from this angle, it seems, Riemann is less irreverent and brash than he may at first appear. Somewhat paradoxically, he tampered with the notation in order to *preserve* the integrity of the music.

Riemann's opening gambit in this analysis is quite remarkable, and it is worth considering the tactical rhetoric that he employed when he introduced the rebarred version: to begin with, he pronounced the first subject to be banal, calling it a 'triviality', caused by the 'dire uniformity' of the motives. Yet he was careful not to blame Beethoven for this trifling subject. Instead, he put forth the Beethoven critic Lenz as a scapegoat. Lenz, who characterised the sonata as a 'comparatively weak work, which belongs in the first period',[3] was scolded by Riemann for having misunderstood the structure of the theme. Clearly, the banality of the theme was not an intrinsic flaw of Beethoven's conception but of the inadequate notation of it and of Lenz's misguided reading. To cleanse the theme of this stigma and to prevent further misunderstanding, Riemann felt justified in proposing his changes.

Riemann amended the barlines, shifting the downbeat by one minim in the manner shown in Example 5.1a, on the basis of his principle of *Auftaktigkeit*, the compulsory upbeat: the downbeat beginning in Beethoven's version is not acceptable, as the harmonic structure goes against the metric stress. As we saw in Chapter 3 above, Riemann's archetypal harmonic–metric model was *T | S D | T*, not *T S | D T*. In other words, the stress falls on the second and fourth functions of the model, not on the first and third. The point of reference for Riemann in this case was the last harmony of the initial four-bar phrase. He complained that cadential effects should not fall on the middle of the bar,

---

[3] Hugo Riemann, *Ludwig van Beethovens sämtliche Klavier-Solosonaten*, 2nd edn (Berlin: Max Hesse, 1920), vol. 2, p. 201.

Example 5.1b The bass line of the opening of the same sonata. Riemann suggests that the same E♭ that ends the phrase should also be imagined as the bass note of the opening chord.

$$T \qquad D_4^6 \qquad \pm \qquad (2) \qquad T$$

but on the accented beginning of it. *Auftaktigkeit* is thus restored. Anything else, he claimed, would be 'bad spelling'. In the rebarred version, the motives, which had previously been bland and banal, are now transformed into something varied and sophisticated – or so Riemann would have it.

The point of *Auftaktigkeit*, however, is not scored easily: Riemann explained that the G of the first full bar is supported by a D_4^6 which is resolved into a $\frac{5}{3}$ in the following beat. To be sure, this model follows the standard rules of a suspension, with the suspension sounded on the strong beat and the resolution on the following weak beat, but where is the preparation? The D_4^6, if we accept this function for the second beat of the sonata, surely also opens the piece. If anything, the dominant effect is even stronger there, as the tonic note E♭ is conspicuously absent from the opening harmony. Yet Riemann insisted that the piece in fact opened with the tonic. To hammer home his point, he had to infer the 'true' meaning of the opening harmony from a later occurrence. As the opening repeats itself after two bars, we find an E♭ in the bass. The same E♭, Riemann explained, should be imagined in the bass of the opening chord. If that is so, it will of course have to be heard as the tonic. The cadence then starts and ends with a tonic statement, just as Riemann postulated in his rules concerning cadences; with the repeat of the entire opening phrase, we have a metrically and harmonically perfect eight-bar period.

Using these strategies, Riemann managed to kill two birds with one stone: he refuted the reproach of triviality that he originally attributed to the theme himself (even if he used Lenz as yet another ventriloquist's dummy for this purpose) by showing how varied the musical structure really is below the faulty notation, and reappraised the apparently banal theme by means of his analysis.[4] And in rebarring Beethoven's sonata, Riemann sought to restore and bring out the flawless musical logic that

---

[4] To be fair, in the current analytical climate it seems that a more palatable solution would have acknowledged the metric ambiguity of Beethoven's sonata, whose alternate stress in the middle of the (original) bars is reminiscent of the Gavotte. For a thoughtful critique of Riemann's rebarring see William Rothstein, 'Beethoven With and Without *Kunstgepräng*': Metric Ambiguity Reconsidered', in *Beethoven Forum* 4 (Lincoln, Nebr.: University of Nebraska Press, 1995), pp. 165–93.

inheres in the work but was obfuscated in the faulty notation. To be sure, his rebarring is not meant as a dig at the authority of the composer; it does not threaten the status of Beethoven, but rather adds a human touch: even a genius can make mistakes in the notation of his thoughts.

I

Riemann appears to have laid out the conceptual framework for his guiding assumptions in his intrusion to Beethoven's scores in a study of 1909, on the spontaneous activity of the composer's imagination and the intellectual work involved in the compositional process. This is all the more remarkable because previously he had dismissed any kind of engagement in the compositional process – notably sketch studies – as 'scavengers' work' that was 'hardly rewarding'.[5] To be sure, he was still doubtful about the knowledge of the composer's imagination that can be gained from sketches: for him, these represent simply fragmentary aides-memoires for the composer, and researchers cannot hope to capture the full sonic impression – the 'fully voiced, multiply shaded, complex whole'[6] – that the composer holds in his imagination right from the beginning. Riemann insisted that what the artist does while composing has very little to do with abstract intellectual work but is rather a silent experiencing of tones, a mental representation of sounds:

We now realise that the composer does not invent notes but tones, and that this invention is a physical internal hearing. It is not exaggerated to assume that this internal hearing has all the traits of real hearing, that for instance the fortissimo of a large orchestra is recaptured by the imagination, and that, likewise, the sweetness of expressive shading and the titillating effects of unusual timbres are part of the internal image too ... It is important to realise, in its full implications, what it means when Beethoven says that he imagines a whole work of music, e.g. a symphonic movement, in all its parts as a completely finished whole, which then merely needs to be written down, which is 'quickly achieved'.[7]

---

[5] Riemann, *Wie hören wir Musik?: Grundlinien der Musikästhetik*, 6th edn (Berlin: Max Hesse, 1923), p. 17. See Michael Arntz, *Hugo Riemann (1849–1919): Leben, Werk und Wirkung* (Cologne: Concerto-Verlag, 1998), p. 149.

[6] Hugo Riemann, 'Spontane Phantasietätigkeit und verstandesmäßige Arbeit in der tonkünstlerischen Produktion', *Jahrbuch der Musikbibliothek Peters* 16 (1909), pp. 37–8.

[7] Ibid., pp. 40–1. 'Wir wissen nun, daß der Komponist nicht Noten, sondern Töne erfindet und daß dieses Erfinden ein leibhaftes inneres Hören ist. Man geht nicht zu weit, wenn man annimmt, daß dieses innere Hören alle Merkmale des wirklichen Hörens hat, daß z. B. auch das Fortissimo eines starken Orchesters mit voller Illusion vorgestellt wird und daß ebenso aller Schmelz ausdrucksvoller Tongebungen und die Reize der Sonder-klangfarben dabei zur Geltung kommen ... Es ist wichtig, sich einmal vollständig klar zu machen, was es heißt, wenn ein Beethoven sagt, daß er [sich] ein ganzes Tonstück, z. B. einen Symphoniesatz, in allen seinen Teilen vollständig fertig als Ganzes vorstellen

If this is so, notation is not only unreliable as a source of authority but also shifts the entire compositional act to what Riemann called here the composer's imagination. The musical idea is worked out in the composer's sonic imagination – not on paper – sometimes over many years, until it is finally fixed in the score. Meanwhile, musical notation, and indeed performance, are only the imperfect and contingent vehicles by which these musical ideas are conveyed to the wider public.

The figure of Beethoven is of particular importance here because the 'internal hearing' which becomes the central category was, famously, his only means of hearing at all. Unlike Thayer, whose Beethoven biography he edited, Riemann felt very strongly that the complexity of Beethoven's late work was not a weakness but rather an admirable consequence of Beethoven's deafness, since it helped him focus on his internal hearing. Indeed, Riemann even suggested that the actual sonic representation of music – or 'receptive hearing' – may be a hindrance to the imagination of tones.[8] This conclusion marks an important paradigm shift in Riemann's thought, where music is now fully internalised and sonic, acoustical events are relegated to the status of a mere by-product of the tone imaginations.

In fact, Riemann spent the final years of his life working out a fully fledged theory of the tone imaginations, which he considered the 'Alpha and Omega of musical artistry'.[9] This term, tone imaginations, is chosen advisedly, since in this conception, 'music' signified for Riemann not merely the sounding phenomenon, but rather the whole process of transplanting the musical thought of the composer into the musical mind of the listener. Sounding music was merely the intermediary stage – the beginning and end of the process were tone imaginations. Jacques Handschin captured the idea of the tone imagination as the noumenon

---

kann, so daß es nur mehr der Niederschrift bedarf, die dann "schnell vonstatten geht".'
It is noteworthy that recent musicological scholarship has been sceptical of the imaginative powers accorded to Beethoven, since the most important document on which this idea rests – namely Schlösser's retrospective account (repeated in Thayer's biography), to which Riemann's article makes reference – has been identified as an unreliable testimony. See Maynard Solomon, 'Beethoven's Creative Process: A Two-Part Invention', in *Beethoven Essays* (Cambridge, Mass.: Harvard University Press, 1988), pp. 126–38.

[8] Riemann, 'Spontane Phantasietätigkeit', p. 46.

[9] Riemann, 'Ideen zu einer "Lehre von den Tonvorstellungen"', *Jahrbuch der Musikbibliothek Peters* 21/22 (1914/15), p. 2. On the difficulty of translating the German *Vorstellung* – vacillating between representation, presentation, imagination and mental image – see Robert W. Wason and Elizabeth West Marvin, 'Riemann's "Ideen zu einer 'Lehre von den Tonvorstellungen'"': An Annotated Translation', *Journal of Music Theory* 36 (1992), p. 72–4; Brian Hyer, 'Reimag(in)ing Riemann', *Journal of Music Theory* 39 (1995), pp. 101–6, and Klaus Mehner, 'Hugo Riemanns "Ideen zu einer 'Lehre von den Tonvorstellungen'"', in Böhme-Mehner and Mehner, eds., *Hugo Riemann*, pp. 49–57.

behind the sounding phenomenon, when he considered Riemann's late work as 'real Kantianism'.[10] The sounding world was fully separated from the psychological processes.

The notion of tone imaginations relies on two basic principles in tandem: on the one hand, the 'economy of imagination', which Riemann found prefigured in Lotze's aesthetics and which seems to feed into the emerging *Gestalt* psychology, and on the other, his old – originally Helmholtzian – idea of *Klang* representation. Both these ideas refer back to the grid of harmonic relations, as shown above in Example 2.4. The tonal image shifts along the axes of the grid of harmonic relations, which explains both the structure of major and minor triads and the relations between triads in succession, just as in Riemann's early conceptions of the dualistic tonal space and *Klang* representation. At the same time, the way the imagination moves across the grid is guided by the principle of the greatest possible economy, ensuring that the simplest route from one *Klang* to the next is chosen. This means that the laws of good intonation may be overruled in favour of greater listening economy. It is on the implicit basis of this principle of economy, as we saw in Chapter 4, that Riemann argued – *pace* Hauptmann – that 'our musical practice does not know two kinds of D' in C major.[11]

In principle Riemann's argument is simple: as a mental construct, music can be imagined as an ideal structure, without the interference of Pythagorean or syntonic commas, just as Beethoven's tone imaginations were apparently in perfect accordance with Riemann's ideal structures, but became somewhat muddled in the score. And in a sense, his earlier statements on mental structures suggest that Riemann was quite happy to leave the precise mechanisms unclear. Thus he had written in 1905, before he completed his theory of tone imaginations:

The precise nature of the ultimate transformations from sound waves to affective stimuli in the central organ will probably be forever beyond scientific proof. At any rate, we are nowadays still far from making any certain assertions on that matter.[12]

As seen before, the virgin territory of music psychology with its emphasis on mental structures was seen by Riemann as an expedient ground to renegotiate his musical ideas. That is not to say, however, that he merely

---

[10] Jacques Handschin, *Der Toncharakter*, intro. Rudolf Stephan (reprint Darmstadt: Wissenschaftliche Buchgesellschaft, 1995), p. 126.

[11] Riemann, 'Ideen zu einer "Lehre von den Tonvorstellungen"', p. 18.

[12] Riemann, 'Das Problem des harmonischen Dualismus', *Neue Zeitschrift für Musik* 51 (1905), p. 25. 'Welcher Art die letzten Umsetzungsformen der Tonschwingungen in Affektionen des Zentralorgans sein mögen, wird sich wohl ewig dem wissenschaftlichen Nachweise entziehen; zum mindesten kann heute von irgend welcher bestimmten Angabe darüber noch gar nicht die Rede sein.'

Example 5.2 Riemann's analysis of Beethoven's Sonata in F major, Op. 10, no. 2. In this extraordinarily complex harmonic and metric analysis, Riemann uses a new function sign, 3^+, to indicate a major-third relation.

transferred his old views to a new territory. In fact, he took some consequences of his new theory that forced him to rethink his old entrenched positions.

The main conceptual changes concerned the understanding of the apparent consonance. Crucially, he introduced new function symbols for major-third relations, $^{\circ}III$ and 3^+, because he felt that the musical reality of Beethoven's sonatas made these additional categories necessary.[13] The first use of this new function sign is found in the analysis of Beethoven's Op. 10, no. 2, as shown in Example 5.2. Riemann explained that the direct major-third relation, expressed in the succession of $e^+ - g^+ - c^+$ that concludes the example, could not adequately be represented with the function labels *(D) [Tp] – D – T* and necessitated the introduction of a new symbol. In admitting these major-third relations, it seems, Riemann had at last stopped 'backpedaling', as our critic had remarked in Chapter 2, though at the expense of theoretical coherence. Thus it is extremely unlikely that he would allow the three modifications that characterise apparent consonances to take place on this new 'harmonic pillar', since these additional complications would cast his system of harmonic function into utter chaos.

His death in 1919 prevented him from further pursuing these ideas – and from closing the incoherences that some of the theoretical innovations brought along. In many ways, the systematic aspect of his musical thought ended in tatters. Yet it is clear that the conception of tone imaginations carried with it a fundamental reshuffling of harmonic relations. It would seem that the relinquishment of the acoustical framework, which he announced as early as 1905, had finally resulted in a reconception of the parameters of his musical thought. What is more, it would seem that Riemann had finally given up the doctrine of harmonic dualism, because he no longer needed it in the realm of tone imaginations. Was that really the case?

---

[13] See *Handbuch der Harmonielehre*, 6th edn (Leipzig: Breitkopf und Härtel, 1917), p. xvii.

II

Beyond this somewhat tentative, though potentially portentous reshuffling of his system of harmonic function, Riemann was evidently prepared to reconsider the foundations of his musical thought in light of his theory of tone imaginations. In 1905 he had still insisted on the transcendent nature of triadic hearing, postulating that 'to hear music as essentially triadic is the be-all and end-all of music. Even simple monody is heard as incomplete harmonies (tonal complexes) by today's listener, and probably by listeners of all times.'[14] It seems that by 1916 these certainties had disappeared, alongside his formerly Eurocentric views:

An introduction to the music of earlier periods or of foreign nations also requires a new approach. If a composition of the thirteenth or sixteenth century sounds strange to us, then this is because many features in it contradict what we are accustomed to... In trying to understand the idiosyncrasies of Hungarian, Nordic, Russian music etc. we make a similar experience: the peculiarity and strangeness recede as soon as one comprehends the internal logic of the music and familiarises oneself with the mentality prevalent in that nation or epoch.[15]

Riemann's rhetoric here is interesting: he grouped temporal and geographic distance together and seemed to equivocate between them, but in doing so it is clear that he was doing no less than to open the possibility for a relativised view of the significance of Western tonal music. In other words, if there are no absolutes – in the sound wave or anywhere else in the physical world – musical logic can be subject to historical or ethnic contingencies: the door would be opened to cultural differences.

From this angle, Riemann went on to expand his publication in non-Western music. In a study of 1916, entitled *Folkloristische Tonalitätsstudien* (*Studies in Folklore Tonalities*), he explored the possibility of conceiving of musical systems other than Western tonality. It is noteworthy that this study marked the inauguration of a series of academic publications from Riemann's Leipzig Institute for musicology. With this

---

[14] Riemann, 'Das Problem des harmonischen Dualismus', p. 26. '[E]in Hören im Sinne von Dreiklängen [ist] das A und O aller Musik. Auch die absolut einstimmige Melodie hört zweifellos der Hörer von heute, wahrscheinlich aber der Hörer aller Zeiten im Sinne von Harmonien (Tonkomplexen).'

[15] Riemann, 'Neue Beiträge zu einer Lehre von den Tonvorstellungen', *Jahrbuch der Musikbibliothek Peters* 23 (1916), pp. 2–3. 'Neue Gesichtspunkte erfordert auch die Einführung in die Musik älterer Epochen oder fremder Nationen. Mutet uns eine Komposition des 13. oder 16. Jahrhunderts fremdartig an, so kommt das daher, daß in derselben sich vieles unsern Gewöhnungen Widersprechende vorfindet... Das Begreifen der Idiotismen des Ungarischen, Nordischen, Russischen usw. – Überall aber macht man wieder die gleiche Erfahrung, daß das Besondere, Befremdliche schwindet, sobald man seine immanente Logik begriffen und sich in den Vorstellungskreis eingelebt hat, welcher die Nation oder die Epoche beherrscht.'

Example 5.3 Riemann's conception of the pentatonic scale, as explored in *Folkloristische Tonalitätsstudien*. A chain of fifths is rearranged symmetrically around a central tone; the upper and lower major thirds are missing.

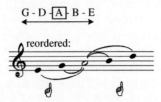

publication – which is surely of some symbolic value – Riemann, who never obtained a tenured professorship, can be said to have finally consolidated his institutional position within musicology by the means available to him.[16] It is wholly appropriate that he should branch out broadly into this new territory.[17]

Folkloristische Tonalitätsstudien is distinguished by being the only study in which Riemann erects a model of music not from a harmonic basis, but on the basis of scales. In fact, he developed a model of music based on the anhemitonic pentatonic scale, which he considered common to Ancient Greek and Japanese, and moreover Scottish and Irish music.[18] The way he introduced these scales was as a series of fifths, expanding symmetrically in both directions, which would then be reordered within the compass of one octave, to form characteristic pentatonic scales, as shown in Example 5.3. The central tone, Riemann suggests, plays the role of the tonic, and it is surrounded by seconds and fourths in each direction. He contended, in a wonderful double negative, that this may sometimes cause problems when examining musical works, but 'eventually turns out not to be quite erroneous'.[19]

[16] Michael Arntz describes the circumstances surrounding this period in Riemann's life in *Hugo Riemann*, pp. 101–10.

[17] Riemann had published some preliminary articles on the topic of non-Western music before. See particularly, the short essay 'Exotische Musik', *Max Hesses deutscher Musikerkalender* 1906, pp. 135–7, and 'Ueber Japanische Musik', *Musikalisches Wochenblatt* 33 (1902), pp. 209–10, 229–31, 245–6, 257–9, 273–4, 289–90.

[18] Riemann, *Folkloristische Tonalitätsstudien* (Leipzig: Breitkopf und Härtel, 1916), p. 1. For modern views of Riemann's ethnomusicological approach, see Peter Revers, 'Zur Theorie und Ästhetik der Harmonisierung exotischer Melodien im frühen 20. Jahrhundert', *Musiktheorie* 7 (1992), pp. 3–24; Dieter Christensen, 'Hugo Riemann and the Shaping of Musicology: An Ethnomusicological Perspective', in Christoph-Hellmut Mahling and Ruth Seibers, eds., *Festschrift Walter Wiora zum 90. Geburtstag* (Tutzing: H. Schneider, 1997), pp. 34–43, and Klaus Wolfgang Niemöller, 'Hugo Riemann und die "exotische Musik": Zum Konflikt von musikalischem Eurozentrismus und Weltmusik', in Klaus Wolfgang Niemöller, Uwe Pätzold and Chung Kyo-Chul, eds., *Lux Oriente: Begegnungen der Kulturen in der Musikforschung* (Kassel: Gustav Bosse, 1995), pp. 467–75.

[19] Riemann, *Folkloristische Tonalitätsstudien*, p. 3.

One consequence of this theoretical approach is particularly noteworthy: as the hands in Example 5.3 indicate, the major thirds – counting up or down from the central pitch, the melodic 'tonic' – are absent from this scale. Riemann commented:

One should consider that the missing tones are just those whose chromatic alteration leads into the next fifth-related positioning of the scale. Also of note is the fact that both tones, below and above, function as leading tones to the major third of the scale [i.e. the interval around the central tone].[20]

The way these observations are channelled – particularly that the non-existence of major thirds is considered as a lack – shows quite clearly that Riemann still considered the anhemitonic scale in relation to the 'fully developed' diatonic scale, as an incomplete and hence inferior version of the basis of Western music. As Riemann saw it, pentatonic music had no way of modulating, in the way that diatonic music did.

Of course this casts the whole approach in a very different light: Riemann's decision to approach non-Western music as melodically based was not founded on an admission of cultural relativism, but it is in fact perfectly in line with his old assumption concerning the role of the major third as the 'wheel of progress'. Where this wheel was missing, triads and hence harmony itself was quite simply not possible; non-Western music had to remain one-dimensional. The above plea for empathy with the music of past eras and different cultures would then be merely an instruction to suspend one's knowledge of the advances of modern music and to adopt a more primitive listening strategy.

Riemann's covert assumptions are finally made explicit at the end of his theoretical introduction, which should be quoted at length, when he returns to familiar ground and brings up the topic of harmonic dualism:

After K. Fortlage (1847) had already pointed out the role of the lower whole-tone (instead of the lower semitone) in the melodic construction of Scandinavian music, Arthur von Oettingen finally uncovered the essence of pure minor harmony. To be sure, the seven-degree minor scale as well as the seven-degree major scale both developed by the insertion of two filling-tones [where scale degrees were 'missing']. At the same time, it cannot be denied that modern music has privileged the major somewhat, and furthermore, that modern music has imposed alien major-mode elements onto the minor mode – so much so that minor melody and harmony have almost receded from consciousness. It was only with the emergence of a national Nordic music (Hartmann, Gade, Grieg), that attention was drawn to the characteristic effects that pertain to the minor mode. The minor dominant, in particular, had disappeared from musicians'

---

[20] Ibid., p. 5. 'Man beachte wohl, daß diese beiden fehlenden Töne gerade diejenigen sind, deren chromatische Veränderung in die nächst quintverwandte Lage der Skala führt. Auch ist zu beachten, daß beide Töne oben und unten als Leittöne an die große Terz der Skala ansetzen.'

view, so that Moritz Hauptmann did not hesitate to declare the major dominant as indispensable to the minor mode, even to derive the minor tonic from it.[21]

In this sense, Riemann's harmonic dualism was 'delivered of its acoustical shackles', as he had proclaimed triumphantly in 1905, but it was clearly still one of his principal preoccupations.[22] It is in this light that his special interest in Scottish and Irish folk songs in *Folkloristische Tonalitätsstudien* must be seen. Oettingen had used some of Beethoven's folk-song settings as the basis of his own reharmonisations in the pure minor mode. Riemann too used this repertoire for some of his own versions. (And one cannot help but feel that this was done in the spirit of one-upmanship: Riemann, the musician, would show Oettingen, the physicist, how such minor-mode harmonisations are done properly – especially when Beethoven's authority looms over the entire project.[23])

One of these examples, the Scottish song 'Enchantress farewell', is particularly striking: Beethoven set the song in A major, while Riemann chose the relative F# minor. Example 5.4 reproduces the cadential points in Beethoven's and Riemann's versions. Riemann's harmonisation shows that is possible to set the whole song as a series of plagal cadences. In fact, this late example presents perhaps the most rigorous application of the consequences of harmonic dualism, and is more faithful to the consequences of the dualistic premise than most other examples in Riemann's analytical observations.

Compare this with a previous practical attempt on Riemann's side to grapple with non-Western music. In 1902 – that is to say, a significant time before he formulated his late theory of the tone imaginations, at roughly the same time as he made his infamous remark about the

---

[21] Ibid., p. 13. 'Nachdem bereits K. Fortlage (1847) auf die Rolle des Unterganztones (statt des Unterhalbtones) in der Melodik der Skandinavier hingewiesen, hat besonders A. von Öttingen das Wesen der reinen Mollharmonik aufgedeckt. Wenn auch die 7stufige Mollskala ebenso wie die 7stufige Durskala aus der Pentatonik durch Einfügung der beiden Fülltöne (Pien) sich entwickelt hat, so ist doch nicht in Abrede zu stellen, daß die neuere Musik die Durskala etwas bevorzugt, daß sie auch Moll mit eigentlich demselben fremden, nach Dur gehörigen Elementen so stark versetzt hat, daß die Mollmelodik und -harmonik fast aus dem Bewußtsein gekommen war und erst die Vordrängung einer nationalen nordischen Musik (Hartmann, Gade, Grieg) wieder auf die eigentümlichen Wirkungen aufmerksam machte, welche dem Moll eignen. Ganz speziell die °D warden Musikern so aus dem Gesichtskreis entschwunden, daß Moritz Hauptmann nicht davor zurückschreckte, die D+ der Molltonart für schlechterdings unentbehrlich zu erklären, ja sogar die Molltonika von ihr abzuleiten.' Riemann's reference is to Carl Fortlage, *Das musikalische System der Griechen in seiner Urgestalt: aus den Tonleitern des Alypius zum ersten Male entwickelt* (Leipzig 1847; reprint Amsterdam: Schippers, 1964).

[22] Riemann, 'Das Problem des harmonischen Dualismus', p. 70.

[23] Oettingen's examples can be found in *Harmoniesystem in dualer Entwickelung* (Dorpat and Leipzig: W. Glässer, 1866), pp. 101–11 and 261, and in *Das duale Harmoniesystem* (Leipzig: C. F. W. Siegel, 1913), pp. 130–7.

Example 5.4a From Beethoven's folk-song setting, 'Enchantress farewell'.

Example 5.4b Riemann's reharmonisation of this song in minor cadences, from *Folkloristische Tonalitätsstudien*.

unreliable quality of non-Western musical performance quoted above in Chapter 4 – he had published a collection of non-Western music, entitled 'Six Original Chinese and Japanese Songs'.[24] His arrangement of these melodies, for piano and violin, supplies all the melodies with a simple chordal, albeit exoticised harmony, and betrays a lot about his notion of what the 'original' nature of these songs entailed.

Among these six 'original' songs, one melody – entitled 'Funeral March (Death Lament)' and reproduced here in Example 5.5a – is particularly distinguished, in that it is harmonised predominantly in terms of subdominant and minor tonic (only bars 16–18 introduce a minor dominant function). Riemann had taken this song from a collection of Chinese songs published in 1884, in which it had already been transcribed into Western notation by the editor.[25] In fact, the editor, J. A. van Aalst, had advised his reader that this piece of music was 'exceedingly original and really worthy of a better interpretation than that afforded by the shrieking clarionet'.[26] In this sense, Riemann had only followed his advice when he set the melody for violin and piano.

[24] Hugo Riemann, ed., *Sechs originale chinesische und japanische Melodien* (Leipzig: Breitkopf und Härtel, 1902).

[25] See Peter Revers, 'Zur Theorie und Ästhetik der Harmonisierung exotischer Melodien', p. 6. Revers rightly points out that of the six arrangements, this one complies best with pentatonicism in Riemann's sense.

[26] J. A. van Aalst, *Chinese Music* (Shanghai: Statistical Department of the Inspectorate General of Customs, 1884), p. 45.

Example 5.5a A Chinese 'Funeral March' in Riemann's harmonised setting for violin and piano, from *Sechs originale chinesische und japanische Melodien*.

Example 5.5b The same melody as transcribed in Riemann's source, J. A. von Aalst's *Chinese Music*, which is slightly different from Riemann's arrangement.

A few things are noticeable in Riemann's harmonisation. The tonal centre of the piece is clearly on A, as Riemann's two-bar introduction makes amply clear: the melodically central pitch A is here surrounded symmetrically by minor tonic (°e) and minor subdominant (°a). At the same time, Riemann appears to cling to this tonal centre for longer than necessary. The melodic structure suggests a shift (to a tonal centre around G) as early as bar 11. However, a new harmony – a minor dominant – is only introduced to mark this shift as late as bar 17. The previous occurrences of G are all considered as passing dissonances. It seems that the harmonisation adds to the 'primitive' nature of the music – while at the same time keeping it somewhat 'pure'.

Furthermore, Riemann made some changes: for one thing, he added some metrical complications (at bars 11 and 16), which are absent from the rather four-square original, partly perhaps to add an exotic flavour, partly to make the metric structure (which in the original transcription consists of forty-three bars of one minim's length) fit in better with his axiom of universal eight-bar periods. At the same time, as shown in Example 5.5b, he changed the first note after the double barline from van Aalst's version: while it is possible that this was merely a transcription error on Riemann's part, it is nonetheless noticeable that if Riemann had kept the original D, a major harmony would have been necessary in the accompaniment; the present harmonisation, which harks back to the harmony of bar 3, would not have been possible with the D. As it

is, however, the F# functions, in Riemann's dualistic framework, as the 'under-seventh' of °e; the pure minor mode of the piece remains uninterrupted. As such, the 'Funeral March' is turned into a textbook example of systematic harmonisation, and becomes an important document in Riemann's evolutionary history of music – from its humble pentatonic beginnings to fully fledged functional harmony – as no less than the proof that pure minor is possible, if only, as it were, at the fringes of civilisation, such as in Chinese culture and in Scottish folk song.

In fact, a similar thought had already been expressed at the very outset of Riemann's career, in the doctoral dissertation, where Riemann asserted that the true minor principle was found in the music of Scotland and Scandinavia (perhaps bearing in mind Goethe's views on dualism and his 'Scandinavian theorist').[27] It would seem, then, that very little actually changed from the beginning. In the context of Riemann's cultural pessimism, it would seem that harmonic dualism, which failed to find its place in the consciousness of contemporary composers, lived on in the purer realms, detached from the European mainstream. There it remained a keepsake of a utopia of music – and, one imagines, of musicology too. While Riemann had realised that harmonic dualism was a hindrance to the functioning of his system of harmony, the idea could live on in his tonal imagination.

III

In harmonising non-Western melodies, Hugo Riemann tapped into an important debate at the beginning of the century, namely the question of whether it was possible to harmonise exotic melodies faithfully.[28] Although Riemann was not uncritical of other scholars' attempts in that field, he was, as we have seen, essentially of the opinion that exotic melodies could well be harmonised. Ethnomusicologists, above all the Berlin school around Carl Stumpf, Otto Abraham and Ernst Moritz von Hornbostel, by contrast, warned not to take apparent analogies with Western music at face value: the idiosyncrasies of these 'exotic' melodies

---

[27] Riemann, *Über das musikalische Hören*, Dr. phil. dissertation (Göttingen University, 1873), publ. as *Musikalische Logik: Hauptzüge der physiologischen und psychologischen Begründung unseres Musiksystems* (Leipzig: C. F. Kahnt, 1874), pp. 46–7.

[28] See on the one hand, Abraham J. Polak, *Harmonisierungen indischer, türkischer und japanischer Musik* (Leipzig: Breitkopf und Härtel, 1905), Georg Capellen, 'Exotische Rhythmik, Melodik und Tonalität als Wegweiser zu einer neuen Kunstentwicklung', *Die Musik* 6 (1906/7), p. 216–27, and on the other, Otto Abraham and Erich Moritz von Hornbostel, 'Über die Harmonisierbarkeit indischer exotischer Melodien', *Sammelbände der Internationalen Musikgesellschaft* 7 (1905/6), pp. 138–41. For a modern commentary on the issues surrounding the debate, see Peter Revers, 'Zur Theorie und Ästhetik der Harmonisierung exotischer Melodien', pp. 3–24.

must not be assimilated according to Western prejudices. In particular, while there are examples of simultaneous singing, there is no evidence supporting the existence of harmony for any music other than Western.[29]

Stumpf and Hornbostel had revolutionised ethnological research into music in so far as they had begun using sound recordings in the service of musicology. In 1902 they had begun what was to become a world-renowned sound archive, a collection of wax cylinder recordings of musical performances from all over the world.[30] It was from the basis of this sounding evidence that they now attacked these attempts to assimilate non-Western musics to Western modes of presentation. This adoption of the phonograph by what was then called 'comparative musicology' severely challenged the accepted musical paradigm for whose establishment Riemann had just worked so hard. Abraham and Hornbostel were only too aware of the dawn of a new period (whose consequences, however, have only penetrated mainstream musicology in the last few decades):

With the introduction of physical–acoustical methods, comparative musicology has entered a new era. The earlier methodology – listening to music during expeditions, describing the emotive impression and making statements about rhythm and pitch based solely on the aural impression – has the disadvantage of lacking any investigative objectivity. *Vis-à-vis* music especially, it is difficult to step outside the boundaries of convention, and one easily makes the mistake of assuming that the foundations of our European music are the foundations of all music. In other words, one applies the wrong yardstick. Our notions of 'major' and 'minor' and others have become such powerful concepts, and our entire musical thought rests on them, that it requires great effort to liberate oneself from them. To any given melody, we imagine – consciously or semi-consciously – corresponding harmonies.[31]

---

[29] Abraham and Hornbostel, 'Über die Harmonisierbarkeit', pp. 138–41. Richard Wallaschek, of the Viennese school of ethnomusicology, had claimed in *Primitive Music* (London: Longmans Green, 1893) that African Bachabin boys had sung to their Western visitors in 'correct harmonies'. As Abraham and Hornbostel are quick to point out, however, this contention is merely based on a report, not on primary evidence.

[30] See Susanne Ziegler, 'Erich M. von Hornbostel und das Berliner Phonogramm-Archiv', in Sebastian Klotz, ed., *Vom tönenden Wirbel menschlichen Tuns* (Berlin, Mirow: Schibri-Verlag, 1998), pp. 146–68, and Dieter Christensen, 'Erich M. von Hornbostel, Carl Stumpf, and the Institutionalization of Comparative Musicology', in Philip V. Bohlman and Bruno Nettl, eds., *Comparative Musicology and Anthropology of Music: Essays in the History of Ethnomusicology* (Chicago: University of Chicago Press, 1991), pp. 201–9.

[31] Otto Abraham and Erich Moritz von Hornbostel, 'Über die Bedeutung des Phonographen für vergleichende Musikwissenschaft', *Zeitschrift für Ethnologie* 36 (1904), pp. 226–7. 'Mit der Einführung physikalisch-akustischer Methoden ist die vergleichende Musikwissenschaft in eine neue Aera eingetreten. Das frühere Verfahren, auf den Forschungsreisen Musik zu hören, den Gefühlseindruck zu schildern und über Rhythmus und Tonhöhe Aussagen zu machen, die rein auf dem Gehörseindruck basieren, hat den Übelstand, dass die Objektivität in der Untersuchung fehlt. Gerade

Note how Hornbostel and Abraham consider their method 'physical–acoustical', which, one would assume, had been the hallmark of Helmholtz or Riemann. In fact, however, by referring to the 'physical–acoustical' domain, the comparative musicologists drew attention to the different status that the sound wave attained thanks to the phonograph: the new technology etched the vibration directly into the wax cylinder, and in this way inscribed the musical performance directly into the material with which the researchers could work. This meant that where previous generations had to theorise acoustical relations in any musical system – most problematically, of course, in Riemann's harmonic dualism – the sound wave itself no longer presented a substantive problem for the comparative musicologists working with the phonograph. In fact, Riemann's tone imaginations can be understood as an alternative approach to circumventing this problem.

At the same time, as Hornbostel and Abraham briefly explain, the phonograph had a profound effect on the memory and transcription work of musicological researchers and ultimately changed the epistemological claims on which this research was conducted. Where previously a transcription had to be made under the impression of the single performance, the memory skill of the researcher had necessarily, as in Riemann's example, to be determined by logical rules; continuous inference from this framework of reference was necessary to process the information at once. By contrast, the phonograph itself functioned as the researcher's memory: the performance could be repeated as often as necessary (or at least, as often as the groove in the wax cylinder allowed); the researcher could even slow down the recording to decode particularly complex rhythms. As a consequence, where Riemann had continuously advocated an 'active' listening, that is for an application of the laws of his musical logic, the phonograph made any such active involvement undesirable, and fostered the non-intrusive attitude of the researcher.

Finally, the parameters of transcription itself underwent a crucial change of significance. Previously musicologists had been dependent on musical notation to convey non-Western music to a wider public, with all its obvious shortcomings: all musics had to be made to comply with a stave of five lines and four spaces, with a limited capacity for recording metric or rhythmic complexities and improvisatory or ornamental freedom, and no scope for notating timbral variations. The recording

der Musik gegenüber kommt man aus den konventionellen Schranken nicht heraus, und man verfällt leicht in den Fehler, die Grundlagen unserer europäischen Musik als Grundlagen der Musik überhaupt anzunehmen, und so mit einem falschen Masstab zu messen. Unsere Begriffe "Dur" und "Moll" und andere haben sich so stark in uns festgesetzt, unser ganzes musikalisches Denken basiert derartig auf ihnen, dass man nur mit grosser Mühe sich von ihnen frei machen kann. Zu allen Melodien denken wir uns bewusst oder halb bewusst Harmonien.'

revolution, however, ensured that the contingencies of notation could be circumvented: the musical samples that the ethnographers would take home were direct sonic imprints of the musical performance, which offered the researcher much greater reliability than a notated example could provide.[32] (This is not to deny that the final stage for comparative musicologists remained transcription of the material.)

By contrast, when looking at the recording revolution from Riemann's angle, it appears that one of the principal consequences was that by avoiding the constraints of writing, nonsense was allowed to be perpetuated.[33] The immediacy of the sound recording provided no filter that would ensure that what was recorded stayed within the limits of acceptable reason – or indeed, to revert to the expression used in the Introduction, that it would remain 'in the truth'. That is what the concluding paragraph of Riemann's *Folkloristische Tonalitätsstudien* was effectively saying:

Studies such as the present one serve in the first place to aid understanding of the structure of melodies. If these are carried on, presumably nothing much will remain of the intervals of 3/4 or 5/4 tones, and of the 'neutral' third, which tone psychologists have begun to hear out of phonographs, but which contradict our musical system.[34]

Forced with a choice between the truth of the musical system and the contradictory evidence that phonographs could provide, Riemann opted for the epistemological framework that his system provided. This is no different from his earlier position, which dismissed performances of non-Western music, including intervals unknown in Western music, as performed with insufficient precision. In this sense, the true significance of the rebarring of the Beethoven sonata discussed initially is as an expression of his belief in the perfectibility of the score.

As we saw earlier in this chapter, Riemann was no defender of notation as a source of authority, certainly not as practised in sketch studies. However, he *did* doubtless believe that the constraints of notation, the regulatory framework that it provided, were fully adequate in conveying the necessary elements of music. As we saw on numerous occasions

[32] See Abraham and Hornbostel, 'Über die Bedeutung des Phonographen', pp. 222–36.

[33] This position is sharply analysed in Friedrich Kittler, *Gramophone, Film, Typewriter*, trans. Geoffrey Winthrop-Young and Michael Wutz (Palo Alto, Calif.: Stanford University Press, 1999), p. 86.

[34] Riemann, *Folkloristische Tonalitätsstudien*, p. 112. 'Untersuchungen wie die vorliegenden dienen auch in erster Linie der besseren Schulung für ein volles Verständnis der Struktur von Melodien. Werden dieselben weitergeführt, so wird vermutlich von den unserm Musiksystem widersprechenden Intervallen von 3/4 oder 5/4-Tönen und von den "neutralen" Terzen, die die Tonpsychologen jetzt aus dem Phonogramm heraushören, nicht allzuviel übrigbleiben.'

throughout this book, on a fundamental level, this concerned particularly the intervals and scales that are possible in the tonal system. (His scorn against his former student Max Reger, briefly revisited in the Introduction, is perhaps the best demonstration that notational concerns were not always of secondary importance to him.) What is more, with the admission of recordings as the objects of musicological enquiry, the distinct possibility existed – apparently starting with Alexander Ellis's postulate of 'neutral thirds'[35] – that theories were going to be erected around these flawed renditions.

Again, nothing less was at stake than the very meaning of that thing called 'music'.[36] However, there is one difference: the previous threats to Riemann's musical thought – manifested in the form of 'degenerate' compositions, and at times French or vocal music – menaced the predominance of his system from the inside, as it were. They could therefore be contained by means of strict pedagogy. By contrast, the persistence of non-Western music threatened to relativise the universal validity of his systematic thought from the outside by proposing alternatives to Riemann's ideas of music. Comparative musicology exacerbated this culture clash that might – and eventually would – dethrone Riemann's beliefs.

A word of caution might be in order, since it would be wrong to think of Hornbostel and Stumpf as cultural relativists in a radical contemporary sense. To be sure, while the comparative musicologists disputed the supremacy of Western music, they shared the music historians' belief in the existence of musical universals, and it was their declared supreme goal to formulate the origin and essence of music. Abraham and Hornbostel, for instance, declared: 'Comparative musicology has to isolate the commonalities and connections of the development of music in all parts of the world, to explain the differences with reference to the particular cultural relations, and finally arrive at conclusions as to the origin of music by extrapolation.'[37] The idea that the origin is identical with any universal features of music is not without problems in itself. What remains, however, is a clash between what these universal features might constitute.

If the image of Riemann's nocturnal experiment to prove the existence of the undertones with which we began this investigation signifies the strange mixture of empiricism and post-Hegelian idealism on which his system was built, then the phonograph is the emblem of the new age

[35] Alexander J. Ellis, 'On the Musical Scales of Various Nations', *Journal of the Society of Arts* 33 (1885), pp. 485–527.

[36] Hornbostel promised in his 'Die Probleme der vergleichenden Musikwissenschaft', *Zeitschrift der Internationalen Musikgesellschaft* 7 (1905), pp. 88, to deal with the fundamental question 'What is music?'

[37] Abraham and Hornbostel, 'Über die Bedeutung des Phonographen', p. 224.

that threatened the universal truth of Riemann's system.[38] In this sense, the epistemological space that demarcated Riemann's truth about music was still determined by roughly the same parameters as Helmholtz's had been in the mid-nineteenth century. While the precise epistemological ground of Riemann's musical thought shifted several times during his career, his fundamental belief that music could somehow be expressed in numerical terms – whether it be the early 'brain oscillations' that aroused Lotze's scepticism, the objective undertones in the sound wave, string divisions, or indeed interval ratios – never wavered. To be sure, Riemann's statement that the object of the study of tone imaginations is not notes but tones, imagined sounds, might seem to mark a move away from these long-held convictions. Yet he was not prepared to accept all the consequences that this paradigm change would have entailed – such as the acceptance of 'neutral thirds' as a possible manifestation of tone imaginations. In any case, his death in 1919 prevented him from resolving the conflicts within his musical system that the new perspective had given rise to.

Ultimately, it seems, Riemann was too committed to his old convictions to jettison his theoretical assumptions – to step beyond the truth in whose service he had laboured so hard. It was ultimately his insistence on musical universals, on his pedigreed certainties, bound up as they were with the universality of tonality and the supremacy of the German canon of instrumental music – even when they were tucked away in the psychological realm – that would show up the limitations of his musical thought.

---

[38] This is not of course to say that Stumpf and Hornbostel's Berlin branch of 'comparative musicology' became the guiding model for musicology. However, their approach provided a methodological framework and a legitimate set of questions that went alongside the continued enquiry into the great works of instrumental music that dominated the musicological discourse for most of the twentieth century.

Epilogue

It is perhaps appropriate that the final word should be given to Friedrich Nietzsche. In 1888 he remarked to his friend Carl Fuchs, with whom he had been in correspondence about Riemann's ideas on phrasing: 'Moral: With your Riemann you are completely on the "right track" – indeed the only one that still exists...'[1] In the context of Nietzsche's critique of Riemann, whom he called a 'schoolmaster' earlier in the same letter, this aphorism must be read with a pinch of salt: the correctness that Nietzsche found in Riemann's views on music was bound up with the corrections that the schoolmaster might demand from his pupils. We have seen how Riemann's normative ideas about music fed into a power struggle between musicological knowledge and compositional production, how the rules of his music-theoretical ideas should ensure that composers would remain in the harmonic 'Garden of Eden', at precisely the time when it became apparent that this Garden of Eden was at stake.

The correctness of Riemann's musical thought is not the transcendent truth that Riemann himself aspired to, but one learned by rote and, where necessary, reinforced by the cane administering correction from the lectern of academic authority. (With regard to Riemann's prominent role in the institutional history of musicology, the Foucauldian double meaning of 'discipline' would apply to the full in this context.) In this sense, the innocuous adverb 'still' becomes the key to Nietzsche's rather sarcastic aphorism. It captures precisely the dilemma between the universal aspirations of Riemann's system, and the historically contingent

---

[1] Friedrich Nietzsche, *Gesammelte Werke*, ed. Karl Schlechta (Darmstadt: Wissenschaftliche Buchgesellschaft, 1997), vol. 3, p. 1313. Nietzsche is more positive about Riemann in a passage in 'Der Fall Wagner', which is sensitively interpreted in Leslie A. Blasius, 'Wagner, Nietzsche, Riemann: When Music Lies,' in *Music Theory and Natural Order from the Renaissance to the Early Twentieth Century*, ed. Suzannah Clark and Alexander Rehding (Cambridge: Cambridge University Press, 2001), pp. 93–107. A detailed study of the correspondence between Fuchs and Nietzsche can be found in Rainer Cadenbach, 'Wie Hugo Riemann sich von Carl Fuchs dabei helfen ließ, "das erlösende Wort" einmal bei Nietzsche zu finden: Zu einer vergessenen Kontroverse über künstlerisches Schaffen und "Phrasierung"', in Tatjana Böhme-Mehner and Klaus Mehner, eds., *Hugo Riemann (1849–1919): Musikwissenschaftler mit Universalanspruch* (Cologne, Weimar, Vienna: Böhlau, 2001), pp. 69–91.

truth of his musical thought – a long time before the frayed edges of Riemann's musical system started to show.

Again, it is easy to forget that despite the soap bubble that encapsulated Riemann's musical thought, the fiction of harmonic dualism, his concept of music went on to be extremely influential in the academy. Above all, his conceit that tonality constitutes a timeless structure supplanted François-Joseph Fétis's earlier, historically contingent, definition of the term, and tonality is still commonly understood in this ahistorical sense in the academy. It was the semblance of scientific rigour, on the basis of which he argued for the timeless validity for this and other aspects of his concept of music, that lent Riemann's musical thought its authority and widespread appeal within the discipline of musicology and beyond. What is more, his systematic musical thought promised to link all the major aspects of the burgeoning discipline of musicology, from acoustics to aesthetics and history (and back again). For the first time, it seemed possible that musicology could indeed stand up to objective, scientific scrutiny: Riemann helped define music as a stable, knowable entity – and, what is more, as an object *worthy* of scientific study. Riemann defined music, down from the most minute detail to the largest historical category.

Riemann, the 'schoolmaster', would have to revert to the cane because his organicist ambitions of building up the whole from the most detailed parts – in his aesthetics of musical form as well as his musicological project as a whole – could not sustain his vision out of the system itself. Whereas we initially considered Riemann's analogy between listening to music and looking at Cologne Cathedral as an emblem of these organicist beliefs, it is worth comparing that passage with a very similar reflection on architectural and musical form, which Riemann wrote around the same time:

It goes without saying that the final result [of aesthetically apprehending a work of music] will be monstrous if the small-scale symmetries are not understood with sufficient clarity. In comprehending the architectural work of art, which begins with a totality, the proportions of the larger parts are apprehended first, and it is particularly for these that strict symmetry is required, while on the level of small-scale detail much asymmetry can be tolerated. In music, by contrast, it is small-scale symmetry that must lead to a comprehension at first of larger proportions. Even strict symmetry of these larger parts is not absolutely necessary, albeit desirable. In any case, their full comprehension requires great power of memory.[2]

---

[2] Riemann, *Systematische Modulationslehre* (Hamburg: J. F. Richter, 1887), pp. 2–3. 'Es ist wohl einleuchtend, dass das Schlussresultat ein monströses sein muss, wenn die Symmetrien im Kleinen nicht mit hinreichender Klarheit verstand worden sind; denn während bei dem zuerst im Ganzen aufgefassten architektonischen Kunstwerk die Proportionen der grössten Theile zunächst verstanden werden und vor allem für diese

While the initial example of the 'musical cathedral' had been constructed bit by bit into an overwhelming whole structure, the emphasis on the aesthetic effect derived from the totality of the musical work is considerably weaker in the latter excerpt. On the most basic level, this difference can be explained with respect to their respective contexts: in a composition treatise (in this case *Systematische Modulationslehre*) Riemann was under much more pressure to explain the totality of the work of music in terms useful for a composer than in an exposé of general aesthetic principles.

The consequences of these differences, however, go much further: its vagueness is an indication that the aspirations to normative rules cannot stand up. While irregularities at the detailed level are demonised as 'monstrous', there is no guideline to prevent large-scale irregularities. Riemann's thoughts on form did not stretch beyond the small-scale level. Thus, in his late *Große Kompositionslehre*, he stated explicitly that he would not explore 'the formal element beyond the eight-bar period'.[3] What may appear as theoretical nonchalance in his handling of overall forms would seem to put a question mark over the organicist claims of Riemann's music aesthetics: it merely remained 'desirable' – in more than one sense – that well-shaped proportions are maintained at the large scale. Ultimately, it is well possible that in practice the musical cathedral remains a ruin – and there was nothing in Riemann's systematic musicological and aesthetic thought to prevent this.

It was the 'small hypothesis' of the undertone series, the scientific fiction of harmonic dualism, that held, in some ways, the whole edifice of Riemann's musical thought together and sustained the holistic illusion of an organic connection between the disparate aspects. This was the token of Riemann's confidence in being 'on the right track' – it was not harmonic dualism itself that made any sense; rather, harmonic dualism was necessary to make sense of and sustain the rest of Riemann's musical thought, to cover up the void at the core of his normative ideas on music. By contrast, the attempts to destabilise this institutionally accepted notion of music, whether it be in the disputes with the comparative musicologists or debates with composers, although fought at the dawn of the twentieth century, did not unfold their full impact until comparatively recently. (And ironically, it seems that Hornbostel's

strenge Symmetrie gefordert wird, während im kleineren Detail vieles Asymmetrische mit hingenommen wird, ist bei der Musik die Symmetrie im Kleinen das zunächst Verständniss der grösseren Proportionen führende und sogar eine strenge Symmetrie der letzteren nicht absolut erforderlich, wenn auch natürlich erstrebenswerth; jedenfalls gehört zu ihrer vollen Erfassung schon eine starke Gedächtniskraft.'

[3] Riemann, *Große Kompositionslehre* (Leipzig: Breitkopf und Härtel, 1902), vol. 1, p. 424. See also Lotte Thaler, *Organische Form in der Musiktheorie des 19. und frühen 20. Jahrhunderts* (Munich and Salzburg: Emil Katzbichler, 1983), pp. 18–54.

contentious 'theory of blown fifths' [*Blasquintentheorie*], would have been a similar Achilles heel, another case of a music-theoretical 'As-if'.)

Nietzsche concluded his assessment of Riemann in his letter to Carl Fuchs by declaring the musicologist a 'decadent'. Whereas Riemann's ideology had been aimed at the eradication of decadence, and the erection of an everlasting – and at times German – musical art, Nietzsche declared that precisely this obsession with detail, the attempt to pin music down to the last facet, was a symptom of the very culture of decadence against which Riemann was battling polemically.[4] To be sure, as Nietzsche hastened to add, this term was not negatively connoted for him.[5] Indeed, it appears this ironic verdict expressed at the same time rejection and a dose of admiration for Riemann's musical thought. In this sense, the epithet 'decadent' hit twice: first, it effectively undermined Riemann's own aesthetic ideas of a renewed, 'healthy' classicism by marking his supposedly timeless system as a product of his own time. And second, the notion of decadence itself was an expression of Nietzsche's conviction that fundamental truths must eventually decay. With this assessment, Nietzsche had completed an incisive critique of Riemann's entire musical system *avant la lettre*, at just the time when his musical thought became accepted in Germany as the institutional doctrine of the young discipline of musicology.

[4] Nietzsche, *Gesammelte Werke*, vol. 3, pp. 1312–13 and 1226.
[5] Ibid., p. 1226. See also Julian Young, *Nietzsche's Philosophy of Art* (Cambridge: Cambridge University Press, 1992), pp. 132–44.

Riemann's key terms as explained in the *Musik-Lexikon* (5th edn, 1900)

Apparent Consonance [*Scheinkonsonant*] is an important term of the speculative theory of music; apparent consonances are those dissonances that, when considered in isolation, coincide with consonances; e.g. the chord consisting of root, third and sixth (instead of fifth), or that consisting of root, fourth and sixth instead of root, third and fifth; any parallel *Klänge*[1] and leading-tone changes are apparent consonances. (Cf. *Dissonance*)

Consonance [*Konsonanz*] (Lat. *Consonantia*, 'sounding together') is the fusion of several tones to a unified significance of the *Klang*. The consonance of the major principle (the major triad) is the sounding together of a principal tone with its upper fifth and upper third; the consonance of the minor principle (the minor triad) is the sounding together of a principal tone with its lower fifth and lower third. Tones are only consonant if and while they *are* actually understood in context as components of one and the same *Klang* (see *Klang, Dissonance*). In deviation from this precise definition of musical consonance, physicists have defined consonant tones as those that *can* be understood as components of the same *Klang*. (Cf. *Apparent consonance*)

Dissonance [*Dissonanz*] (Lat. *Dissonantia*, 'sounding apart') is the disturbance of the unified conception (consonance) of those tones pertaining to one *Klang* by one or several tones that must be understood as representatives of different *Klänge*. There are therefore no dissonant intervals, but only dissonant tones. Which tone is dissonant within a physically (acoustically) dissonant interval depends on the *Klang* in whose context the interval is heard (take C–D: in the context of a C major triad, D is dissonant; in the context of a G major triad, C is dissonant). Musically speaking, even acoustically consonant intervals can be found to be dissonant (e.g. C–G in the context of an A♭ major chord with G as an appoggiatura to A♭). One must stress that the identification of

---

[1] I follow Ian Bent in leaving the untranslatable word *Klang* in the original. The German *Klang* can denote variously 'tone' (but different from *Ton*) or 'chord' (likewise for *Akkord*) and sometimes something between the two depending upon context. 'Sonority' would seem the closest English equivalent. The anglicised 'clang', which is sometimes used, does nothing to clarify the multiple meanings of this concept and has the additional disadvantage of sounding ugly.

dissonant tones by means of *Klang* representation is not based on equivalent, or coordinated, *Klänge* but is rather understood as subordinate to one dominant *Klang*, so that it seems advisable to define any dissonant chords in the sense of the dominating *Klang*. Rameau already recognised that certain dissonant additional tones help us characterise a *Klang* in its position within the tonality. Therefore we distinguish the following dissonances: *A. Characteristic dissonances:* 1) minor seventh of the major triad, which lends the chord the significance of a dominant, e.g. C–E–G|B♭ = dominant of F major or F minor. 2) The major sixth of the major triad, which characterises the chord as a subdominant; e.g. C–E–G|A = subdominant of G major. 3) The lower seventh of the minor triad, by means of which the chord appears as a subdominant, e.g. A|C–E♭–G = subdominant of G minor. 4) The lower sixth of the minor triad, which identifies the chord as a dominant, e.g. B♭|C–E♭–G = dominant of F minor. *Vis-à-vis* these four characteristic dissonances (D^7, S^6, S^{VII}, D^{VI}), which play a major part in key recognition in general as well as in modulations in particular, any other dissonances appear as merely coincidental embellishments, caused by lively movement in one of the parts, or conversely by delaying a progression in one of the parts. The former cause the so-called *B. Passing Dissonances,* e.g. when one part traverses one or several pitches while the others remain still (in C major: c **d** e, e **f** g, g **a b** c, or the same progressions backwards). These so-called passing notes are easier to understand when they fall on metrically light beats than on heavy beats, and most difficult when they do not begin with a complete melodic connection but rather enter by leap (fictive passing note). Some of these passing dissonances may occasionally result in *apparent consonances*, whose momentary conception as real *Klänge* provides some charming and mysterious effects of harmony, such as: a) the sixth of the major triad and the lower sixth of the minor triad without the fifth (standing in for it), results in the *parallel* of the *Klang* concerned and represents it within the tonality. In C major, the apparent consonances of A minor (***Tp***), D minor (***Sp***) and E minor (***Dp***) are created in this way. b) Sounding the leading-tone (in the major principle, the lower leading-tone, in the minor the upper leading-tone) instead of the principal tone results in the equally charming harmony of another representative apparent consonance, the *leading-tone change* (in C major: 𝔗 = E minor, 𝔖 = A minor, 𝔇 = B minor (!), in A minor: 𝔗 = F major, 𝔇 = C major, 𝔖 = B♭ major (!).) The retardation of one voice results in *C. Suspension dissonances* of various kinds are achieved by deferring the entry of the third by tying over the fourth from the previous harmony, likewise the suspension of the second from the root, the second from the third, the sixth from the fifth (which again results in the *parallel,* unless the fifth is also present in a different part) etc. Furthermore, several suspensions can occur simultaneously, or be

combined with characteristic dissonances and passing notes. The fourth and final group of dissonances is that of the so-called D. *Altered chords*. These result from chromatic alteration of the tones pertaining to the *Klang*; such a dramatic change may have the character of a passing motion, e.g. when an augmented fifth is inserted between fifth and sixth (G# after G in the C major triad, if an F major chord follows with an A in the same part); depending on the metric weight and the duration of the tone such an altered chord tone may have various effects. Any alteration forces the harmony to move to another one; the strongest effect, however, is achieved by those that simultaneously urge toward a new key ... (Cf. *Functions*)

Dualism, harmonic [*Dualismus, harmonischer*], broadly speaking, the assumption of a twofold (dual) basis of harmony, the major consonance (from the principal tone upwards) and the minor consonance (from the principal tone downwards). (Cf. *Klang*)

Functions [*Funktionen*] (tonal functions of harmony) describe, in the terminology of the author of this lexicon, the various significances that chords possess, depending on their position to the tonic, for the logic of the composition [*Tonsatz*]. The problem, which he strove to solve right from his early book *Musikalische Logik* (1873) onwards, he finally solved in his *Vereinfachte Harmonielehre oder Lehre von den tonalen Funktionen der Harmonie* (German 1893, English 1895, French 1899), namely that of developing a taxonomy in which the most complicated dissonant formations and deceptive progressions are presented as more or less modified versions of the three only essential harmonies: Tonic (*T*), Subdominant (*S*) and Dominant (*D*). In the major mode, these three harmonies are major triads (T^+, S^+, D^+), in the minor mode they are minor triads (^oT, ^oS, ^oD), but the subdominant in the major mode may be a minor triad (^oS) and the dominant in the minor mode may be a major triad (D^+). The dissonant forms of the dominants that contain more than three tones are in the first instance: S^6, D^7, S^{VII}, D^{VI} (cf. *Dissonance A*, also *Klang shorthand*). In addition, the forms of apparent consonances, which represent the *Klang* as one of the opposite harmonic gender, namely the replacement of the fifth by the sixth ($^6_5$), the *parallels*: *Tp*, *Sp*, *Dp*, ^oTp, ^oSp, ^oDp, and the replacement of the root by the second in the opposite direction, the *leading-note changes*: 𝍫, 𝍬, 𝍭, 𝍮, 𝍯, 𝍰, with the former three replacing the principal tone of the major principle with the lower minor second, the latter three replacing the principal tone of the minor principle with the upper minor second, e.g. in A minor: 𝍯 = D F Bb instead of D F A, in C major: 𝍫 = B E G instead of C E G etc. – Crucial to the precise denomination of these chords is the derivation from the principal *Klänge* that they represent. Chromatic harmonies are usually represented as dominants of subsequent simpler

harmonies and are labelled as such, e.g. the ones in parentheses in the following example.

$$T \quad (D) \quad Sp \quad (D^7) \quad D \quad .. \quad T$$

Further abbreviations are the dominant of the dominant as $\mathcal{D}$ and the secondary minor subdominant as $\overset{\circ}{_{m}\!S}$. Ellipses (omission of expected chords) after chromatic harmonies are indicated briefly by the chord of the expected resolution in square brackets, e.g. in C major the succession $T (D^7) \mid [Tp] (S^{VII} D^7) \mid [Sp] S^{VII} D^7 \mid T$ appears as in the following example:

$$(\text{Fig. bass}) \quad \substack{6\!\!\!/\\4\\3} \quad \substack{6\natural\\4\\3} \quad \substack{7\\\#} \quad \substack{6\natural\\4\\\natural} \quad 7$$

Modulation always appears as the reinterpretation of one function into another one, e.g. in C major: $T_{\underset{3}{\cdot\cdot}} = S \mid D_{4\cdot\cdot}^{6+} \mid T$

$$(\text{Fig. bass}) \quad 6 \quad \substack{6\#\\4} \quad \substack{5\#\\3\#} \quad \substack{5\#\\\#}$$

Since this kind of taxonomy is not bound to a specific key, it is highly suitable for analytical purposes as well as an aid for transposition.

Klang, or sonority, we call the audible vibration of elastic bodies, that is to say, *Klang* is the scientific name for what the layman calls 'tone'. One says equally that an instrument has a good '*Klang*' or 'tone'. Acoustical science differentiates between *Klang* and noise, and by the latter it means an aural impression created by irregular vibrations, by the former one created by regular vibrations. Regular vibrations are those that repeat at regular speed and pace, as the pendulum of the clock. Pitch (or height) of the perceived tone depends on the velocity of the succession (period) of the individual vibrations, therefore vibrations of constant periods result in tones or *Klänge* of constant pitch. Since it has become known that the *Klänge* of our musical instruments are not simple tones but are rather composed from a series of simple tones – which may be discernible

with sufficient concentration but are not normally distinguished – the word *Klang* has received a more general and all-encompassing meaning in scientific usage, while 'tone' denotes the simple tone as a part of the *Klang*. As a rule, the pitch of a *Klang* is determined by the lowest and usually the strongest of its tones, which are often called partial tones, or harmonic series. Since all other partials are higher than the fundamental tone, which lends the *Klang* its pitch name, these partials are usually called overtones (note, though, that the second overtone is not the third of the series, but rather the second)... The series of the first sixteen partials for the tone C is:

Those tones written in minims are all components of the major triad of the fundamental (C major triad). For this reason that it was believed that the consonance of the major triad (consonance of the major principle) had to be explained by means of the overtone series, so that a major triad, no matter in which inversion, should always be conceived as a *Klang* in which these overtones (which correspond to the actually sounding tones of the triad) are enhanced. Obviously, this explanation has some serious problems. Those partials marked with an * above do not correspond exactly with the pitches of the notes of our tonal system, with which they are represented here; if these tones are produced as part of the chord, they are not understood in the sense of the overtone series, but rather in the sense of roughly corresponding tones related according to the minor principle (see below). This is true for all tones that both correspond to those from the seventh partial upwards and whose ordinal numbers are prime numbers. Those whose ordinal numbers are product numbers ($9 = 3 \times 3, 15 = 3 \times 5, 25 = 5 \times 5$ etc.), can be understood as overtones of overtones, as secondary overtones, that is as integrating components of the primary (the 9th as the 3rd of the 3rd; the 15th as the 5th of the 5th etc.). If these are represented in the chord, that is produced at the same volume as the primary ones, they will obviously sound dissonant; the primary overtone, to which these secondary overtones relate as direct partials, will then appear itself as fundamental, so that two *Klänge* are present at the same time. The sole exception is the simplest ratio, 2:1, the octave relation, whose exponentials never form a dissonance. Also, any interval can be enlarged or shortened by one or more octaves without changing its harmonic significance. Thus, on deleting the primary overtones from the 7th onwards, as well as all those corresponding to product numbers (including all octaves), the only remaining components of the

consonance of the principle, of the over-*Klang*, are the root or primary tone (1), the twelfth (3) and the seventeenth (5); the primordial shape of the major chord is therefore not actually the triad in close position but in wide spacing.

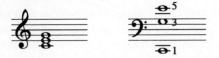

The ordinal numbers of the partials represent at the same time the ratios, or relative numbers of vibrations, for the interval formed between them; e.g. the ratio between the 15th and 16th overtones (leading-tone relation B:C) = 15:16.

The consonance of the minor triad cannot be explained from the over-tone series, and any attempts to do this nonetheless (Helmholtz) had to result in musically inadequate explanations. By contrast, an explanation that approaches the issue from opposites is more successful. Long before the discovery of the overtones, the consonance of the major chord was related to the division of strings $1-\frac{1}{6}$ (i.e. 1 is the length of the string of the fundamental, $\frac{1}{2}$ that of the octave, $\frac{1}{3}$ that of the twelfth, etc. up to the 6th partial). The consonance of the minor principle, on the other hand, was related to the inversion of that series, that is the string lengths 1–6, i.e. 1 is the fundamental, 2 the *lower* octave, 3 the *lower* twelfth etc. This understanding of the consonance of the minor principle as a polar opposite to that of the major principle is first found, as far as is known, in Zarlino in the thirtieth chapter of *Institutioni armoniche* [sic] (1558), was then promoted by Rameau (since 1737) and Tartini (1754 and 1767), two of the most learned and intelligent theorists. In more recent times, since M. Hauptmann (1853), this approach is explained, more or less consis-tently, in a great number of young theorists (O. Kraushaar, O. Tiersch, O. Hostinsky), as well as in full sharpness and to all its consequences by A. v. Oettingen and the author of this lexicon. The consonance of the minor principle is related to an undertone series in exactly the way the consonance of the major principle is related to the overtone series. The acoustical phenomena justifying the postulate of this undertone se-ries are those of sympathetic vibration [*Mittönen*] and of combination tones. A sounding tone causes sonorous bodies to resonate in sympa-thetic vibration, if their resonance pitch corresponds to one of its un-dertones, or – which is the same thing – if it is an overtone of their resonance pitch. The lowest combination tone of an interval is always the first common undertone of both interval tones, e.g. for e′:g′ = C, for c″:d″ also = C, etc. Taking c″ as a starting point, the series of the sixteen first undertones is:

The ordinal numbers of the undertones represent the relative string lengths of these tones. The ratios of vibrations would be expressed by the series of simple fractions: 1, $\frac{1}{2}$ $\frac{1}{3}$ etc., just as, conversely, the ratios of string lengths for the tones of the overtone series could be represented by the series of simple fractions; e.g in the sense of the overtones series the octave c:c′ (c → c′; letting c = 1) can be represented as 1:2 (with the view to the ratio of vibrations) or as $1{:}\frac{1}{2}$ (with the view to string lengths). In the sense of the undertone series, by contrast (c ← c′; letting c′ = 1), the octave must be represented as $1{:}\frac{1}{2}$ with the view to the ratio of vibrations, and as 1:2 with the view to string lengths. The undertone series must be simplified by means of analogous manipulations as in the overtone series, to prove the consonance of the minor principle. First all octave repetitions are deleted (all tones corresponding to even numbers). Just as the equivalent partials of the overtone series, the 7th, 11th and 13th undertones (and any prime-number undertone beyond the 7th) do not correspond to tones in our musical system. Those relating to product numbers ($9 = 3 \times 3$, $15 = 3 \times 5$ etc.) are secondary undertones, and hence just as dissonant against the fundamental of the main *Klang* as the secondary overtones against the principal tone of the over-*Klang*. Thus the only remaining chief components ar 1:3:5 for $c^3{:}f^1{:}a\flat$ (F minor chord). According to the latest trend in musicology (cf. *Stumpf*), the proof of the principles of tone relations, that is of consonance and dissonance, by means of acoustical phenomena, has been given up. Musicologists now merely consider them as illustrations of the primordial laws on which the fundamental facts of musical hearing rest, namely the more or less perfect agreement or fusion [*Vereinbarkeit oder Verschmelzung*] of tones. In this notion of agreement, tight boundaries are drawn for musical hearing, and certain degrees have been demonstrated to exist, for which acoustical phenomena provide no clues. The latest trends in musicology thus move the foundation of music theory from the domain of mathematical, physical and physiological demonstration to that of psychology. The four degrees of fusion, which have to be regarded as fundamental for music theory, are: 1) octave fusion (expanded notion of tone) 2) consonant intervals (to be reduced to third and fifth on the basis of the notion of 'active listening') 3) the concept of *Klang* (interval fusion, possible in two forms: major *Klang* and minor *Klang*) 4) *Klang* fusion (including distinction of *Klänge*, dissonance, depending on the the ratio of the coinciding *Klänge*). *Klänge* not recognised by their degree of relation to each other, form the unmusical 'discordance'. (See *Succession of Klänge, Dissonance*)

Klang representation [*Klangvertretung*] is a term of contemporary theory of harmony, related to the particular significance that a tone or interval obtains, depending on whether it is understood in the sense of this or that *Klang*; e.g. any tone C has a very different significance for the logic of the composition [*Tonsatz*] according to whether it is imagined as the third of the Ab major triad or as the third of the A minor triad (°e; cf. *Klang shorthand*). In the former case it is closely related to Db and the Db major triad, in the latter to B and the E major and minor triads. Each tone can pertain to six different *Klänge* as an essential component (cf. *Klang*), namely e.g. the tone C to the C over-*Klang* (C major triad) as the major principal tone, to the F over-*Klang* as the upper fifth (or fifth of the major principle), the Ab under-*Klang* as the major third (upper third), the C under-*Klang* (F minor triad) as the minor principal tone, the G under-*Klang* (C minor triad) as lower fifth (fifth of the minor principle), and finally the E under-*Klang* (A minor triad) as the lower third (major third of the minor principle).

Even when the tone C appears as a dissonant addition to another *Klang* or instead of one of the usual tones of that chord (as a suspension or altered tone), its significance must still be determined in the sense of one of these six *Klänge*, namely that most closely related to it.

Klang shorthand [*Klangschlüssel*] is the new chord taxonomy, developed by the author of this lexicon in his theoretical writings and used there exclusively, which he hopes will replace figured bass because this old practice does not allow a clear enough recognition of the meaning of the chords as *Klänge*. Just as in figured bass, in the *Klang* shorthand the figures 1–10 are used, but the intervals are not counted from the bass tone, but from the principal tone of the *Klang* in which sense the chord is understood. For major chords, Arabic figures are used, for minor chords Roman figures; the former indicate intervals reckoned upwards from the principal tone, the latter indicate intervals reckoned downwards from the principal tone. The principal tone is notated by letter (c, a, etc.). The figures have the following meaning: 1 (I) principal tone, 2 (II) major second, 3 (III) major third, 4 (IV) perfect fourth, 5 (V) perfect fifth, 6 (VI) major sixth, 7 (VII) minor seventh, 8 (VIII) octave (used in exceptional cases, for instance after 9 (IX)), 9 (IX) major ninth, 10 (X) major tenth. All figures except 1, 3, 5, 8 (I, III, V, VIII) indicate dissonant tones, for only principal tone, third and fifth are components of the major or minor *Klang* (see *Klang*). The chromatic change of the remaining seven

intervals listed above are indicated by means of < for the sharpening and > for the flattening by a semitone. Double sharpenings or flattenings are musically unthinkable. The major triad (over-*Klang*) is marked by the abbreviation sign + instead of $^5_3$, the minor chord (under-*Klang*) by the sign ° instead of $|^{\text{III}}_{\text{V}}$. However, the sign + is only used in opposition to and in alternation with °; if no extra sign is given, we assume the over-*Klang* of the given tone. Unlike figured bass, *Klang* shorthand is not bound to the bass part, but can be used for any part; indeed, it does not require any given part at all. While the student of figured bass has no opportunity to learn how to write a good bass line, he can do so to the maximum using *Klang* shorthand. For the more exact names of dissonant chords, cf. *Dissonance*. Instead of using the concrete names of the *Klänge* according to their principal tone (c^+, °e, etc.), the author has recently introduced a more general taxonomy, the letters indicating the tonal function of harmonies: *T* (tonic), *D* (dominant), *S* (subdominant), with + and ° for major and minor. This taxonomy is completely independent of pitch, and provides highly important means of assisting the development of harmonic thought. See his *Vereinfachte Harmonielehre* (London 1893, English 1895, French 1899) as well as 3rd edn of *Handbuch der Harmonielehre* (1898). (Cf. *Functions*)

Succession of Klänge [*Klangfolge*] is the succession of two chords with the view to their meaning as *Klänge*. To be able to speak of a succession of *Klänge*, one must first of all conceive of all chords, including dissonant ones, in the sense of *Klänge* and name them. Also, if we want to arrive at general conclusions, we will require a terminology that does not focus on special cases, but is rather applicable to a greater number of cases. The beginnings of such a terminology have been commonly found since G. Weber. The triads of all the scale degrees are given ordinal numbers, which are designated as capital Roman numerals for major chords, and small ones for minor chords; those for diminished chords are marked with a small zero, augmented ones sometimes with a small dash (E. F. Richter).

The label V–I denotes the succession of two major triads, of which the first is the dominant of the second. V–ı means the transition from one major chord to a minor chord, of which the former is the dominant of the latter, etc. Meanwhile, this terminology has proven inadequate for more liberated harmonies; the succession of C major – Ab major – D major – G major – C major, which forms a clearly intelligible musical

unit, can hardly be explained with this terminology. While it does not introduce a modulation to another key at any stage, one would still have to explain the A♭ major triad in the sense of F minor or C minor and the D major triad in the sense of G major:

For such successions of *Klänge* a terminology that orientates itself by the diatonic scale is not possible. They belong to the free kind of tonality (see there), which has only been recognised recently, and whose boundaries far surpass those of harmonies derived from the diatonic scale. Tonality does not know of tones pertaining to and foreign to the scale [*leitertreu und leiterfremd*] but only one principal *Klang* and related *Klänge*. For the above example, the C major triad remains the principal *Klang* throughout, and the remaining ones are related to it; the A♭ major triad is its lower-third *Klang* (parallel of its minor subdominant: °*Sp*; cf. *Functions*), the D major triad is the *Klang* of its second upper fifth (2nd dominant; 𝄐), the G major triad is that of the first upper fifth. The first harmonic succession from C major to A♭ major reaches for the undertone side, the second one jumps over to the overtone side (A♭ major – D major), the third and fourth lead back to the principal *Klang*. The succession of A♭ major – D major is therefore not incomprehensible, because in its continued relation to the principal *Klang* it is implicitly broken down into its components – a third relation and a double-fifth relation (whole-tone relation) – or A♭ – C – [G] – D. The whole is the cadence: *T* – °*Sp* – 𝄐 – *D* – *T*. A rational, general terminology for harmonic successions must approach the issues from the relations between principal tones, among which fifth relations, third relations, whole-tone relations, minor-third relations, leading-tone relations, tritone relations etc. are to be distinguished. Moreover, it must be considered whether both *Klänge* are the same harmonic mode (major or minor), or whether it changes. While we call the successions of chords in the same mode 'step' [*Schritt*], those that switch from one harmonic mode to the other we call 'change' [*Wechsel*]. Thus there are four types of successions in which the principal tones are in a fifth relation. For tonality it makes a big difference whether a harmonic move from the tonic follows the

overtone or the undertone side (cf. *Klang*); starting from a major triad, the latter implies a contradiction, an opposition to the principle on which the *Klang* is based (starting from the minor triad, the former move produces the equivalent effect). Therefore steps and changes to *Klänge* of the opposite side are usefully determined by the addition of 'opposite' [*Gegen-*]. The succession C major – G major, and A minor – D minor (E under-*Klang* – A under-*Klang*) respectively, is thus a (plain) fifth step [*(schlichter) Quintschritt*]; C major – F major, and A minor – E minor (E under-*Klang* – B under-*Klang*; or simply: under-E – under-B, according to the terminology explained in *Klang* shorthand = ^{o}e – ^{o}b) respectively, an opposite fifth step [*Gegenquintschritt*]; C major – C minor (^{o}g) and A minor (^{o}e) – A major is a (plain) fifth change [*(schlichter) Quintwechsel*]; and C major – B♭ minor (^{o}f) and A minor (^{o}e) – B major is an opposite fifth change [*Gegenquintwechsel*]. In any of these types of successions, as in these examples, the 'plain' changes are very easily understandable, the 'opposite' changes, however, are always very difficult to follow. Successions involving thirds include: (plain) third step C major–E major, and A minor–F minor (^{o}e – ^{o}c); opposite third step C major–A♭ major, and A minor–C# minor (^{o}e – ^{o}g#); (plain) third change C major–A minor (^{o}e) and A minor (^{o}e)–C major; finally the opposite third change C major–D♭ minor (^{o}a♭), and A minor (^{o}e)–G# major. A systematic account of this terminology can be found in H. Riemann's theoretical writings. (Cf. *Klang, Klang representation, Klang shorthand,* and *Functions*)

Tonality [*Tonalität*] (*Tonalité*) is the peculiar significance that chords obtain on account of their relation to a principal *Klang*, the *Tonic*. The notion of tonality (*centre harmonique*) was brought into theory by Rameau (1722); the name tonality was proposed by Fétis. The older theory is essentially based on the scale, and means by 'tonic' the beginning and concluding tone, whereas the new theory of harmony, which is nothing but the theory of the significances of the chords for the logic of the composition [*Logik des Tonsatzes*] (cf. *Functions*), proposes a major or minor chord as a tonic. Thus the tonality of C major is prevalent, as long as all harmonies are understood in their position to the C major chord.

This bold but forceful and sweet-sounding succession cannot be defined in the sense of a tonality of the older kind; in the sense of the C major tonality it is: Tonic – opposite third-*Klang* – Tonic – plain third-*Klang* – Tonic [*Tonika – Gegenterzklang – Tonika – schlichter Terzklang – Tonika*]. That

is to say, the tonic is only juxtaposed with related *Klänge* (cf. *Succession of Klänge*). A change of the tonality is called modulation.

Tone relations [*Tonverwandtschaft*], a term from modern speculative theory, which relates to the belongingness of tones in *Klänge*. Tones are related in the first degree (directly related) if they belong to one and the same *Klang* (cf. *Klang*). Related to C in the first degree are G, F, E, A♭, A and E♭; for C:G pertains to the C major or minor triads, C:F to the F major or minor triads, C:E to the C-major or A minor triads; C:A♭ to the A♭ major or F minor triads, C:A to the F major or the A minor triads, C:E♭ to the A♭ major or the C minor triads. Tones related in the first degree are consonant, but only if they are *heard* in the sense of a *Klang* to which they both pertain (cf. *Apparent Consonances*). Tones are related in the second degree if they do not pertain to the same *Klang*, and therefore cannot be related directly to each other (e.g. C is related to D via G, which is in a fifth relation to both). It is unnecessary to assume third or fourth or even further degrees of relation, since any tones that are not directly related to each other are dissonant. The varying quality of dissonances depends on the kind of mediation, on which intelligibility of the interval depends; such mediation is not based on tones but rather on *Klänge*, so that *Klang* relation becomes the real issue. Tones pertaining to *Klänge* related to each other in the first degree are more easily intelligible than those pertaining to *Klang* relations of the second degree. *Klänge* related to each other in the first degree are: 1) those of the same harmonic gender (both major or minor) whose principal tones are related to each other in the first degree; 2) those of different harmonic gender in which one is the changing *Klang* of a chord tone of the other, that is for the major triad the minor triad (under-*Klang*) of the principal tone, fifth tone, or third tone. ... In general it is noteworthy that minor relations have been exploited by composers to a much lesser degree than major relations, which is no doubt in part a consequence of the imperfect theoretical knowledge of the essence of the minor mode in the older theory of harmony. Even Moritz Hauptmann still denied the minor keys the same relations as the major ones possess.

Undertones [*Untertöne*] (Undertone series) we call the series of tones that extends downwards, in reciprocal relation to the overtone series. Just as the overtone series serves to explain the consonance of the major triad, so one must draw on the undertone series to explain the consonance of the minor triad (cf. *Klang*). The author of this lexicon has repeatedly attempted to prove the actual existence of the undertones, as corresponding to overtones. In his *Musikalische Logik* (1873), he demonstrated their subjective production in the ear, he believed he had to conclude their objective existence from various clues (cf. 'Die objective Existenz der Untertöne', 1876 [sic], and *Musikalische Syntaxis*, 1877). In *Katechismus*

der Musikwissenschaft, p. 79, he finally offered the scientific proof as to why, despite the commensurability of vibration forms, a tone cannot produce the undertone series by means of summation of its vibrations. With this, the question is finally settled. (Each tone necessarily produces the whole series of undertones, but each undertone is produced multiple times, in accordance with its ordinal number – the second twice, the third three times, etc. – just so that they necessarily cancel each other out by means of interference.)

Upbeat [*Auftakt*] describes an apparently incomplete bar that begins a composition or a phrase, for instance in:

it is the lone quaver that begins the piece. Since our notation always places the barline before that part of the bar that marks the centre of gravity of the bar-motive, all metrical elements (bar-motives) beginning with a light part become upbeats, that is the barline cuts through them. Nothing can be more misguided than to remove such an 'upbeat' from what follows and to consider the tonal content between two barlines as a motive. On the contrary, one can claim in general that one has to consider in compositions beginning with the full bar (on the downbeat: 'one') how much of the end of the bar should be counted as an upbeat to the following. For the upbeat is not only a possible form but rather the actual vantage point, the primeval form of all musical creation. The statement that any figuration is in the first instance the renewal of upbeat values is – in this concision – the intellectual property of the author of this lexicon. See his *Metrik and Agogik* (1884), where the gradual decline of the superior theory of rhythm of the previous century is documented.

BIBLIOGRAPHY

Aalst, J. A. van. *Chinese Music* (Shanghai: Statistical Department of the Inspectorate General of Customs, 1884).

Abraham, Gerald. *The Concise Oxford History of Music* (London: Oxford University Press, 1979).

Abraham, Otto, and Ernst M. von Hornbostel. 'Über die Bedeutung des Phonographen für vergleichende Musikwissenschaft', *Zeitschrift für Ethnologie* 36 (1904), pp. 222–36.

'Über die Harmonisierbarkeit indischer exotischer Melodien', *Sammelbände der Internationalen Musikgesellschaft* 7 (1905/06), pp. 138–41.

Adler, Guido. 'Umfang, Methode und Ziel der Musikwissenschaft', *Vierteljahrsschrift für Musikwissenschaft* 1 (1885), pp. 5–20.

Studie zum Ursprung der Harmonie, in *Sitzungsberichte der (kaiserlichen) Akademie der Wissenschaften in Wien, philosophisch-historische Klasse* 98 (1886), pp. 781–830.

Adler, Guido ed. *Wiener Instrumentalmusik vor und um 1750. Vorläufer der Wiener Klassiker* (Vienna: Artaria, 1908).

Handbuch der Musikgeschichte (Frankfurt: Frankfurter Verlagsanstalt, 1924).

Anderson, Benedict. *Imagined Communities*, revised edn (New York and London: Verso, 1991).

Apfel, Erwin, and Carl Dahlhaus. *Studien zur Theorie und Geschichte der musikalischen Rhythmik und Metrik*, 2 vols. (Munich: Dr. Emil Katzbichler, 1974).

Arens, Katherine. *Structures of Knowing: Psychologies of the Nineteenth Century* (Dordrecht: Klüver, 1989).

Arndt, Ernst Moritz. *Werke*, ed. Heinrich Meisner, 14 vols. (Leipzig: Karl Fr. Pfau, 1892–1909).

Arntz, Michael. '"Nehmen Sie Riemann ernst?": Zur Bedeutung Hugo Riemanns für die Emanzipation der Musik', in Tatjana Böhme-Mehner and Klaus Mehner, eds., *Hugo Riemann (1849–1919)*, pp. 9–16.

Hugo Riemann (1849–1919): Leben, Werk und Wirkung (Cologne: Concerto-Verlag, 1999).

Bent, Ian. *Music Analysis in the Nineteenth Century*, 2 vols. (Cambridge: Cambridge University Press, 1995).

Berlin, Isaiah. *Vico and Herder: Two Essays in the History of Ideas* (London: Hogarth Press, 1976).

Besseler, Heinrich. 'Das musikalische Hören der Neuzeit', in *Bericht über die Verhandlungen der (königlich) Sächsischen Akademie der Wissenschaften zu Leipzig, philologisch-historisch Klasse* 104 (1959), pp. 1–11.

Bibliography

Blasius, Leslie D. 'Nietzsche, Riemann, Wagner: When Music Lies', in Suzannah Clark and Alexander Rehding, eds., *Music Theory and Natural Order from the Renaissance to the Early Twentieth Century* (Cambridge: Cambridge University Press, 2001), pp. 93–107.

Böhme-Mehner, Tatjana, and Klaus Mehner, eds., *Hugo Riemann (1849–1919): Musikwissenschaftler mit Universalanspruch* (Cologne, Weimar, Vienna: Böhlau, 2001).

Boisitz, Barbara. 'Hugo Riemann – Guido Adler: Zwei Konzepte von Musikwissenschaft vor dem Hintergrund geisteswissenschaftlicher Methodendiskussionen um 1900', in Tatjana Böhme-Mehner and Klaus Mehner, eds., *Hugo Riemann (1849–1919)*, pp. 17–29.

Borchmeyer, Dieter. 'Anwalt der kleinen Terz: Goethe und die Musik', in Thomas Daniel Schlee, ed., *Beethoven, Goethe und Europa: Almanach zum Internationalen Beethovenfest Bonn 1999* (Laaber: Laaber-Verlag, 1999), pp. 41–62.

Boyd, Richard. 'Realism, Approximate Truth and Philosophical Method', in David Papineau, ed., *The Philosophy of Science* (Oxford: Oxford University Press, 1996), pp. 215–55.

Brendel, Franz. 'Zur Anbahnung einer Verständigung', *Neue Zeitschrift für Musik* 50 (1859), pp. 265–73.

'Zur Eröffnung des 50. Bandes der Zeitschrift', *Neue Zeitschrift für Musik* 50 (1859), pp. 1–2.

Geschichte der Musik in Italien, Deutschland und Frankreich, 4th edn (Leipzig: Breitkopf und Härtel, 1867).

Bruckmüller, Ernst. 'The National Identity of the Austrians', trans. Nicholas T. Parsons, in Mikuláš Teich and Roy Porter, eds., *The National Question in Europe in Historical Context* (Cambridge: Cambridge University Press, 1993), pp. 196–227.

Bujić, Bojan, ed. *Music in European Thought 1851–1912* (Cambridge: Cambridge University Press, 1988).

Burnham, Scott. 'Method and Motivation in Hugo Riemann's History of Music Theory', *Music Theory Spectrum* 14 (1992), pp. 1–14.

'Musical and Intellectual Values: Interpreting the History of Tonal Theory', *Current Musicology* 53 (1993), pp. 76–88.

Beethoven Hero (Princeton: Princeton University Press, 1995).

Burstayn, Shai. 'Gerald of Wales and the Sumer Canon', *Journal of Musicology* 2 (1983), pp. 135–50.

Cadenbach, Rainer. 'Wie Hugo Riemann sich von Carl Fuchs dabei helfen ließ, "das rettende Wort" einmal bei Nietzsche zu finden: Zu einer vergessenen Kontroverse über künstlerisches Schaffen und "Phrasierung"', in Tatjana Böhme-Mehner and Klaus Mehner, eds., *Hugo Riemann (1849–1919)*, pp. 69–91.

Cahan, David. 'Helmholtz and the Civilizing Power of Science', in *Hermann von Helmholtz and the Foundations of Nineteenth-Century Science* (Berkeley and Los Angeles: University of California Press, 1993), pp. 559–601.

Calinescu, Matei. *Five Faces of Modernity* (Durham, NC: Duke University Press, 1987).

Bibliography

Capellen, Georg. 'Die Unmöglichkeit und Ueberflüssigkeit der dualistischen Molltheorie Riemann's', *Neue Zeitschrift für Musik* 68 (1901), pp. 529–31, 541–3, 553–5, 569–72, 585–7, 601–3, 617–19.

'Exotische Rhythmik, Melodik und Tonalität als Wegweiser zu einer neuen Kunstentwicklung', *Die Musik* 6 (1906/07), pp. 216–27.

Caplin, William. 'Tonal Function and Metrical Accent: A Historical Perspective', *Music Theory Spectrum* 5 (1983), pp. 1–14.

Cassirer, Ernst. *Geist und Leben* (Leipzig: Reclam Leipzig, 1993).

Chamberlain, Houston Stewart. *Die Grundlagen des neunzehnten Jahrhunderts*, 2 vols., 3rd edn (Munich: Bruckmann, 1901).

Christensen, Dieter. 'Erich M. von Hornbostel, Carl Stumpf, and the Institutionalization of Comparative Musicology', in Philip V. Bohlman and Bruno Nettl, eds., *Comparative Musicology and Anthropology of Music: Essays in the History of Ethnomusicology* (Chicago: University of Chicago Press, 1991), pp. 201–9.

'Hugo Riemann and the Shaping of Musicology: An Ethnomusicological Perspective', in Christoph-Hellmut Mahling and Ruth Seibers, eds., *Festschrift Walter Wiora zum 90. Geburtstag* (Tutzing: H. Schneider, 1997), pp. 34–43.

Christensen, Thomas. *Rameau and Musical Thought in the Enlightenment* (Cambridge: Cambridge University Press, 1993).

Chua, Daniel K. L. *Absolute Music and the Construction of Meaning* (Cambridge: Cambridge University Press, 1999).

Clark, Suzannah. 'From Nature to Logic in Schubert's Instrumental Music', Ph.D. dissertation (Princeton University, 1997).

'Seduced by Notation: Oettingen's Topography of the Major-minor System', in Suzannah Clark and Alexander Rehding, eds., *Music Theory and Natural Order from the Renaissance to the Early Twentieth Century* (Cambridge: Cambridge University Press, 2001), pp. 161–80.

'Terzverwandtschaften in der "Unvollendeten" von Schubert und der "Waldstein"-Sonate von Beethoven – Kennzeichen des neunzehnten Jahrhunderts und theoretisches Problem', *Schubert durch die Brille* 20 (1998), pp. 122–30.

Clark, Suzannah, and Alexander Rehding, eds. *Music Theory and Natural Order from the Renaissance to the Early Twentieth Century* (Cambridge: Cambridge University Press, 2001).

Cone, Edward T. *Musical Form and Musical Performance* (New York: Norton, 1968).

Cook, Nicholas. 'Schenker's Theory of Music as Ethics', *Journal of Musicology* 7 (1989), pp. 415–439.

'Epistemologies of Music Theory', in Thomas Christensen, ed., *The Cambridge History of Western Music Theory* (Cambridge: Cambridge University Press, 2002), pp. 78–105.

Craig, Gordon A. *German History 1866–1945* (Oxford: Oxford University Press, 1981).

Dahlhaus, Carl. 'Terminologisches zum Begriff der harmonischen Funktion', *Die Musikforschung* 28 (1975), pp. 197–202.

'Über den Begriff der tonalen Funktion', in Martin Vogel, ed., *Beiträge zur Musiktheorie des neunzehnten Jahrhunderts* (Regensburg: Gustav Bosse, 1966), pp. 93–102.

'War Zarlino Dualist?', *Die Musikforschung* 10 (1957), pp. 286–90.

'Was heißt "Geschichte der Musiktheorie"?', in Frieder Zaminer, ed., *Ideen zu einer Geschichte der Musiktheorie* (Darmstadt: Wissenschaftliche Buchgesellschaft, 1985), pp. 8–39.

Die Musiktheorie im 18. und 19. Jahrhundert; Erster Teil: Grundzüge einer Systematik (Darmstadt: Wissenschaftliche Buchgesellschaft, 1984).

Die Musiktheorie im 18. und 19. Jahrhundert; Zweiter Teil: Deutschland, ed. Ruth E. Müller (Darmstadt: Wissenschaftliche Buchgesellschaft, 1989).

Foundations of Music History, trans. J. Bradford Robinson (Cambridge: Cambridge University Press, 1983).

Klassische und Romantische Musikästhetik (Laaber: Laaber-Verlag, 1988).

Studies on the Origin of Harmonic Tonality, tr. Robert O. Gjerdingen (Princeton: Princeton University Press, 1990).

The Idea of Absolute Music, trans. Roger Lustig (Chicago and London: University of Chicago Press, 1989).

Dahlhaus, Carl, and Lars Ulrich Abraham. *Melodielehre* (Cologne: Heinz Gerig, 1972).

Deathridge, John. 'Germany: the Special Path', in Jim Samson, ed., *The Late Romantic Era from the Mid-nineteenth Century to World War I* (Basingstoke: Macmillan, 1991), pp. 50–73.

Einstein, Alfred. 'Hugo Riemann zum 70. Geburtstag', *Zeitschrift für Musikwissenschaft* 1 (1919), pp. 569–70.

Ellis, Alexander J. 'On the Musical Scales of Various Nations', *Journal of the Society of Arts* 33 (1885), pp. 485–527.

Falck, Robert. 'Emancipation of the Dissonance', *Journal of the Arnold Schoenberg Institute* 6 (1982), pp. 106–11.

Fechner, Gustav Theodor. *Elemente der Psychophysik*, 2 vols. (Leipzig: Breitkopf und Härtel, 1860).

Vorschule der Aesthetik, 2nd edn (Leipzig: Breitkopf und Härtel, 1897).

Fichte, Johann Gottlieb. *Reden an die deutsche Nation*, intro. Reinhardt Lauth (reprint Hamburg: Felix Meiner, 1978).

Fleischer, Otto. 'Ein Kapitel vergleichender Musikwissenschaft', *Sammelbände der Internationalen Musikgesellschaft* 1 (1899/1900), pp. 1–53.

Forkel, Johann Nikolaus. *Allgemeine Geschichte der Musik*, 2 vols. (Leipzig: Schwickert, 1788).

Forster, Wolf von. 'Heutige Praktiken im Harmonielehreunterricht an Musikhochschulen und Konservatorien', in Martin Vogel, ed., *Beiträge zur Musiktheorie des neunzehnten Jahrhunderts* (Regensburg: Gustav Bosse, 1966), pp. 257–79.

Fortlage, Carl. *Das musikalische System der Griechen in seiner Urgestalt: aus den Tonleitern des Alypius zum ersten Male entwickelt* (Leipzig 1847; reprint Amsterdam: Schippers, 1964).

Frantz, Constantin. *Die Wiederherstellung Deutschlands* (Berlin: Ferdinand Schneider, 1865).

Fukac, Jiri. 'Hugo Riemann, Guido Adler und ihr Einfluß auf die Pardigmenwechsel der Musikwissenschaft', in Tatjana Böhme-Mehner and Klaus Mehner, eds., *Hugo Riemann (1849–1919)*, pp. 59–68.

Gellner, Ernest. *Nations and Nationalism* (Oxford: Blackwell, 1983).

Relativism and the Social Sciences (Cambridge: Cambridge University Press, 1985).

Giddens, Anthony. *Modernity and Self-Identity* (Cambridge: Polity Press, 1991).

Goethe, Johann Wolfgang von. *Sämtliche Werke, Briefe, Tagebücher und Gespräche*, ed. Dieter Borchmeyer et al., 40 vols. (Frankfurt/Main: Deutscher Klassiker-Verlag, 1985–99).

Gosman, Alan. 'Rameau and Zarlino: Polemics in the *Traité de l'harmonie*', *Music Theory Spectrum* 22 (2000), pp. 44–59.

Grimm, Hartmut. '"Ästhetik von unten" – Hugo Riemanns Konzept der Musikästhetik', in Tatjana Böhme-Mehner and Klaus Mehner, eds., *Hugo Riemann (1849–1919)*, pp. 117–30.

Gurlitt, Willibald. 'Hugo Riemann (1849–1919)', *Veröffentlichungen der Akademie der Wissenschaften und der Literatur, Mainz: Abhandlungen der geistes- und sozialwissenschaftlichen Klasse* 25 (1950), pp. 1865–1901.

'Hugo Riemann und die Musikgeschichte', *Zeitschrift für Musikwissenschaft* 1 (July 1919), pp. 571–87.

Habermas, Jürgen. *The Philosophical Discourse of Modernity*, trans. Frederick G. Lawrence (Cambridge, Mass.: MIT Press, 1987).

Haken, Boris von. 'Brahms und Bruckner', *Musiktheorie* 10 (1995), pp. 149–57.

Handschin, Jacques. *Der Toncharakter*, intro. Rudolf Stephan (reprint Darmstadt: Wissenschaftliche Buchgesellschaft, 1995).

Harrison, Daniel. *Harmonic Function in Chromatic Music* (Chicago and London: University of Chicago Press, 1994).

Hauptmann, Moritz. *Die Natur der Harmonik und Metrik: Zur Theorie der Musik* (Leipzig: Breitkopf und Härtel, 1853); English trans. and ed. William E. Heathcote as *The Nature of Harmony and Metre* (London: Swan Sonnenschein, 1893; reprint New York: Da Capo Press, 1991).

Hayes, Paul. 'France and Germany: Belle Epoque and Kaiserzeit', in Paul Hayes, ed., *Themes in Modern European History 1890–1914* (London: Routledge, 1992), pp. 24–54.

Heinz, Rudolf. *Geschichtsbegriff und Wissenschaftscharakter in der Musikwissenschaft in der zweiten Hälfte des 19. Jahrhunderts* (Regensburg: Gustav Bosse, 1968).

Helmholtz, Hermann von. *On the Sensations of Tone*, trans. Alexander J. Ellis (London, 1885; reprint New York: Dover, 1954).

Henseler, Theodor A. *Das musikalische Bonn* (Bonn: n. p., 1959).

Herder, Johann Gottfried. *Sämmtliche Werke*, ed. Bernhard Suphan, 33 vols. (Berlin: n. p., 1877–1913).

Heuß, Alfred. 'Über die Dynamik der Mannheimer Schule', in Carl Mennicke, ed., *Riemann-Festschrift* (Leipzig: Max Hesse, 1909), pp. 433–55.

'Zum Thema "Mannheimer Vorhalt"', *Zeitschrift der Internationalen Musikgesellschaft* 8 (1908), pp. 273–80.

Hobsbawm, Eric J. *Nations and Nationalism since 1780*, 2nd edn (Cambridge: Cambridge University Press, 1990).

Hohendahl, Peter Uwe. *Literarische Kultur im Zeitalter des Liberalismus 1830–1870* (Munich: C. H. Beck, 1985).

Hornbostel, Ernst Moritz von. 'Die Probleme der vergleichenden Musikwissenschaft', *Zeitschrift der Internationalen Musikgesellschaft* 7 (1905), pp. 85–97.

Humboldt, Wilhelm von. *Über die Verschiedenheit der menschlichen Sprachbaues und ihren Einfluss auf die geistige Entwicklung des Menschengeschlechts*, ed. Andreas Flintner and Klaus Giel, 8th edn (Darmstadt: Wissenschaftliche Buchgesellschaft, 1996); trans. into English by Peter Heath as *On Language*, intro. Hans Aarsleff (Cambridge: Cambridge University Press, 1988).

Hutchinson, John. *The Dynamics of Cultural Nationalism* (London: Allen and Unwin, 1987).

Hyer, Brian. 'Reimag(in)ing Riemann', *Journal of Music Theory* 39 (1995), pp. 101–36.

'The Concept of Function in Riemann', unpublished paper (AMS/SEM/SMT Meeting Oakland, Calif., 1990).

'Tonal Intuitions in *Tristan und Isolde*', Ph.D. dissertation (Yale University, 1989).

Imig, Renate. *Systeme der Funktionsbezeichnung seit Hugo Riemann* (Düsseldorf: Verlag der Gesellschaft zur Förderung der systematischen Musikwissenschaft, 1971).

James, Harold. *A German Identity 1770–1990*, revised edn (London: Weidenfeld and Nicolson, 1990).

Jardine, Nicholas. *The Scenes of Inquiry* (Oxford: Clarendon Press, 1991).

John, Eckhard. *Musikbolschewismus: Die Politisierung der Musik in Deutschland 1918–38* (Stuttgart and Weimar: Metzler, 1994).

Jorgenson, Dale A. 'A Résumé of Harmonic Dualism', *Music and Letters* 44 (1963), pp. 31–42.

Moritz Hauptmann of Leipzig (Lewiston, NY: E. Mellen Press, 1986).

Kahl, Willy. 'Der "obskure" Riemann: Ein Brief F. Chrysanders', in *Studien zur Musikgeschichte des Rheinlandes* (Cologne: Arno Verlag, 1956), pp. 54–6.

Kittler, Friedrich. *Gramophone, Film, Typewriter*, trans. Geoffrey Winthrop-Young and Michael Wutz (Palo Alto, Calif.: Stanford University Press, 1999).

Klumpenhouwer, Henry. 'Dualistic Tonal Space and Transformation in Nineteenth-Century Musical Thought', in Thomas Christensen, ed., *The Cambridge History of Western Music Theory* (Cambridge: Cambridge University Press, 2002), pp. 456–76.

'Structural Relations between Riemann's Function Theory and his Dualism', unpublished article.

Knight, David. *The Age of Science* (Oxford: Blackwell, 1986).

Koch, Heinrich Christoph. *Versuch einer Anleitung zur Composition*, 4 vols. (Leipzig: Adam Friedrich Böhme, 1787–93; reprint Hildesheim: Georg Olms, 1969).

Kohn, Hans. *Prelude to the Nation States: The French and German Experience 1789–1815* (Princeton, New Jersey: D. van Nostrand, 1967).

Kopp, David. 'A Comprehensive Theory of Chromatic Mediant Relations in Mid-Nineteenth-Century Music', Ph.D. dissertation (Brandeis University, 1995).

Koselleck, Reinhart. 'Zur historisch-politischen Semantik asymmetrischer Gegenbegriffe', in Harald Weinrich, ed., *Positionen der Negativität* (Munich: Wilhelm Fink, 1975), pp. 65–105; reprinted (in excerpts) in Michael Jeismann and Henning Ritter, eds., *Grenzfälle: Über alten und neuen Nationalismus* (Leipzig: Reclam Leipzig, 1993), pp. 174–93.

Kragh, Helge. *An Introduction to the Historiography of Science* (Cambridge: Cambridge University Press, 1987).

Krebs, Harald. *Fantasy Pieces: Metric Dissonance in the Music of Robert Schumann* (New York: Oxford University Press, 1999).

Kuhn, Thomas. *The Structure of Scientific Revolutions*, 2nd edn (Chicago and London: University of Chicago Press, 1970).

Kurth, Ernst. *Die Voraussetzungen der theoretischen Harmonik*, afterword by Carl Dahlhaus (Munich: Dr. Emil Katzbichler, 1973).

La Mara C. [pseudonym: Maria Lipsius] *Briefe hervorragender Zeitgenossen an Franz Liszt*, 3 vols. (Leipzig: Breitkopf und Härtel, 1895–1904).

Langbehn, Julius. [pseudonym: 'Ein Deutscher'] *Rembrandt als Erzieher*, 42nd edn (Leipzig: n. p., 1893).

Larsen, Jens Peter. 'On the Importance of the "Mannheim School"', in *Handel, Haydn and the Viennese Classical Style* (Ann Arbor, London: University of Michigan Press, 1988), pp. 263–8.

Laurencin, Franz P., Graf. 'Erklärende Erläuterung und musikalisch-theoretische Begründung der durch die neuesten Kunstschöpfungen bewirkten Umgestaltung und Weiterbildung der Harmonik', *Neue Zeitschrift für Musik* 54 (1861), pp. 4–5, 9–14, 21–4, 29–34, 41–3, 53–5, 61–4.

Leichtentritt, Hugo. *Music, History and Ideas* (Cambridge, Mass.: Harvard University Press, 1947).

Lederer, Victor. *Über Heimat und Ursprung der mehrstimmigen Tonkunst* (Leipzig: C. F. W. Siegel, 1906).

Lewin, David. 'A Formal Theory of Generalized Tonal Functions', *Journal of Music Theory* 26 (1982), pp. 23–100.

'Amfortas's Prayer to Titurel and the Role of D in *Parsifal*: The Tonal Spaces of the Drama and the Enharmonic C♭/B', *Nineteenth-Century Music* 7 (1984), pp. 336–49.

Generalized Musical Intervals and Transformations (New Haven: Yale University Press, 1987).

Lichtenstein, A. 'Lotze und Wundt: Eine vergleichende philosophische Studie', *Berner Studien zur Philosophie und ihrer Geschichte* 24 (1900), pp. 1–80.

Lotze, Hermann R. *Grundzüge der Logik und Encyclopädie der Philosophie* (Leipzig: S. Hirzel, 1883).

System der Philosophie; Erster Theil: Logik, 2nd edn (Leipzig: S. Hirzel, 1880).

System der Philosophie; Zweiter Theil: Metaphysik, 2nd edn (Leipzig: S. Hirzel, 1884).

Louis, Rudolf. *Der Widerspruch in der Musik* (Leipzig: Breitkopf und Härtel, 1893).

Die deutsche Musik der Gegenwart (Munich and Leipzig: Georg Müller, 1909).

Mayer, Verena. *Gottlob Frege* (Munich: C. H. Beck, 1996).

Mehner, Klaus. 'Hugo Riemanns "Ideen zu einer 'Lehre von den Tonvorstellungen'"', in Tatjana Böhme-Mehner and Klaus Mehner, eds., *Hugo Riemann (1849–1919)*, pp. 49–57.

Meinecke, Friedrich. *Weltbürgertum und Nationalstaat* (Munich: R. Oldenburg, 1962).

Mennicke, Carl. 'Eine biographische Skizze nebst einem Verzeichnis seiner Werke', *Riemann-Festschrift*, ed Carl Mennicke (Leipzig: Max Hesse, 1909), pp. vii–xxviii.

Mickelsen, William C. *Hugo Riemann's Theory of Harmony, and History of Music Theory, Part III* (Lincoln, Nebraska: University of Nebraska Press, 1977).

Mooney, M. Kevin. 'The "Table of Relations" and Music Psychology in Hugo Riemann's Harmonic Theory', Ph.D. dissertation (Columbia University, 1996).

Moos, Paul. *Moderne Musikästhetik in Deutschland* (Leipzig: Horst Seemann Nachfolger, 1902).

Philosophie der Musik (reprint of 2nd edn, Hildesheim: Georg Olms, 1975).

Moser, Hans Joachim. 'Die harmonischen Funktionen in der tonalen Kadenz', *Zeitschrift für Musikwissenschaft* 1 (1919), pp. 515–23.

Motte-Haber, Helga de la, and Carl Dahlhaus. *Systematische Musikwissenschaft* (Wiesbaden: Akademische Verlagsgesellschaft Athenaion, 1982).

Münnich, Richard. 'Von [der] Entwicklung der Riemannschen Harmonielehre und ihrem Verhältnis zu Oettingen und Stumpf', in Carl Mennicke, ed., *Riemann-Festschrift* (Leipzig: Max Hesse, 1909), pp. 60–76.

Niemöller, Klaus Wolfgang. 'Hugo Riemann und die "exotische Musik": Zum Konflikt von musikalischem Eurozentrismus und Weltmusik', in Klaus Wolfgang Niemöller, Uwe Pätzold and Chung Kyo-Chul, eds., *Lux Oriente: Begegnungen der Kulturen in der Musikforschung* (Kassel: Gustav Bosse, 1995), pp. 467–75.

Nietzsche, Friedrich. *Gesammelte Werke*, ed. Karl Schlechta, 3 vols. (Darmstadt: Wissenschaftliche Buchgesellschaft, 1997).

Nowak, Adolf. 'Wandlungen des Begriffs "Musikalische Logik" bei Hugo Riemann', in Tatjana Böhme-Mehner and Klaus Mehner, eds., *Hugo Riemann (1849–1919)*, pp. 37–48.

Oettingen, Arthur von. *Das duale Harmoniesystem* (Leipzig: C. F. W. Siegel, 1913).

Harmoniesystem in dualer Entwickelung (Dorpat: W. Glässer, 1866).

Olender, Maurice. *The Languages of Paradise*, trans. Arthur Goldhammer (Cambridge, Mass.: Harvard University Press, 1992).

Pedersen, Holger. *Linguistic Science in the Nineteenth Century*, trans. John W. Spargo (Cambridge, Mass.: Harvard University Press, 1931).

Polak, Abraham J. *Hamonisierungen indischer, türkischer und japanischer Musik* (Leipzig: Breitkopf und Härtel, 1905).

Rameau, Jean-Philippe. *Génération harmonique* (Paris, 1737), ed. E. Jacobi (reprint New York: American Institute of Musicology, 1968).

Treatise on Harmony, trans. and ed. Philip Gossett (New York: Dover, 1971).

Rehding, Alexander. 'The Quest for the Origins of Music in Germany circa 1900', *Journal of the American Musicological Society* 53 (2000), pp. 345–85.

'Trial Scenes at Nuremberg', *Music Analysis* 20 (2001), pp. 239–67.

Reinecke, Hans Peter. 'Hugo Riemanns Beobachtung von "Divisionstönen" und die neueren Anschauungen zur Tonhöhenwahrnehmung', in Wilfried

Brennecke and Hans Haase, eds., *Hans Albrecht in Memoriam* (Kassel: Bärenreiter, 1962), pp. 232–41.

Renan, Ernest. *Qu'est-ce qu'une nation?* (Paris: Ancienne Maison Michel Lévy Frères, 1882).

Revers, Peter. 'Zur Theorie und Ästhetik der Harmonisierung exotischer Melodien im frühen 20. Jahrhundert', *Musiktheorie* 7 (1992), pp. 3–24.

Riemann, Hugo [pseudonym: Hugibert Ries]. 'Aesthetische Essays über das Dreikunstwerk', *Neue Zeitschrift für Musik* 66 (1870), pp. 93–5, 197–9, 320–1.

'Das chromatische Tonsystem', in *Präludien und Studien* (reprint: Hildesheim: Georg Olms, 1967), vol. 1, pp. 183–219.

'Das Problem des harmonischen Dualismus', *Neue Zeitschrift für Musik* 51 (1905), pp. 3–5, 23–6, 43–6, 67–70.

'Degeneration und Regeneration in der Musik', *Max Hesses deutscher Musikerkalender* 23 (1908), pp. 136–8.

'Der gegenwärtige Stand der musikalischen Aesthetik', in *Präludien und Studien* (reprint Hildesheim: Georg Olms, 1967), vol. 2, pp. 46–55.

'Die Musik seit Wagners Heimgang: Ein Totentanz (1897)', in *Präludien und Studien* (reprint Hildesheim: Georg Olms, 1967), vol. 2, pp. 33–41.

'Die Natur der Harmonik', *Waldersees Sammlung musikalischer Vorträge* 4 (1882), pp. 159–90.

'Die Neugestaltung der Harmonielehre', *Musikalisches Wochenblatt* 22 (1891), pp. 513–14, 529–31, 541–3.

'Die objective Existenz der Untertöne in der Schallwelle', *Allgemeine deutsche Musikzeitung* 2 (1875), pp. 205–6, 213–15.

'Ein vergessener Großmeister', *Max Hesses deutscher Musikerkalender* 18 (1903), pp. 139–41.

'Exotische Musik', *Max Hesses deutscher Musikerkalender* (1906), pp. 135–7.

'Hie Wagner! Hie Schumann!', in *Präludien und Studien* (reprint Hildesheim: Georg Olms, 1967), vol. 3, pp. 204–14.

'Ideen zu einer "Lehre von den Tonvorstellungen"', *Jahrbuch der Musikbibliothek Peters* 21/22 (1914/15), pp. 1–26.

[pseudonym: Hugibert Ries]. 'Musikalische Logik', in *Präludien und Studien* (reprint Hildesheim: Georg Olms, 1976), vol. 3, pp. 1–22.

'Neue Beiträge zu einer Lehre von den Tonvorstellungen', *Jahrbuch der Musikbibliothek Peters* 23 (1916), pp. 1–21.

'Spontane Phantasietätigkeit und verstandesmäßige Arbeit in der tonkünstlerischen Produktion', *Jahrbuch der Musikbibliothek Peters* 16 (1909), pp. 33–46.

'Stamitz – oder Monn?', *Blätter für Haus- und Kirchenmusik* 9 (1907/08), pp. 97, 113.

'Ueber Japanische Musik', *Musikalisches Wochenblatt* 33 (1902), pp. 209–10, 229–31, 245–6, 257–9, 273–4, 289–90.

'Wohin steuern wir?', in *Präludien und Studien* (reprint Hildesheim: Georg Olms, 1967), vol. 2, pp. 42–5.

'Zur Theorie von Konsonanz und Dissonanz', in *Präludien und Studien* (reprint Hildesheim: Georg Olms, 1967), vol. 3, pp. 31–46.

Allgemeine Musiklehre: Handbuch der Musik, 8th edn (Berlin: Max Hesse, 1922).

Catechism of Musical Aesthetics, trans. Hans Bewerunge (London: Augener, 1895).

Die Elemente der musikalischen Aesthetik (Berlin and Stuttgart: W. Spemann, 1900).

Folkloristische Tonalitätsstudien (Leipzig: Breitkopf und Härtel, 1916).

Geschichte der Musik seit Beethoven (1800–1900) (Leipzig and Stuttgart: W. Spemann, 1901).

Geschichte der Musiktheorie, 2nd edn (Berlin: Max Hesse, 1921; reprint Hildesheim: Georg Olms, 1990).

Große Kompositionslehre, 3 vols. (Stuttgart: W. Spemann, 1902–13).

Grundriß der Musikwissenschaft (Leipzig: Quelle und Meyer, 1908).

Handbuch der Akustik (Musikwissenschaft), 3rd edn (Berlin: Max Hesse, 1921).

Handbuch der Fugenkomposition, 3 vols., 8th edn (Berlin: Max Hesse, n.d).

Handbuch der Harmonielehre, 6th edn (Leipzig: Breitkopf und Härtel, 1917).

Handbuch der Musikgeschichte, 4 vols. (Leipzig: Breitkopf und Härtel, 1904–13).

Ludwig van Beethovens sämtliche Klavier-Solosonaten, 3 vols., 2nd edn (Berlin: Max Hesse, 1920).

Musikalische Syntaxis (Leipzig: Breitkopf und Härtel, 1877; reprint Niederwalluf: Dr. Martin Sändig, 1971).

Musikgeschichte in Beispielen, ed. Arnold Schering, 4th edn (Leipzig: Breitkopf und Härtel, 1929).

Musik-Lexikon, 3rd edn (Leipzig: Max Hesse, 1887).

Musik-Lexikon, 4th edn (Leipzig: Max Hesse, 1894).

Musiklexikon, 5th edn (Leipzig: Max Hesse, 1900).

Musiklexikon, 6th edn (Leipzig: Max Hesse, 1905).

Musiklexikon, 7th edn (Leipzig: Max Hesse, 1909).

Neue Schule der Melodik (Hamburg: Karl Gradener und J. F. Richter, 1883).

Skizze einer neuen Methode der Harmonielehre (Leipzig: Breitkopf und Härtel, 1880).

Studien zur Geschichte der Notenschrift (Leipzig: Breitkopf und Härtel, 1878).

Systematische Modulationslehre (Hamburg: J. F. Richter, 1887).

Über das musikalische Hören, Dr. phil. dissertation (Göttingen University, 1873), publ. as *Musikalische Logik: Hauptzüge der physiologischen und psychologischen Begründung unseres Musiksystems* (Leipzig: C. F. Kahnt, 1874).

Vereinfachte Harmonielehre (London: Augener, 1893).

Wie hören wir Musik?: Grundlinien der Musikästhetik, 6th edn (Berlin: Max Hesse, 1923).

Riemann, Hugo, ed. *Sechs originale chinesische und japanische Melodien* (Leipzig: Breitkopf und Härtel, 1902).

    ed. *Sinfonien der Pfalzbayerischen Schule (Mannheimer Schule)*, 3 vols. (Leipzig: Breitkopf und Härtel, 1902–7).

Robertson, Alec, and Denis Stevens, eds., *The Pelican History of Music*, 4 vols. (Harmondsworth: Penguin, 1960–8).

Rosen, Charles. *The Classical Style*, revised edn (London: Faber and Faber, 1976).

Rothstein, William. 'Beethoven with and without *Kunstgepräng*': Metric Ambiguity Reconsidered', in *Beethoven Forum* 4 (Lincoln, Nebraska: University of Nebraska Press, 1995), pp. 165–93.

Rummenhöller, Peter. 'Moritz Hauptmann, der Begründer einer transzendental-dialektischen Musiktheorie', in Martin Vogel, ed., *Beiträge zur Musiktheorie im 19. Jahrhundert* (Regensburg: Gustav Bosse, 1966), pp. 11–36.

Moritz Hauptmann als Theoretiker: eine Studie zum erkenntniskritischen Theoriebegriff in der Musik (Wiesbaden: Breitkopf und Härtel, 1963).

Musiktheoretisches Denken im 19. Jahrhundert (Regensburg: Gustav Bosse, 1967).

Sadie, Stanley and Alison Latham, eds., *The Cambridge Music Guide* (Cambridge: Cambridge University Press, 1990).

Santayana, George. *Lotze's System of Philosophy*, ed. Paul G. Kuntz (Bloomington, London: Indiana University Press, 1971).

Schaffer, Simon. 'Glass Works', in I. Bernhard Cohen and Richard S. Westfall, eds., *Newton: Texts, Backgrounds, Commentaries* (New York: Norton, 1995), pp. 202–17.

Schafhäutl, Karl von. 'Moll und Dur', *Allgemeine Musikalische Zeitung* 13 (1878), cols. 1–6, 22–7, 38–42, 53–7, 69–73, 87–92, 101–5, 115–20, 132–7.

Schama, Simon. *Landscape and Memory* (London: Fontana, 1996).

Schenker, Heinrich. *Der freie Satz*, 2nd edn (Vienna: Universal Edition, 1956).

Der Tonwille, intro. Hellmut Federhofer (reprint Hildesheim: Georg Olms, 1990).

Harmonielehre (reprint Vienna: Universal Edition, 1978); English trans. by Elizabeth Mann Borgese as *Harmony* (Cambridge, Mass.: MIT Press, 1973).

Scherber, Ferdinand. 'Degeneration und Regeneration', *Neue Musikzeitung* 29 (1908), pp. 233–6.

Schlee, Thomas Daniel. 'Zelter hatte doch recht: Parerga zur großen Terz', in Thomas Daniel Schlee, ed., *Beethoven, Goethe und Europa: Almanach zum Internationalen Beethovenfest Bonn 1999* (Laaber: Laaber-Verlag, 1999), pp. 63–8.

Schlegel, Friedrich. *Sprache und Weisheit der Indier*, ed. E. F. K. Koerner, intro. and trans. J. Peter Maher (Amsterdam: John Benjamins, 1977).

Schmalzriedt, Siegfried. 'Kadenz', in Hans Heinrich Eggebrecht and Albrecht Riethmüller, eds., *Handwörterbuch der musikalischen Terminologie* (Stuttgart: Franz Steiner, n.d.).

Schnädelbach, Herbert. *Philosophy in Germany 1831–1933*, trans. Eric Matthews (Cambridge: Cambridge University Press, 1984).

Schneider, Albrecht. *Analogie und Rekonstruktion* (Bonn: Verlag für systematische Musikwissenschaft, 1984).

Schoenberg, Arnold. *Style and Idea*, ed. Leonard Stein, trans. Leo Black (London: Faber and Faber, 1975).

Theory of Harmony, trans. Roy E. Carter (London: Faber and Faber, 1978).

Schumann, Andreas. 'Glorifizierung und Enttäuschung: Die Reichsgründung in der Bewertung der Literaturgeschichtsschreibung', in Klaus Amann and Karl Wagner, eds., *Literatur und Nation: Die Gründung des Deutschen Reiches 1871 in der deutschsprachigen Literatur* (Vienna: Böhlau, 1996), pp. 31–43.

Sechter, Simon. *Die Grundsätze der musikalischen Komposition*, 4 vols. (Leipzig: Breitkopf und Härtel, 1853–54).

Seidel, Elmar. 'Die Harmonielehre Hugo Riemanns', in Martin Vogel, ed., *Studien zur Musiktheorie des neunzehnten Jahrhunderts* (Regensburg: Gustav Bosse, 1966), pp. 39–92.

Seidel, Wilhelm. 'Riemann und Beethoven', in Tatjana Böhme-Mehner and Klaus Mehner, eds., *Hugo Riemann (1849–1919)*, pp. 139–51.

Seidl, Arthur. *Das Erhabene in der Musik: Prolegomena zu einer Ästhetik der Tonkunst*, Inaugural Dissertation (Regensburg: M. Warner, 1887).

Shigihara, Susanne. *'Die Konfusion in der Musik': Felix Draesekes Kampfschrift von 1906 und die Folgen* (Bonn: Gudrun Schröder, 1990).

Sievers, Gerhard. 'Max Regers Kompositionen in ihrem Verhältnis zu der Theorie Hugo Riemanns', *Die Musikforschung* 3 (1950), pp. 212–23.

Die Grundlagen Hugo Riemanns bei Max Reger, Dr. phil. dissertation (University of Hamburg, 1949).

Simon, W[alter] M. *European Positivism in the Nineteenth Century* (Port Washington, NY, and London: Kennikat Press, 1972).

Smith, Anthony D. 'Chosen Peoples: Why Ethnic Groups Survive', in J. Hutchinson and A. D. Smith, eds., *Ethnicity* (Oxford: Oxford University Press, 1996), pp. 189–97.

Snarrenberg, Robert. 'Competing Myths: The American Abandonment of Schenker's Organicism', in Anthony Pople, ed., *Theory, Analysis and Meaning in Music* (Cambridge: Cambridge University Press, 1994), pp. 29–56.

Solomon, Maynard. *Beethoven Essays* (Cambridge, Mass.: Harvard University Press, 1988).

Soper, Kate. *What is Nature?* (Oxford: Blackwell, 1995).

Stefan, Rudolf. '"Klassizismus" bei Hugo Riemann', in Tatjana Böhme-Mehner and Klaus Mehner, eds., *Hugo Riemann (1849–1919)*, pp. 131–7.

Stern, Fritz. *The Politics of Cultural Despair* (Berkeley and Los Angeles: University of California Press, 1961).

Stumpf, Carl. 'Konsonanz und Konkordanz: Nebst Bemerkungen über Wohlklang und Wohlgefälligkeit musikalischer Zusammenhänge', *Zeitschrift für Psychologie und Physiologie der Sinnesorgane, 1. Abt., Zeitschrift für Sinnesforschung* 58 (1911), pp. 321–55.

Tonpsychologie, 2 vols. (Leipzig: S. Hirzel, 1883–90).

Taruskin, Richard. 'Chernomor to Kashchei: Harmonic Sorcery; or Stravinsky's "Angle"', *Journal of the American Musicological Society* 38 (1985), pp. 72–142.

Taubmann, Otto. Review of Riemann's *Präludien und Studien*, *Allgemeine Musikzeitung* 23 (1896), pp. 671–2.

Thaler, Lotte. *Organische Form in der Musiktheorie des 19. und frühen 20. Jahrhunderts* (Munich and Salzburg: Dr. Emil Katzbichler, 1983).

Treitler, Leo. 'Gender and Other Dualities in Music History', in Ruth A. Solie, ed., *Musicology and Difference* (Berkeley and Los Angeles: University of California Press, 1993), pp. 23–45.

Ullmann, Hans-Peter. *Das deutsche Kaiserreich* (Darmstadt: Wissenschaftliche Buchgesellschaft, 1997).

Vaihinger, Hans. *Philosophie des Als-Ob* (Berlin: Reuther und Reichard, 1911).

Vogel, Martin. 'Arthur v. Oettingen und der harmonische Dualismus', in Martin Vogel, ed., *Beiträge zur Musiktheorie des neunzehnten Jahrhunderts* (Regensburg: Gustav Bosse, 1966), pp. 103–32.

Wallaschek, Richard. *Primitive Music* (London: Longmans Green, 1893).

Wason, Robert W. 'Progressive Harmonic Theory in the Mid-Nineteenth Century', *Journal of Musicological Research* 8 (1988), pp. 55–90.

Viennese Harmonic Theory from Albrechtsberger to Schenker and Schoenberg (Rochester, NY: University of Rochester Press, 1985).

Wason, Robert W. and Elizabeth West Marvin, 'Riemann's "Ideen zu einer 'Lehre von den Tonvorstellungen' "': An Annotated Translation', *Journal of Music Theory* 36 (1992), pp. 69–116.

Webster, James. *Haydn's 'Farewell' Symphony and the Idea of Classical Style* (Cambridge: Cambridge University Press, 1991).

Weitzmann, Carl. 'Erklärende Erläuterung und musikalisch-theoretische Begründung der durch die neuesten Kunstschöpfungen bewirkten Umgestaltung und Weiterbildung der Harmonik', in *Neue Zeitschrift für Musik* 52 (1860), pp. 1–3, 9–12, 17–20, 29–31, 37–9, 45–6, 53–4, 65–6, 73–5.

Wienke, Gerhardt. *Voraussetzungen der Musikalischen Logik bei Hugo Riemann*, Dr. phil. dissertation (Freiburg/Br., 1952).

Willey, Thomas E. *Back to Kant: The Revival of Kantianism in German Social and Historical Thought 1860–1914* (Detroit, Mich.: Wayne State University Press, 1978).

Williams, Raymond. *Problems in Culture and Materialism*, 2nd edn (New York: Verso, 1997).

Wolff, Eugene K. *The Symphonies of Johann Stamitz* (Utrecht: Bohn, Scheltema & Holkema/The Hague: Martinus Nijhoff, 1981).

Young, Julian. *Nietzsche's Philosophy of Art* (Cambridge: Cambridge University Press, 1992).

Zarlino, Gioseffo. *Le istitutioni harmoniche* (Venice, 1573); English trans. by Claude V. Palisca and Giulio A. Marco as *The Art of Counterpoint* (New Haven, Conn.: Yale University Press, 1968).

Ziegler, Susanne. 'Ernst M. von Hornbostel und das Berliner Phonogramm-Archiv', in Sebastian Klotz, ed., *Vom tönenden Wirbel menschlichen Tuns* (Berlin, Mirow: Schibri-Verlag, 1998), pp. 146–68.

Zimmermann, Petra. '"Erlaubt sich der Komponist einen üblen Scherz?": Fragen an Max Regers Klavierlied *Ein Drängen* (Op. 97, Nr. 3)', *Jahrbuch des Staatlichen Instituts für Musikforschung Preußischer Kulturbesitz* 1999, pp. 137–52.

INDEX

Aalst, J. A. van 173, 175
Abraham, Otto 176–8, 180
Acoustics 2, 8, 15, 17, 20–3, 27, 31–2, 34, 48,
    53, 70, 80, 89–90, 116, 133, 166, 168,
    172, 177–8, 183
Adler, Guido 1, 2, 5, 122, 141–6, 148–9
Aesthetics 2–3, 9–10, 20–1, 27, 31–2, 44, 65,
    87, 89, 108, 121–2, 158–9, 167, 183–5
    bottom-to-top 2, 3, 16 see also Fechner
Anacrusis 73, 198 see also upbeat, metre
Analysis, musical 36–9, 59–61, 68, 73–5,
    162–4 see also music theory, Riemann
Anderson, Benedict 143, 156
'Anonymous 4' 132
Apparent consonance see consonance
Archaeology 18
Aristotle 18
Arndt, Ernst Moritz 127
Arntz, Michael 4
Asymmetrical opposite, see symmetry
Atom 83–5
Auftaktigkeit, see metre
Austria 142–5, 148–9

Bach, Johann Sebastian 40, 43, 114, 152, 162
    The Art of Fugue 65
    Well-Tempered Clavier 65, 162
Baroque 92, 98
Bass
    figured 92, 139
    fundamental 95
Bebel, August 63
Beethoven, Ludwig van 38–40, 61, 65, 110,
    114, 145–6, 147–9, 152, 155, 157, 160,
    162–8, 172
    Scottish folk-song settings 172
    Sonata Op. 10, no. 2 168
    Sonata 'quasi una fantasia' Op. 27, no. 1
        162, 164, 179
    Sonata Op. 54 76
    Sonata Op. 109 148

Symphony no. 9 3
    'Waldstein' Sonata 36–9, 59, 62, 75
Berlin 176
Berlioz, Hector 40–1, 152–6, 158
    Benvenuto Cellini 150, 152
Bielefeld 4
Biography 5–6
Bismarck, Otto von 63, 127
Bohemia 139, 142–3, 147
Bonn 145–6
Boole, George 118
    Algebra 118
Bopp, Franz 119–20
Brendel, Franz 42–3
Bromberg 4
Burnham, Scott 8

Cadence 38, 60, 67–73, 75–8, 80–2, 91, 100,
    103–4, 106–7, 114, 151, 153–5, 172
    interrupted 75, 82
Celts 131
Chamberlain, Houston Stewart 131
    Die Grundlagen des neunzehnten
        Jahrhunderts 131
Chemistry 83
China 173, 176
Chomsky, Noam 121
Chopin, Frédéric 40
    Nocturne in E♭ major 73
Chromaticism 39, 50, 58, 62–3, 66, 104, 106,
    123, 150, 171
    'chromatic movement' 63–4
Classicism 100, 102–3, 110–2, 137–42, 144,
    147–9, 157–8, 185
Cologne 145
    Cathedral 3, 6, 154, 183
Comma, syntonic/Pythagorean 167
Consonance 23, 52–5, 72, 88, 90, 108, 186
    apparent 20, 55, 76, 110, 115, 168, 186
    'concordance' 109
Counterpoint 131–2

Index

Dahlhaus, Carl 28–31, 56, 61, 78–9
Dalton, John 83
Darwinism 93
Decadence 185 *see also* Nietzsche
Degeneration 11, 98, 138, 180
Denkmäler
   Deutscher Tonkunst 142–3, 146–7
   Der Tonkunst in Österreich 142
Dialectics 24–5, 41, 68–71, 78–9, 114
Diatonicism 58, 64, 108, 125, 137, 171
   diatonic scale 50, 97–8, 121–6, 158, 170–2

Discantus (*déchant*) 133–4, 141
Dissonance 23, 52–5, 90, 108, 186
   characteristic dissonances 94–6, 187
   'discordance' 109
   emancipation of 155
Dittersdorf, Karl Ditters von 140
Draeseke, Felix 64, 137
Dualism, harmonic 7–9, 14–20, 22, 26–33,
      35–7, 39, 47–8, 51–5, 60, 65–6, 68, 78–9,
      80–2, 96, 102, 104–7, 109, 111–12,
      132–3, 160, 167–8, 171–2, 176, 178,
      183–4, 188
   vs harmonic function 7–9, 52–4
Dvořák, Antonin
   String Quintet in G major 56

Ear 3, 33, 47, 123, 151, 159
'Economy of imagination' 167
Einstein, Alfred 1, 2, 5, 14
Ellis, Alexander 180
Empiricism 16, 82, 84, 90, 123, 180
England 7, 130–2, 160
Enlightenment 117
Epistemology, musical 9, 13, 19, 31–2, 35,
      82, 87, 160, 178–9, 181–2
Evolution of art 43–4

Fauxbourdon 132, 134–42, 158–60
Fechner, Theodor 2, 20, 84, 90
   bottom-to-top aesthetics *see* aesthetics
   'psycho-physical parallelism' 84, 90
Fétis, François-Joseph 183
Fichte, Johann Gottlieb 70, 128–30, 133–6,
   146, 149, 156
   Reden an die deutsche Nation 128, 134
Fiction 86, 88, 101, 107–8, 160, 183–4
Figured bass *see* bass
Forkel, Johann Nikolaus 116–17
Forms, musical 3, 6, 39, 99, 110, 149, 154,
   157, 183–4

Fortlage, Karl 171
Foucault, Michel 121, 182
France 97, 117, 119, 133–4, 154, 156, 180
Frankfurt 128
Franz, Constantin 127
Frege, Gottlob 118
Fuchs, Carl 182, 185
Function *see* Harmony
Fusion *see* Klang
Future 9, 45–6, 105–6, 110, 123, 137, 157,
   180

Gade, Niels W. 171
Gellner, Ernest 30–1
Genius 11, 44, 88–9, 165
   genius loci 144–6
Gerald of Wales (Giraldus Cambrensis)
   131
   Descriptio Cambriae 131
Gerhard, Charles 84
Germany 2, 4, 7, 17, 20, 22, 31, 35, 39–40,
      43, 65, 82, 84, 111, 117–20, 127–40,
      142–50, 155–6, 158, 160–1, 181, 185
   Holy Roman Empire of the German
      Nation 143
   'New German School' 42
   Wilhelmine 7, 9, 14, 19, 35, 63, 137, 147,
      149, 159
Giddens, Anthony 45
Göttingen 33, 83
Goethe, Johann Wolfgang von 6, 26–8, 128,
   176–7
   Faust 128
   Von deutscher Baukunst 7
Grabner, Hermann 7
Grammar 120
   musical 116–17, 121, 126, 150 *see also*
      language
   of Port-Royal 121
Gramophone 177
Grieg, Edvard 171

Hahn, Albert 63–4
Hamburg 4
Handschin, Jacques 166
Hanslick, Eduard 1
Harmony 1, 12, 14, 20–1, 23–4, 26, 35, 40–3,
      45–8, 50–2, 58–9, 61–3, 67, 73–4, 76,
      78–80, 92–3, 95–6, 100, 103, 105–6,
      108–11, 116–17, 123–4, 126, 131–3, 135,
      137–8, 149, 151–6, 158–60, 163–4,
      170–1, 173–7

Harmony (*cont.*)
  and metre 72–3, 75, 77, 100, 102
  and scale 122
  as Garden of Eden 105–11, 124, 136–7,
    156, 182
  grid of harmonic relations 48, 50–2, 56,
    58–60, 106, 133, 167
  harmonic function 7–9, 17, 37–8, 51–9,
    60–1, 70, 73–82, 87, 94–5, 100, 103–4,
    110, 122, 125, 137, 139, 141, 150–6, 158,
    163–4, 168–9, 176, 188
  harmonic pillars 51, 55–8, 94, 168
  harmonic space 50–1, 55, 58, 61, 76,
    105–7, 109, 167
  Harmonieschritte see root
  Roman-numeral taxonomy 7, 57
Hartmann, Johan Peter Emilius 171
Hauptmann, Moritz 22–7, 31, 35, 41, 47,
  68–9, 71, 104, 114–16, 122, 133, 136,
  167, 172
  Die Natur der Harmonik und Metrik 23
  'triad of triads' *see* triad
Haydn, Joseph 110, 139–40, 142, 144, 147–8

Haydn, Michael 142
Hearing 2–3, 5, 9, 15–17, 19, 32–3, 35–6, 47,
  86–7, 92, 103, 105, 130, 154, 159, 165–7,
  169, 171, 177 *see also* ear, listener
  as logical activity 3, 178
  deafness 166
Hegel, Georg Wilhelm Friedrich 24, 35,
  40–1, 45, 82, 109–10, 112, 180
Helmholtz, Hermann von 20–3, 27, 31–3,
  48, 70–1, 79, 82–3, 108, 167, 178, 181
  On the Sensations of Tone 20
Herbart, Johann Friedrich 2
Herder, Johann Gottlieb 117, 119, 126, 128,
  157
Heterophony 132
Heuß, Alfred 148
History 17–18, 27–8, 130, 143, 144
  and music theory/musicology 3, 35, 39,
    41, 43–6, 62, 64, 91–3, 96, 98–100, 107,
    110, 111, 125–6, 130–1, 139–40, 148–9
  as detrimental force 110–11, 138
  genealogy 93
  Hegelian 109
  historical logic 41, 86, 92, 98–9, 107 *see*
    also logic
  historical relativism 53, 117–18, 159, 169,
    171, 180
  pre-history 98

  primordial 130
  Whiggish 93, 96
Hoffmann, Leopold 140
Hornbostel, Erich Moritz von 176–8, 180,
  184
  Blasquintentheorie 185
Humboldt, Wilhelm von 119–22, 125–7
  Kawi Introduction 119–20
Hyer, Brian 61, 71

Idealism 24, 82–5, 121, 129–30, 180
  'idealism of values' 85 *see also* Lotze
Indy, Vincent d' 31
Intonation, pure/equi-tempered 115,
  123–4, 167
Ireland 170, 172
Irrationalism 85

Jadassohn, Salomon 2
Japan 170, 173

Kantianism 167 *see also* neo-Kantianism
Karlsruhe 84
Kirnberger, Johann Philipp 117
Klang 21, 47–8, 50–1, 54, 70–1, 80, 89,
  114–15, 121–3, 167, 189
  fusion (*Klangverschmelzung*) 53–4, 81, 86,
    108–9
  representation (*Klangvertretung*) 48, 89,
    167, 193
  shorthand (*Klangschlüssel*) 51, 80, 152,
    193
  succession of *Klänge* 194
Koch, Heinrich Christoph 116–17

Language 113–21, 125–9, 145–7, 149, 156,
  158, 161
  and logic 114–18
  German *see* Germany
  Greek 120, 150
  Hebrew 119
  Latin 120, 133–4
  original *see* origin
  Sanskrit 119–21
Laurencin, Franz Peter Graf 40–3, 45–7, 51,
  63–4, 105
Laws 44, 67, 88–9, 91–2, 105, 114, 124,
  146–7, 178 *see also* music
Leibniz, Gottfried Wilhelm 118
Leipzig 4, 33, 169
Lenz, Wilhelm von 163–4
Lévi-Strauss, Claude 126

Listener 3, 9, 12, 56, 63, 163, 166, 169
Liszt, Franz 19, 26, 40–1, 152, 154, 158
   Faust Symphony 41, 150, 158
Logic 84–6, 117–19, 121
   and language 114–18
   historical 41, 86, 91, 98–9, 107
   musical 39, 42, 44, 46–7, 51, 67–8, 72,
      76–9, 89, 91–3, 98–100, 103–7, 110–11,
      113–17, 139, 150–4, 156, 163–4, 169,
      178
Lotze, Hermann Rudolf 33, 83–4, 87, 103,
   109, 167, 181
Louis, Rudolf 63

Maler, Wilhelm 7
Mannheim School 139–44, 146, 148–9,
   157
   'Mannheim sigh' 157
Marburg 83
Marx, Adolf Bernhard 133
Memory 178, 183
Metre 1, 23, 72–3, 75–7, 100, 125, 153, 163
   and harmony 72–3, 75, 77, 100, 102
   Auftaktigkeit 163–4, 198
   rebarring *see* Riemann
Mimesis 20
Mode, major/minor 20–1, 25, 27, 31, 62,
   79–80, 82, 88, 90, 92, 94–5, 103–4, 108,
   171–2, 176–7
   medieval 97–9
Modernity 42–3, 45–6
Monism 7–8, 19, 29–30, 52
Monn, Georg 141
Monody 169
Mozart, Leopold 140, 145
Mozart, Wolfgang Amadeus 142, 144, 148
Music
   absolute 156–8, 181
   and universal laws 10, 20, 42, 44, 62, 65,
      89, 92, 111, 121, 138, 160, 180–2 *see also*
      laws
   as language 113, 117, 121–2, 126, 130,
      150, 156–8, 161
   essential elements of 2, 5–6, 9–10, 13, 33,
      91–2, 107–8, 124, 134, 149, 158, 163,
      167, 177, 179–80
   folk music 135, 144, 169–70, 172, 176
   musical object 2, 36, 41, 59, 62, 96, 98,
      180, 183
   musicology's definition of 10–11, 13,
      21, 34–5, 43, 62–3, 166, 169, 180–1,
      183–4

non-Western 97, 123, 126, 169–73, 176,
   178–80
vocal 157–8, 180
Western or German repertoire 14, 62,
   64–6, 98, 100, 102, 111, 125–6, 131,
   135–6, 148, 150, 156, 160, 169, 171,
   176–7, 180
Musicology 1–2, 4–7, 9–10, 13–19, 31–2, 89,
   122, 130, 156, 170, 176–8, 182, 185
   as science 6, 14, 19, 59, 62, 65, 68, 73, 82
      see also science
   chairs of 1–2, 4
   ethnomusicology 124–5, 176–80, 184
   history of 1, 182–3
   Riemann's system of 2, 5, 7–9, 15, 32, 39,
      63, 98–9, 103, 110, 130, 137–8, 150, 152,
      168, 176, 179–83, 185
   systematic 5, 168, 184
Music history 2, 5–6, 10, 13–14, 43, 63,
   66, 98–9, 135, 139, 141, 148, 159, 180,
   183
   end of 13–14, 64, 112, 155–6
Music theory 5–7, 9, 14, 21, 34–6, 39–46,
   62–4, 82, 88–9, 91–3, 123, 133, 135–6,
   156
   and analysis 36, 59–61, 65, 162 *see also*
      analysis *and* Riemann
   history of 17, 96, 98, 107, 135
   implicit/explicit 42–5, 61
   legitimation of 32, 34, 42–3, 46, 62, 88,
      90–3, 125
   practical/speculative 2, 35, 65, 103
Myth of ethnic election 129–30, 133,
   158–60

Napoleon Bonaparte 134
Nationhood, nationalism 14, 117–18, 121,
   125–31, 134–8, 142–7, 149–50, 156,
   158–61, 169, 171
   Kulturnation 127
Nature 12, 14–15, 18, 20–1, 23, 27, 35, 64,
   78–9, 85, 87–93, 98–100, 103, 107–9,
   114–15, 121–4, 126, 128, 130, 134–5,
   144, 147, 150, 158
   second nature 24, 158
Neo-Kantianism 83, 85, 107
Nietzsche, Friedrich 182, 185
Nonsense 179
Normativity 9–10, 62, 73, 103, 106, 182,
   184
Notation 13, 163–6, 173, 178–80
   sketch studies 165, 179

Index

Oettingen, Arthur von 15, 22–3, 26, 35, 37, 47–8, 68, 79, 136, 171–2
phonicity/tonicity 23
Phonica, Regnante, Oberregnante 79
Ontology 84–5
Organicism 6–7, 44, 120, 183–4
Origin 119, 130, 140, 142, 158, 173
  of music 130, 132, 135–7, 158–60, 180
  original language 118–19, 128–9, 149
Overtones 15, 22, 26, 32, 47–8, 70, 79–80, 86, 108 *see also* undertones

Palestrina, Giovanni Pierluigi da 40
Partials *see* overtones
Pedagogy 2, 9–11, 41, 65, 99, 103, 136–7, 180
Pentatonicism 125, 170–1, 176
Perception 2, 47, 84, 160
Period, eight-bar 38, 73, 77, 100, 139, 149, 164, 184
Pessimism, cultural 137–8
Pestalozzi, Johann Heinrich 136
Philology 6, 118–20
Philosophy 82–5, 117
Phonicity *see* Oettingen
Phrasing 162, 182
Physics 2, 15, 20–2, 31, 80, 83, 89–91, 107, 124, 165, 169, 172, 177–8
Physiology 2, 20, 84, 89–90, 107–8, 123
Pitch-class set theory 63
Port-Royal 121
Positivism 82–3
Pragmatism 83, 85
Progress 40–3, 45, 63, 92, 100, 106, 111, 123–4, 133, 135, 137, 158, 160
Psychology 2, 33–4, 52, 89–91, 107, 109, 124, 160–2, 167, 171, 179, 181
  Gestalt psychology 167
Purity 118–19, 123–4, 126, 128–9, 158, 171, 175–6

Rameau, Jean-Philippe 33, 78, 93–7
  Double emploi 95
  Génération harmonique 33, 95
  Fundamental bass *see* bass
Ratner, Leonard 158
Reality, realism 83–6, 98, 107–10
Reger, Max 10–14, 138, 180
  'Ein Drängen' Op. 97, no. 3 12
Renan, Ernest 143–4
  Qu'est-ce qu'une nation? 143

Responsibility 9–10, 13–14, 46, 51, 59, 61–6, 103–6
Riemann, Elisabeth 11
Riemann, Hugo
  and musical analysis 36–9, 68, 73–5, 150–5, 162–4, 172 *see also* analysis and music theory
  and other dualists 26–31, 35
  Auftaktigkeit see anacrusis
  career 1–2, 4, 7, 10, 13, 15–19, 33, 35, 61, 169, 176
  criticisms of 7–8, 10, 16–18, 67–74, 86, 91, 98–100, 102–3, 168
  'Degeneration und Regeneration' 11
  doctoral dissertation (*Über das musikalische Hören/Musikalische Logik*) 33, 47, 68, 113, 176
  experiment with undertones 15–17, 21, 28, 32–3, 35, 87, 180
  Festschrift (1919) 1, 4, 6
  Folkloristische Tonalitätsstudien 169–72, 179
  Geschichte der Musiktheorie 88, 92, 130, 146–7, 159
  Große Kompositionslehre 12, 100, 103, 139, 184
  Handbuch der Akustik 123
  Handbuch der Harmonielehre 17, 51, 75–6
  Handbuch der Musikgeschichte 155, 159
  historical significance of 1, 4, 18–19, 170, 182–3
  inaugural dissertation (*Studien zur Geschichte der Notenschrift*) 5
  Ludwig van Beethovens sämtliche Klavier-Solosonaten 76, 147–8, 160, 162
  'Musikalische Logik' 46–7, 68, 114
  Musikalische Syntaxis 18, 48, 63, 105, 113–14, 136
  Musik-Lexikon 1, 11, 48, 88, 103, 110
  'Die Natur der Harmonik' 89, 91, 124
  Phrasierungsausgaben 162
  rebarring 162, 164, 179
  Sechs originale Chinesische and Japanische Lieder 173, 176
  Systematische Modulationslehre 72, 77, 79, 82, 99, 184
  system of musicology 2, 5, 7–9, 15, 32, 39, 98–9, 103, 110, 130, 137–8, 150, 152, 168, 176, 179–83, 185
  theory of harmony 1, 7–8, 17, 35, 59, 61–2, 65–7, 72–3, 75, 87, 99, 106–7, 110–12, 114, 121, 124, 150, 153, 168, 176

216

theory of metre 1, 72–3, 75, 100, 121, 163
tone imaginations/representations
　(*Tonvorstellungen*) 72, 75–7, 161, 165–9,
　172, 176, 178, 181
Vereinfachte Harmonielehre 17, 51, 82, 103
'Ein vergessener Großmeister' 140
views on music aesthetics 3, 9, 13–14,
　22, 87, 103, 156, 183–5 *see also*
　aesthetics
views on music history 5, 14, 99, 109,
　137–9, 155–6, 176 *see also* music
　history
Wie hören wir Musik? 3, 9
Romanticism 111
Rome 4, 129, 133
Root, triadic 26, 47, 54–5, 60, 67–74, 92
'root-interval progression' 50, 54, 56, 58,
　79–80
Rosen, Charles 100–1, 158

Sachs, Melchior 63–4
Scandinavia 27, 131, 171, 176
Scale *see* diatonicism, pentatonicism
Schenker, Heinrich 7, 100, 162
Five Graphic Analyses 162
Schlegel, Friedrich 119–20
Sprache und Weisheit der Indier 119
Schoenberg, Arnold 43–4, 100, 155–6
Harmonielehre 44
Schubert, Franz 40
'Im Frühling' 56
Schumann, Robert 40–1
Schütz, Heinrich 138
Science 16–17, 19–21, 23, 27, 31–2, 35, 82–6,
　89–93, 96, 99, 108–9, 125, 132, 167
musicology as 6, 14, 19, 59, 62, 65, 68, 73,
　82, 183–4
Scotland 170, 172, 176
Social Democrats 63–4
Sondershausen 4
Sound archive 177
Sound wave 2, 15, 17, 33–4, 70, 86, 167,
　169, 178, 181
Spengler, Oswald 111 *see also* pessimism,
　cultural
Spitta, Philipp 5
Staël, Anne Louise Germaine de 136
Stamitz, Johann 139, 146–9, 157 *see also*
　Mannheim School
Structure
　architectural 3, 183
　language 120–1

musical 2–3, 5, 25, 34, 39, 43, 62–3, 98,
　100, 152, 158, 161, 163–4, 167, 184
Strasbourg 2, 7
Strauss, Richard 155
Also sprach Zarathustra 155
Elektra 155
Salome 155
Stumpf, Carl 52–4, 81, 86, 108–9, 176–7, 180
concordance/discordance *see*
　consonance *and* dissonance
fusion *see* Klang
Style 2, 6, 92, 106–7, 139, 157
Symmetry 3, 7, 15, 20, 24–8, 36–8, 72–3, 80,
　100, 158, 175, 183
asymmetrical opposite 150
Syntax, musical 113 *see also* language

Tacitus 130
De Germania 130
Teleology 92, 98
Thayer, Alexander 166
Tonality 13, 43–5, 48, 51–4, 58, 64, 66,
　68–70, 72, 81, 103–6, 108, 110–12, 115,
　130, 136, 152, 154–6, 169, 180–1, 183,
　196
Tone relation 197
Tonicity *see* Oettingen
Tonvorstellungen see Riemann
Tradition 28, 41, 44, 63–4, 66, 137, 149
Triads, major/minor 7, 9, 15, 19–29, 31–2,
　47, 50–5, 68–72, 81, 92, 96, 108–9, 115,
　122–6, 133–4, 137, 150–1, 154, 159, 167,
　169, 171–2 *see also* mode
'triad of triads' 68–9, 71 *see also*
　Hauptmann
Trivium 113, 118
Tuning 50, 115, 124

Undertones, undertone series 15, 17, 19,
　32, 34–5, 47–8, 50, 59, 80, 82, 86–8, 103,
　106–8, 180–1, 184, 197
Universality 27–8, 62, 65–6, 88, 92, 98–9,
　114, 118, 121, 124–7, 130, 150, 158,
　180–2
University 4, 33, 83
Upbeat 73, 198 *see also* anacrusis, metre
Utopia 9, 63, 66, 99, 107, 136–7, 149, 157,
　176

Vaihinger, Hans 85–6, 88, 107–8
Die Philosophie des Als-ob 85
Vienna 1, 139–6, 148

Index

Vincent, Heinrich 63–4
Vogel, Martin 19

Wagenseil, Johann Christoph 140
Wagner, Richard 12, 40–3, 137, 157
   Lohengrin 40
   Die Meistersinger von Nürnberg 137,
    157
   Tannhäuser 157
   Tristan und Isolde 62, 103
Wales 131–2
Weimar 145

Weitzmann, Carl 40–3, 45–7, 51, 63–4, 105
Wiesbaden 4
Winckelmann, Johann Joachim 140
Work, musical 3, 9–10, 34, 40, 42–3, 62–3,
   65, 98–100, 107, 144, 158, 165, 170,
   183–4
Wundt, Wilhelm 161
   Völkerpsychologie 161

Zarlino, Gioseffo 28–31
   Istitutioni harmoniche 29
Ziehn, Bernhard 37